Paris

a Lonely Planet city guide

**Daniel Robinson
Tony Wheeler**

Paris
1st edition

Published by
Lonely Planet Publications

Head Office:	PO Box 617, Hawthorn, Vic 3122, Australia
Branches:	155 Filbert St, Suite 251, Oakland, CA 94607, USA
	10 Barley Mow Passage, Chiswick, London W4 4PH, UK
	71 bis rue du Cardinal Lemoine, 75005 Paris, France

Printed by
Colorcraft Ltd, Hong Kong

Photographs by
Rachel Black, Simon Bracken, Bethune Carmichael, Olivier Cirendini, Greg Elms, Richard Everist, James Lyon, Richard Nebesky, Tony Wheeler

Front cover: Sign to Metro entrance (Richard Nebesky)
Title page: Time out in the sun, Hôtel de Ville (Bethune Carmichael)

First Published
November 1996

Although the authors and publisher have tried to make the information as accurate as possible, they accept no responsibility for any loss, injury or inconvenience sustained by any person using this book.

National Library of Australia Cataloguing in Publication Data

Robinson, Daniel.
  Paris.

  1st ed.
  Includes index.
  ISBN 0 86442 431 0.

  1. Paris (France) – Guidebooks. I. Wheeler, Tony, 1946-.
  II. Title. (Series: Lonely Planet city guide.)

  914.43604839

Daniel Robinson

Daniel was raised in the USA (the San Francisco Bay area and Glen Ellyn, IL) and Israel. He holds a BA from Princeton University in Near Eastern Studies (Arab and Islamic history and the Arabic language) and has travelled extensively in the Middle East and South, South-East and East Asia.

His previous work for Lonely Planet includes the 1st edition of *France – travel survival kit* and the Vietnam and Cambodia sections of *Vietnam, Laos & Cambodia – travel survival kit*. Daniel lives in Tel Aviv and is currently working on a PhD in history at Tel Aviv University.

Tony Wheeler

Tony was born in England but grew up in Pakistan, the Bahamas and the USA. He returned to England to do a degree in engineering at Warwick University, worked as an automotive design engineer, returned to London Business School to complete an MBA, then set out on an Asian overland trip with his wife, Maureen. That trip led to Tony and Maureen founding Lonely Planet Publications in Australia in 1973, and they've been travelling, writing and publishing guidebooks ever since. In 1996 they moved to Paris, with their children Tashi and Kieran, for a one-year stay.

From the Authors

Daniel Robinson It is a rare treat for an LP author to work in a country with its very own LP office, and I was doubly fortunate that Zahia Hafs' staff in the Latin Quarter included Laurence Billiet, Marina Bonnamy, Jean-Noël Doan, Caroline Guilleminot, Philippe Maitre and Isabelle Muller. Their support, both logistical and moral, was invaluable. I also had the pleasure of working with those highly professional LP veterans Steve Womersley and Adrienne Costanzo.

Finally, I would like to express my heartfelt thanks to Sara Vered, Professor Aharon Oppenheimer and the faculty of Tel Aviv University's Department of Jewish History, whose patience, understanding and forbearance saved my academic career from turning into a burnt, smouldering pile of missed deadlines.

Tony Wheeler Thank you to the staff of LP France who, sometimes a little reluctantly, revealed the identities of their favourite bars, restaurants and assorted Parisian secrets. In particular, thanks must go to Laurence Billiet, Caroline Guilleminot, Zahia Hafs and Isabelle Muller. Thanks also to Christophe Corbel and Michel Macleod for an enormous amount of telephone checking and cross-checking.

From the Publisher

This book was edited by Janet Austin, proofed by Diana Saad and laid out by Cathy Oliver. The beautiful maps were drawn by Chris Love, Matt King, Andrew Tudor and Rachel Black; Rachel also handled the book's design and layout. The editor wishes to thank Steve Womersley and Adrienne Costanzo for their invaluable assistance and buck-passing skills, and to Jane Hart for her help in checking layout. Thanks also go to Christophe Corbel and Michel Macleod in the Paris office for their research.

Warning & Request

Things change: prices go up, schedules change, good places go bad and bad places go bankrupt – nothing stays the same. So if you find things better or worse, recently opened or long since closed, please write and tell us and help make the next edition better.

Your letters will be used to help update future editions and, where possible, important changes will also be included in an Update section in reprints.

We greatly appreciate all information that is sent to us by travellers. Back at Lonely Planet we employ a hard-working readers' letters team – Julie Young and Shelley Preston in Australia, Simon Goldsmith in the UK,

Arnaud Lebonnois in France and Sacha Pearson in the USA – to sort through the many letters we receive. The best ones will be rewarded with a free copy of the next edition or another Lonely Planet guide if you prefer. We give away lots of books, but, unfortunately, not every letter/postcard receives one.

Contents

Map Contents

Introduction

Paris has just about exhausted the superlatives that can reasonably be applied to any city. Notre Dame and the Eiffel Tower – at sunrise, at sunset, at night – have been described countless times, as have the Seine and the subtle (and not-so-subtle) differences between the Left and Right banks. But what writers have been unable to capture is the grandness and even magic of strolling along the city's broad avenues, which lead from impressive public buildings and exceptional museums to parks, gardens and esplanades. Paris probably has more landmarks familiar to people who've never visited the place than any other city in the world. As a result, first-time visitors often arrive in the French capital with all sorts of expectations: of grand vistas, of intellectuals discussing weighty matters in cafés, of romance along the Seine, of naughty nightclub revues, of rude people who won't speak English. If you look hard enough, you can probably find all of the above. But another approach is to set aside the preconceptions of Paris that are so much a part of English-speaking culture, and to explore the city's avenues and backstreets as if the tip of the Eiffel Tower or the spire of Notre Dame weren't about to pop into view at any moment.

Paris is enchanting almost everywhere, at any time, in every season. And you too may find yourself humming that old Cole Porter favourite (inimitably covered by the group Les Négresses Vertes in 1989) as you walk the streets: 'I love Paris in the springtime, I love Paris in the fall...'

Facts about Paris

HISTORY

The Romans & the Gauls

The Celtic Gauls moved into what is now France between 1500 and 500 BC. Some time during the 3rd century BC members of a Celtic tribe called the Parisii set up a few huts on what is now the Île de la Cité. Centuries of conflict between the Gauls and Rome ended between 55 and 52 BC when Julius Caesar's legions took control of the territory and the settlement on the Seine became a Roman town. A temple to Jupiter was established where Notre Dame now stands, and the Roman town spread to the south bank, with Rue Saint Jacques and Rue Soufflot (M14), near the Panthéon and the Jardin du Luxembourg, as the principal crossroads. Traces of this Roman Paris can be seen in the Crypte Archéologique (M14) under the square in front of Notre Dame, in the Arènes de Lutèce (M12) and at the Roman baths in the Musée National du Moyen Age, formerly known as the Musée de Cluny (M14).

Christianity was introduced early in the 2nd century AD, and the Roman period ended in the 5th century when the Franks and other Germanic groups, under their leader Merovius, overran the country. In 508 AD, Merovius' grandson, Clovis I, made Paris his capital, naming it after the original Parisii tribe.

The Middle Ages

The city's strategic riverside situation ensured its importance through the Middle Ages, although settlement remained centred on the Île de la Cité and the Left Bank. North of the Seine the Marais area was exactly what its name suggests: a waterlogged marsh.

In 1163 work started on the cathedral of Notre Dame (M12), the greatest creation of medieval Paris, and construction continued for nearly two centuries. This was a time of frenetic activity in the city. The marshes of the Marais were drained and settlement finally moved to the north bank of the Seine, the area known today as the Right Bank. The food markets at Les Halles (M12) first came into existence around 1110, the Sorbonne (M14) was opened in 1253, the beautiful Sainte Chapelle (M14) on the Île de la Cité was consecrated in 1248 and the

14

Louvre (M12) began its existence as a riverside fortress in the 1200s.

The Scandinavian Vikings (also known as the Norsemen, ie Normans) had begun raiding France's western coast in the 9th century. Eventually they controlled all of the north and west of the region and in 1066 mounted a successful invasion of England. Three centuries of conflict commenced between the Capetian dynasty, founded in 987 with Paris and Orléans as its principal centres, and the Normans of England and Normandy. This bitter struggle degenerated into the Hundred Years War, fought on and off from 1337 to 1453. The Black Death in 1348 killed about a third of the country's population but only briefly interrupted the fighting.

After the French forces were defeated at Agincourt in 1415, the English took control of Paris in 1420. Two years later King Henry IV of England, then an infant, became king of France, but a 17-year-old peasant girl known to history as Jeanne d'Arc (Joan of Arc) surfaced in 1429 and rallied the French troops to defeat the English at Orléans. In 1430 she was captured, convicted of heresy by a court of French ecclesiastics and burned at the stake two years later. However, with the exception of Calais, the English were expelled from French territory in 1453.

The Renaissance & the Reformation

When the English finally withdrew, Paris was a disaster zone. Conditions improved with the arrival of the culture of the Italian Renaissance at the end of the 1400s and the reign of Louis XI. The magnificent Place des Vosges (M15), built in the Marais in the early 1600s, was a prime example of the new era of town planning. The Marais remains the best area for spotting reminders of Renaissance Paris, with gentlemen's mansions, or *hôtels particuliers*, from this era such as the Hôtel Carnavalet (M15). South of the Seine, the Hôtel de Cluny, now the Musée National du Moyen Age (M14), is another fine example. Renaissance-era churches include the Tour Saint Jacques (M14) and Saint Eustache (M12) on the Right Bank, and Saint Étienne du Mont (M14) on the Left. The oldest bridge in Paris, the Pont Neuf (M14), or New Bridge, is another prime example of the architecture of the period.

The Wars of Religion (1562-98) involved three groups: the Huguenots (French Protestants who received help from the English), the Catholic League and the Catholic monarchy. The fighting severely weakened the position of the king and brought the French state close to disintegration. The most deplorable massacre took place in

Paris in 1572, when some 3000 Huguenots who had
come to Paris to celebrate the wedding of Henri of
Navarre were slaughtered at what is now called the Saint
Bartholomew's Day Massacre (23-24 August). Henri of
Navarre, a Huguenot who had embraced Catholicism,
eventually became King Henri IV. In 1598 he promul-
gated the Edict of Nantes, which guaranteed the
Huguenots freedom of conscience and many civil and
political rights. He was succeeded by Louis XIII (ruled
1610-43), whose ruthless chief minister, Cardinal Richelieu, is best known for his untiring efforts to establish an
absolute monarchy in France and French supremacy in
Europe.

Louis XIV & the Ancien Régime

Le Roi Soleil (the Sun King) ascended the throne in 1643
at the age of five and ruled until 1715. He involved
France in a long series of costly wars that gained it
territory but terrified its neighbours and nearly bank-
rupted the treasury with extravagances like the palace
at Versailles, 23 km south-west of Paris. Other examples
of the grandiose architecture of the period include the
Palais du Luxembourg (M14) and the Church of the
Dôme (M11). Louis' country residence allowed the
monarch to sidestep the endless intrigues of the capital,
by then a city of 500,000 people. He quashed the ambitious, feuding aristocracy and created the first
centralised French state. He also mercilessly persecuted
the Protestants, and in 1685 revoked the Edict of Nantes.
His successor, Louis XV (ruled 1715-74), was followed

TONY WHEELER

Palais du Luxembourg

by the incompetent – and later universally despised and powerless – Louis XVI.

As the 18th century progressed, new economic and social circumstances rendered the old order *(ancien régime)* dangerously out of step with the needs of the country. The regime was further weakened by the anti-establishment and anticlerical ideas of the Enlightenment, whose leading lights included Voltaire, Rousseau and Montesquieu.

The Seven Years' War (1756-63) was only one of a series of ruinous wars which had been pursued by Louis XV, and it had led to the loss of France's flourishing colonies in Canada, the West Indies and India. It was in part to avenge these losses that Louis XVI sided with the colonists in the American War of Independence, which only helped to disseminate in France the radical democratic ideas of the American Revolution.

The French Revolution & the First Republic

By the late 1780s, Louis XVI and his queen, Marie-Antoinette, had alienated virtually every segment of society – from enlightened groups to conservatives. When the king tried to neutralise the power of the more reform-minded delegates the urban masses took to the streets and, on 14 July 1789, a Parisian mob stormed the Bastille prison – the ultimate symbol of the despotism of the *ancien régime*.

France was declared a constitutional monarchy and various reforms were made, including the adoption of the Declaration of the Rights of Man. But as the masses armed themselves against the external threat to the new government posed by Austria, Prussia and the many exiled French nobles, patriotism and nationalism mixed with revolutionary fervour and popularised and radicalised the Revolution. It was not long before the moderate republican Girondins lost power to the radical Jacobins, led by Robespierre, Danton and Marat, who established the First Republic in 1792 after Louis XVI proved unreliable as a constitutional monarch. In January 1793 the king, who had tried to flee the country with his family, was convicted of 'conspiring against the liberty of the nation' and guillotined at what is now Place de la Concorde (M7). In March the Jacobins set up the notorious Committee of Public Safety. This body had virtual dictatorial control over the country during the Reign of Terror (September 1793 to July 1794), which saw religious freedoms revoked, churches desecrated and closed and cathedrals turned into 'Temples of Reason'.

By autumn, the Reign of Terror was in full swing, and by the middle of 1794 some 17,000 people nationwide had been beheaded. In the end, the Revolution turned on its own, and many of its leaders, including Robespierre and Danton, followed their victims to the guillotine.

Napoleon & the First Empire

The post-revolutionary government was far from stable, and in 1799 a dashing young Corsican general by the name of Napoleon Bonaparte stepped into the chaos and assumed power. At first he took the title of First Consul, but in 1802 he became 'consul for life' and in 1804 the Pope crowned him Emperor of the French. Napoleon then set out on a seemingly endless series of wars in which France came to control most of Europe. In 1812, in an attempt to do away with his last major rival on the continent, the tsar, Napoleon invaded Russia. Although his Grande Armée captured Moscow, it was wiped out shortly thereafter by the brutal Russian winter. Less than two years after this fiasco, the Russian army entered Paris. Napoleon abdicated and left France for the tiny Mediterranean island-kingdom of Elba.

At the Congress of Vienna (1814-15), the House of Bourbon was restored to the French throne and Louis XVI's brother was installed as Louis XVIII. But in March 1815, Napoleon escaped from Elba, landed in southern France and gathered a large army as he marched northward toward Paris. His 'Hundred Days' back in power ended with defeat by the English Duke of Wellington at Waterloo in Belgium. The English exiled Napoleon to the remote South Atlantic island of Saint Helena, where he died in 1821.

Few of Napoleon's grand plans for Paris were completed, but the Arc de Triomphe (M6), the Arc de Triomphe du Carrousel (M11) and La Madeleine (M7) date from this period.

The Second Republic & the Second Empire

Between 1815 and 1848 the reigns of Louis XVIII, Charles X and Louis-Philippe were periods of conflict and inept rule, finally terminated by the February Revolution of 1848 and the establishment of the Second Republic. In presidential elections held that year, Napoleon's useless nephew Louis Napoleon Bonaparte was overwhelmingly elected. Legislative deadlock led Louis Napoleon to lead a coup d'état in 1851, after which he was proclaimed Emperor Napoleon III.

The Second Empire lasted from 1852 until 1870. During this period, France enjoyed significant economic growth and Paris was transformed under Baron Haussmann, appointed Prefect of the Seine by Napoleon III. In 17 years he oversaw the construction of a new city of wide boulevards, fine public buildings and beautiful parks, serviced, not insignificantly, by a modern sewerage system. The 12 avenues leading out from the Arc de Triomphe (M6) and the parkland of the Bois de Boulogne (M1) were both his work.

Unfortunately, just like his uncle, Napoleon III embroiled France in a number of conflicts, including the disastrous Crimean War (1853-56). In 1870, Prussian prime minister Bismarck goaded Napoleon III into declaring war on Prussia. Within months the thoroughly unprepared French army was defeated and the emperor taken prisoner. When news of the debacle reached the French capital, the Parisian masses took to the streets and demanded that a republic be declared.

The Third Republic & the Belle Époque

As the Prussians advanced on Paris, the Third Republic began as a provisional government of national defence. A four-month siege was followed by an armistice but in the subsequent elections the republicans, who had called for continued resistance, lost to the monarchists, who had campaigned on a peace platform. When ordinary Parisians heard of the harsh terms of the treaty which the monarchist-controlled National Assembly had ratified in 1871, they revolted. The Communards, as the supporters of the Paris Commune were known, took over the city but were slowly pushed back in bloody fighting in which several thousand rebels were killed. A further 20,000 or so Communards, mostly from the working class, were summarily executed.

Despite this disastrous start, the Third Republic ushered in the glittering *belle époque* (beautiful age), with Art Nouveau architecture, the Eiffel Tower (M10), a whole field of artistic 'isms' from Impressionism onwards (best seen at the Musée d'Orsay, M11) and advances in science and engineering, including the construction of the first metro line. The Paris of nightclubs and artistic cafés made its first appearance around this time.

RACHEL BLACK

The Eiffel Tower in autumn

WW I & WW II

Obsession with revenge for the disastrous Franco-Prussian War was a prime cause of France's entry into WW I, but the eventual victory was achieved at a terrible cost in lives. The 1920s and 1930s saw Paris as a centre of the avant-garde, with artists pushing into the new fields of cubism and surrealism, Le Corbusier rewriting the architectural style book, foreign writers like Ernest Hemingway attracted by the city's liberal atmosphere, and nightlife establishing a cutting-edge reputation for everything from jazz clubs to striptease.

Following Germany's invasion of Poland in 1939, France and Britain declared war on Germany. By June 1940 France had capitulated, Paris was occupied, and

French Jews and other minorities were rounded up for deportation to Auschwitz and other death camps. The liberation of France began with the Allied landings in Normandy on D-day (6 June 1944). After a brief insurrection by the Resistance, Paris was liberated on 25 August by an Allied force spearheaded by Free French units, sent in ahead of the Americans so the French would have the honour of liberating the capital.

The Fourth & Fifth Republics

After the war General Charles de Gaulle, leader of the Free French Forces in exile, set up a provisional government, but in January 1946 he miscalculated his support and fell from power when a referendum approved a new constitution and the Fourth Republic. Unstable governments, defeat in Vietnam and a bitter independence struggle in Algeria provoked chaos in France and led to the return of de Gaulle in 1958. His new Fifth Republic, which continues to this day, gives much more power to the president at the expense of the National Assembly.

Paris maintained its position as an artistic and creative centre, and the 1960s saw large parts of the Marais (M15) beautifully restored. In early 1968 student-led anti-Vietnam War protests spread to an all-out attack on the government in the Spring Uprising. Students occupied the Sorbonne (M14), barricades were erected in the Latin Quarter and unrest spread to other universities. Workers joined in the protests and about nine million people participated in a general strike, virtually paralysing the country. The alliance between workers and students couldn't last long, and de Gaulle took advantage of this division and appealed to people's fear of anarchy. Stability was restored but the government made a number of immediate changes, including the decentralisation of the higher-education system and the introduction of reforms, such as lowering the voting age to 18.

1969 to the Present

In 1969 Gaullist leader Georges Pompidou became president and was in turn succeeded by Valéry Giscard d'Estaing in 1974. François Mitterrand, long-time head of the Parti Socialiste (PS; Socialist Party), was elected president in 1981 and immediately set out to nationalise banks, industrial groups and other parts of the economy. Political necessity forced him to take an opposite tack from the mid-1980s, particularly after the right-wing opposition led by Jacques Chirac won a National Assembly majority in the 1986 parliamentary elections.

During this period the leaders' passion for nominal immortalisation through great works *(grands projets)* took hold, starting with the Centre Pompidou (M15). Mitterrand took the enthusiasm to great heights, with the Opéra Bastille (M13), the Grande Arche de La Défense (M1), the Cité des Sciences (M1), the Musée d'Orsay (M11) and the questionable Bibliothèque Nationale de France (M1) all on his building list.

In 1995 Jacques Chirac walked away with a comfortable electoral victory. However, after only two years in power Chirac decided to call an early in election in June 1997, and subsequently lost. He remains as president but Socialist Lionel Jospin is the new prime minister after forming a coalition with the Communists and Greens.

Although it is only early in his term, Jospin is concentrating on controlling the spiralling budget deficit and putting France back on track to meeting European monetary union criteria.

GEOGRAPHY

The city of Paris, which is both the national capital and that of the historic Île de France region, measures approximately 9.5 km (north to south) by 11 km (west to east), not including the Bois de Boulogne and the Bois de Vincennes; its total area is 105 sq km. Within central Paris (which the French call *intra-muros* – meaning, within the walls), the Rive Droite (Right Bank) is north of the Seine, while the Rive Gauche (Left Bank) is south of the river.

Paris is a relatively easy city to come to terms with. The ring road known as the Périphérique makes a neat oval containing the whole central area. The Seine cuts an arc across the oval, and the terrain is so flat that the Montmartre hill, in the central north of the city, comes as a real surprise.

CLIMATE

The Paris basin lies midway between Brittany and Alsace, and is affected by the climates of both. The Île de France region records the nation's lowest annual precipitation (about 575 mm) but rainfall patterns are erratic: you're just as likely to be caught in a heavy spring or autumn downpour as in a sudden summer cloudburst. Paris' average yearly temperature is 12°C, but the mercury sometimes drops below zero in January and can climb to the mid-30s or higher in August.

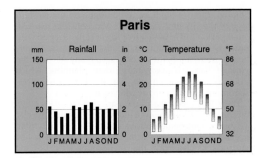

ECOLOGY & ENVIRONMENT

The French are regularly criticised for being somewhat less than environmentally sensitive – they've embraced nuclear power without a thought for the dangers, strung unsightly power lines across beautiful country and blithely tested their nuclear weapons in other peoples' backyards.

In Paris, environmental apathy is most clearly revealed in poor air quality. Fly over Paris on the wrong day and you'll see an LA-style brown cloud hanging ominously over the city. Too many cars is the primary cause of this problem, and there's a curious reluctance to confront car pollution. Parking restrictions appear to be very feebly enforced; enormous numbers of parking attendants, usually working in packs of two or three, scatter parking tickets like confetti, but Parisian drivers seem to simply ignore them. Perhaps the fees are so low that the odd parking ticket is not worth worrying about. Despite its relative flatness, the city is not very bicycle-friendly, certainly in comparison to northern European centres like Amsterdam or Berlin.

On the brighter side, some positive steps are being taken. There are riverside bicycle and pedestrian-only routes on Sundays, and a 50-km network of inner-city bicycle lanes should be in place by 1997. Steady efforts have been made to clean up the Seine; these days it's muddy rather than dirty.

FLORA & FAUNA

At first glance Paris does not appear to have much parkland. There are no great inner-city parks like London's Hyde Park or New York's Central Park, although there is the Bois de Boulogne on the western edge of the city and the Bois de Vincennes to the east. Other parks tend to be small or formal affairs, often with more statuary, fountains and paths than grass. Nevertheless, there are splashes of green, many of them the work of Baron Haussmann's urban planning, which produced interesting parks like the Parc des Buttes-Chaumont and the Parc de Monceau.

There is some fauna in the parks on the city's edge, but the only wildlife you're likely to see around the city are pigeons, those ubiquitous rats-on-wings. In winter, seagulls are sometimes seen on the Seine and a few hardy ducks also brave the river's often swift-flowing waters. Year round, small birds nest in the towers of Notre Dame, and there are crayfish in the city's little-used canals.

Notre Dame's Kestrels
Bird watchers estimate that about 40 pairs of kestrels currently nest in Paris, preferring tall old buildings like Notre Dame. Four or five pairs of kestrels regularly breed in convenient cavities high up in Notre Dame, and once a year, usually in late June, local ornithologists set up a public kestrel-watching station behind the cathedral, with telescopes and even a video camera transmitting close-up pictures of one of the kestrels' nesting sites. The birds form their partnerships in February, eggs are laid in April, the kestrel chicks hatch in May and are ready to depart by early July. In late June, bird watchers may spot the adult kestrels returning to their young with a tasty mouse or sparrow. Unfortunately, Paris' pigeons are too large for a kestrel! ■

GOVERNMENT & POLITICS

The city is run by the Mayor of Paris *(maire)* who is elected by the 163 members of the Conseil de Paris (Council of Paris), who are elected for six-year terms. The mayor has 18 *adjoints* (deputy mayors) and his office is the Hôtel de Ville, or city hall.

The first mayor of Paris to be elected with real powers was Jacques Chirac in 1977. Before that date, as Paris was considered a dangerous and revolutionary city, the mayor was nominated by the government. Since the election of Chirac in 1995 as President of the Republic, the Council of Paris has elected Jean Tiberi – a man who

TONY WHEELER

Parc des Buttes-Chaumont

is very close to the president and is from the same party, Rassemblement pour la République (RPR; the Assembly for the Republic). Tiberi was the former mayor of the 5e *arrondissement* (district) and former deputy mayor for housing.

The mayor has many powers but they do not include control of the police; that office is handled by the Préfet de Police, part of the Ministry of the Interior. Ever since Chirac's election in 1977, the Council of Paris has been run by right-wing parties, either the Union for French Democracy (UDF) or, more frequently, the RPR.

Paris is a *département* (department or county) as well as a city and the mayor is also the head of that division. The city is divided into 20 arrondissements and each has its own *maire d'arrondissement* (mayor of the arrondissement) and *conseil d'arrondissement* (council of the arrondissement) which are also elected for six-year terms. They have very limited powers, principally administering local cultural, sporting and social activities.

ECONOMY

About one-fifth of all economic activity in France takes place in the Paris region. Because of the centralised bureaucracy, the capital also counts 40% of the nation's white-collar jobs.

The European-wide recession hit France especially hard in the early 1990s and unemployment *(chômage)* has stayed firmly stuck at around three million, 12% of the workforce. Estimates number the homeless on Paris' streets at upwards of 50,000.

Although a privatisation programme is in operation, the government still plays a dominant role in banking and finance. State control of the Banque de France, the country's central bank, and the three largest commercial banks – Crédit Lyonnais, Société Générale and Banque Nationale de Paris – began in 1946. Most of the country's other banks were nationalised by the Socialists in the early 1980s. As a result of this heavy state involvement, the banks totter between being over-cautious and wildly extravagant. The Crédit Lyonnais racked up multi-billion-franc losses in the 1980s and 1990s, requiring a massive government bale out, and to top this story of misfortune its headquarters burnt down in mid-1996. France's capital markets are weak and underdeveloped, and the Paris stock market is much smaller than its counterparts in London or Frankfurt.

La Défense, one of the world's most ambitious urban construction projects, was begun in the late 1950s. During the mid-1970s, when skyscrapers fell out of favour, office space in La Défense became hard to sell or lease: whole buildings stood empty and the entire project appeared in jeopardy. But things picked up in the 1980s, and now La Défense is home to many of France's leading multinational firms.

In the late 1980s Mitterrand dreamt of transforming Paris into a financial centre to match London, Tokyo and New York. As old buildings were demolished to make way for office blocks the dream turned sour. Today, many of these buildings, like those of La Défense in the 1970s, lie empty, still awaiting the financial boom. To add to these woes Chirac's moves to restrict welfare payments led to the largest protests since 1968. For three weeks in late 1995 Paris was crippled by public sector strikes, leaving the economy battered and increasing the uncertainty about France's likelihood of qualifying for scheduled European economic and monetary union. To qualify, the government needs to peg back the deficit from 5 to 3% of GDP by the end of 1997.

POPULATION & PEOPLE

The population of Paris is about 2.2 million, although the Île de France, the greater metropolitan area of Paris, has about 10 million inhabitants, or about 20% of France's total population of 58 million people. Paris today is a very cosmopolitan city with many residents from other nations of the European Union (EU) and a large English-speaking constituency.

France has had waves of immigration, particularly from former French colonies in North Africa and French-speaking sub-Saharan Africa. During the late 1950s and early 1960s, over one million French settlers returned to metropolitan France from Algeria, other parts of Africa and Indochina.

In recent years there has been a racist backlash against the country's non-white immigrant communities, especially Muslims from North Africa. In 1993, the French government changed its immigration laws to make it harder for immigrants to get French citizenship or bring their families into the country.

ARTS

Dance

The first *ballet comique de la reine* (dramatic ballet) in France was performed at an aristocratic wedding at the French court in 1581. In 1661 Louis XIV founded the Académie Royale de Danse (Royal Dance Academy), from which ballet around the world developed.

By the end of the 1700s choreographers like Jean-Georges Noverre became more important than the musicians, poets and dancers themselves. In the early 19th century, romantic ballets such as *Giselle* and *Les Sylphides* were more popular than opera in Paris.

Between 1945 and 1955, Roland Petit created such innovative ballets as *Turangalila*, with music composed by Olivier Messiaen. Maurice Béjart shocked the public with his *Symphonie pour un Homme Seul* (danced in black, 1955), *Le Sacre du Printemps* and *Le Marteau sans Maître*, with music by Pierre Boulez.

Music

In the 17th and 18th centuries, French baroque music influenced and informed much of the European musical output. Composers François Couperin and Jean Philippe Rameau were two major players in this field.

France produced and cultivated a number of musical luminaries in the 19th century. Among these were Hector Berlioz, Charles Gounod, César Franck, Camille Saint-Saëns and Georges Bizet. Berlioz was the founder of modern orchestration, while Franck's organ compositions sparked a musical renaissance in France that would produce such greats as Gabriel Fauré and the Impressionists Claude Debussy and Maurice Ravel. Two contemporary composers include Olivier Messiaen, who combines modern, almost mystical music with natural sounds such as birdsong, and his student, the

The many faces of Paris

RICHARD NEBESKY

Men playing boules, Les Halles

RACHEL BLACK

Boys playing basketball, Jardin du Luxemborg

radical Pierre Boulez, who includes computer-generated sound in his compositions.

Jazz hit Paris in the 1920s with a bang and has remained popular ever since. France's contribution to the world of jazz has been great: the violinist Stéphane Grappelli and the legendary three-fingered Gypsy guitarist Django Reinhardt.

The most appreciated form of indigenous music is the *chanson française*, with a tradition going back to the troubadours of the Middle Ages. French songs have always favoured lyrics over music and rhythm, which partially explains the enormous popularity of rap in France today.

The chanson tradition was revived from the 1930s by such singers as Edith Piaf and Charles Trenet. In the 1950s singers such as Georges Brassens, Léo Ferré, Claude Nougaro, Jacques Brel and Barbara became national stars. Today's popular music has come a long way since the *yéyé* (imitative rock) of the 1960s sung by Johnny Halliday – though you might not think so listening to middle-of-the-roaders Vanessa Paradis and Patrick Bruel. Watch out for rappers M C Solaar, Reg'lyss and I Am from Marseille. Evergreen balladeers/folk singers include Francis Cabrel, Julien Clerc, Jean-Jacques Goldman and Jacques Higelin, while the late Serge Gainsbourg remains enormously popular. Some people like the New Age space music of Jean-Michel Jarre; others say his name fits his sound.

France's claim to fame over the past decade has been *sono mondial* (world music) – from Algerian *raï* (Cheb Khaled, Zahouania) and Senegalese *mbalax* (Youssou N'Dour) to West Indian *zouk* (Kassav, Zouk Machine). La Mano Negra and Les Négresses Vertes are two bands that combine many of these elements – often with brilliant results.

Sculpture

By the 14th century, sculpture was increasingly commissioned for the tombs of the nobility. In Renaissance France, Pierre Bontemps decorated the beautiful tomb of François I at Saint Denis, and Jean Goujon created the Fontaine des Innocents in central Paris. The baroque style is exemplified by Guillaume Coustou's *Horses of Marly* at the entrance to the Champs-Élysées.

In the 19th century, memorial statues in public places came to replace sculpted tombs. One of the best artists in the new mode was François Rude, who sculpted the statue of Marshall Ney outside the Closerie des Lilas and the relief on the Arc de Triomphe. Another sculptor was

Jean-Baptiste Carpeaux who began as a romantic, but whose work such as *The Dance* on the Opéra Garnier and his fountain in the Luxembourg Gardens look back to the warmth and gaiety of the baroque era.

At the end of the 19th century, Auguste Rodin's work overcame the conflict of neoclassicism and romanticism. His sumptuous bronze and marble figures of men and women did much to revitalise sculpture as an expressive medium. One of Rodin's most gifted pupils was Camille Claudel, whose work can be seen along with that of Rodin in the Musée Rodin.

Braque and Picasso experimented with sculpture, and in the spirit of Dada, Marcel Duchamp exhibited 'found objects', such as a urinal, which he titled *Fountain* and signed.

One of the most influential sculptors to emerge after WW II was César Baldaccini. He began using iron and scrap metal to create his imaginary insects and animals but later graduated to pliable plastics.

Architecture

A religious revival in the 11th century led to the construction of a large number of *roman* (Romanesque) churches, so-called because their architects adopted many architectural elements (eg vaulting) from Gallo-Roman buildings still standing at the time. Châteaux built during this era tended to be massive, heavily fortified structures that afforded few luxuries to their inhabitants.

The Gothic style originated in the mid-12th century in northern France, whose great wealth enabled it to attract the finest architects, engineers and artisans. Gothic structures are characterised by ribbed vaults carved with great precision, pointed arches, slender verticals, chapels (often built by rich individuals or guilds) along the nave and chancel, refined decoration and large stained-glass windows. The first Gothic building was the basilica in Saint Denis, which initiated a new kind of structural support in which each arch counteracted and complemented the next. Cathedrals built in the early Gothic style were majestic but lacked the lightness and airiness of later works.

In the 14th century, the Rayonnant (Radiant) Gothic style – named after the radiating tracery of the rose windows – developed, with interiors becoming even lighter thanks to broader windows and more translucent stained glass.

The Renaissance, which began in Italy in the early 1400s, set out to realise a 'rebirth' of classical Greek and Roman culture. The French Renaissance introduced a variety of classical components and decorative motifs which were blended with the rich decoration of Flamboyant Gothic.

Mannerism began around 1530, when François I hired Italian architects and artists – many of them disciples of Michelangelo or Raphael – to design and decorate his new château at Fontainebleau. Over the following decades, French architects who had studied in Italy took over from their Italian colleagues. In 1546 Pierre Lescot designed the richly decorated south-western corner of the Louvre's Cour Carrée.

During the baroque period, which lasted from the end of the 1500s to the late 1700s, painting, sculpture and classical architecture were integrated to create structures and interiors of great subtlety, refinement and elegance.

Salomon de Brosse, who designed Paris' Palais du Luxembourg, set the stage for François Mansart, designer of the classical wing of the Château de Blois, and his younger rival, Louis Le Vau, the first architect of Versailles. Jules Hardouin-Mansart, Le Vau's successor at Versailles, also designed the Église du Dôme at the Invalides in Paris, considered the finest church built in France during the 17th century.

Rococo, a derivation of baroque, was popular during the Enlightenment (1700-80). This style was confined almost exclusively to the interiors of private residences and had a minimal impact on churches, châteaux and façades.

Neoclassical architecture, which emerged in about 1780 and remained popular until the mid-19th century, was a search for order, reason and serenity through the adoption of the forms and conventions of Graeco-Roman antiquity: columns, simple geometric forms and traditional ornamentation.

France's greatest 18th-century neoclassical architect was Jacques-Germain Soufflot, who designed the Panthéon. Napoleon used neoclassicism extensively for monumental architecture. Well-known Paris sights designed (though not necessarily executed) during the First Empire (1804-14) include the Arc de Triomphe, La Madeleine, the façade of the Palais Bourbon, the Arc du Carrousel at the Louvre, and the Bourse.

Art Nouveau developed in the 1890s and is characterised by sinuous curves and flowing, asymmetrical forms reminiscent of tendrilous vines, water lilies, the patterns on insect wings and the flowering boughs of trees.

Paris is still graced by Hector Guimard's Art Nouveau metro entrances. There are some fine Art Nouveau interiors in the Musée d'Orsay, an Art Nouveau glass roof

BETHUNE CARMICHAEL

Art Nouveau interiors in the Musée d'Orsay

over the Grand Palais and, on Rue Pavée in the Marais, a synagogue designed by Guimard.

France's most celebrated architect this century, Le Corbusier, was born in Switzerland but settled in Paris in 1917 at the age of 30. A radical modernist, he tried to adapt buildings to their functions in industrialised society without ignoring the human element.

France's leaders have long sought to immortalise themselves by erecting huge public edifices – known as grands projets – in Paris. In recent years, the late president Georges Pompidou commissioned the once-reviled but now much-loved Centre Beaubourg in 1977 (better known as the Centre Pompidou) and his successor, Giscard d'Estaing, was instrumental in transforming a derelict train station into the glorious Musée d'Orsay, which opened in 1986.

But François Mitterrand surpassed them both with his monumental commissions. Since the early 1980s, Paris has seen the construction of such projects as I M Pei's glass pyramid at the Louvre, an architectural cause célèbre in the late 1980s; the city's new opera house, Opéra Bastille; the Grande Arche in the skyscraper district of La Défense; the huge science museum and park at La Villette; Parc André Citroën in the western corner of the 15e arrondissement; the new Finance Ministry offices in Bercy; and the controversy-plagued new home of the Bibliothèque Nationale (the national library).

Literature

The great landmarks of French Renaissance literature are the works of Rabelais, La Pléiade and Montaigne. François Rabelais' exuberant narrative blends coarse humour with encyclopedic erudition in a vast fresco that seems to include every kind of person, occupation and jargon to be found in mid-16th-century France.

During the 17th century, known as *le grand siècle*, François de Malherbe brought a new rigour to the treatment of rhythm. Transported by the perfection of Malherbe's verses, Jean de La Fontaine recognised his vocation and went on to write his charming *Fables* in the manner of Aesop. The mood of classical tragedy permeates *La Princesse de Clèves* by Marie de La Fayette, which is widely regarded as the first major French novel.

The literature of the 18th century is dominated by philosophers, among them Voltaire and Jean-Jacques Rousseau. Voltaire's political writings, in which it is argued that society is fundamentally opposed to nature, were to have a profound and lasting influence. Rousseau's sensitivity to landscape and its moods anticipates romanticism, and the insistence on his own singularity in *Les Confessions* makes it the first modern autobiography.

The 19th century brought Victor Hugo, widely acclaimed for his poetry as well as for his novels *Les Misérables* and *Notre-Dame de Paris*. Hugo is the key figure of French romanticism.

Other 19th-century novelists include Stendhal, Honoré de Balzac, Aurore Dupain, better known as George Sand, and of course Alexandre Dumas the elder, who wrote *Le Comte de Monte-Cristo*, *Les Trois Mousquetaires* and other swashbuckling adventures.

In 1857 two landmarks of French literature appeared: *Madame Bovary* by Gustave Flaubert and *Les Fleurs du*

Mal by Charles Baudelaire. Both writers were tried for the supposed immorality of their works. Flaubert won his case, and his novel was distributed without cuts. Baudelaire was obliged to cut several poems from *Les Fleurs du Mal*, and he died in poverty, practically unknown.

Émile Zola's aim was to convert novel writing from an art to a science by the application of experimentation. His theory may seem naive, but his work influenced all the significant French writers of the late 19th century and is reflected in much 20th-century fiction as well.

Paul Verlaine and Stéphane Mallarmé created the symbolist movement, which strove to express states of mind rather than simply detail daily reality. Arthur Rimbaud, apart from crowding an extraordinary amount of rugged, exotic travel into his 37 years and having a tempestuous homosexual relationship with Verlaine, produced two enduring pieces of work: *Illuminations* and *Une Saison en Enfer* (A Season in Hell).

Marcel Proust dominated the early 20th century with his giant seven-volume novel, *À la Recherche du Temps Perdu* (Remembrance of Things Past); it is largely auto-biographical and explores in evocative detail the true meaning of past experience recovered from the unconscious by 'involuntary memory'. André Gide found his voice in the celebration of homosexual sensuality and, later, left-wing politics. *Les Faux-Monnayeurs* (The Counterfeiters) exposes the hypocrisy and self-deception with which people try to avoid sincerity – a common theme with Gide.

André Breton ruled the surrealist group and wrote its three manifestoes, although the first use of the word 'surrealist' is attributed to the writer Guillaume Apollinaire, a fellow traveller. As a poet, Breton was overshadowed by Paul Éluard and Louis Aragon, both of whom later joined the Communist Party.

Colette enjoyed tweaking the nose of conventionally moral readers with titillating novels that detailed the amorous exploits of such heroines as the schoolgirl Claudine.

After WW II, existentialism, a significant literary movement, developed around Jean-Paul Sartre, Simone de Beauvoir and Albert Camus, who worked and conversed in the cafés of Saint Germain des Prés. All three stressed the importance of the writer's political engagement. De Beauvoir, author of the ground-breaking study *The Second Sex*, had a profound influence on feminist thinking.

In the late 1950s, some younger novelists began to look for new ways of organising the narrative. The so-called new novel *(nouveau roman)* refers to the works of

Nathalie Sarraute, Alain Robbe-Grillet, Boris Vian, Julien Gracq and Michel Butor, among others. However, these writers never formed a close-knit group, and their experiments have taken them in divergent directions. Today the nouveau roman is very much out of favour in France.

In 1980 Marguerite Yourcenar, best known for memorable historical novels such as *Mémoires d'Hadrien*, became the first woman to be elected to the French Academy.

Marguerite Duras came to the notice of a larger public when she won the prestigious Prix Goncourt for her novel *L'Amant* (The Lover) in 1984. She was also noted for the screenplays of *India Song* and *Hiroshima Mon Amour*, described by one critic as part nouveau roman, part Mills & Boon.

Philippe Sollers was one of the editors of *Tel Quel*, a highbrow, then left-wing review which was very influential in the 1960s and early 1970s. His 1960s novels were forbiddingly experimental, but with *Femmes* (Women) he returned to a conventional narrative style.

Another of the editors of *Tel Quel* was Julia Kristeva, best known for her theoretical writings on literature and psychoanalysis. Recently she has turned her hand to fiction, and *Les Samurai*, a fictionalised account of the heady days of *Tel Quel*, is an interesting document on the life of the Paris intelligentsia. Roland Barthes and Michel Foucault are other authors and philosophers associated with this period.

More accessible authors who enjoy a wide following include Françoise Sagan, Patrick Modiano, Yann Queffélec, Pascal Quignard and Denis Tillinac. The *roman policier* (detective novel) has always been a great favourite with the French and among its greatest exponents has been the Belgian-born Georges Simenon and his novels featuring Inspector Maigret.

Cinema

France's place in the film history books was firmly noted when the Lumière brothers organised the world's first paying (1FF) public movie screening – a series of two-minute reels – in Paris' Grand Café on the Blvd des Capucines on 28 December 1895.

In the 1920s and 1930s avant-garde directors such as René Clair, Marcel Carné and the intensely productive Jean Renoir, son of the famous artist, searched for new forms and subjects.

In the late 1950s a large group of new-generation directors burst onto the scene with a new genre, the *nouvelle vague* (new wave).

JAMES LYON

A hallmark of Paris, the *colonne maurice*

This group included Jean-Luc Godard, François Truffaut, Claude Chabrol, Eric Rohmer, Jacques Rivette, Louis Malle and Alain Resnais. This disparate group of directors believed in the primacy of the film-maker, giving rise to the term *film d'auteur*.

A ream of films followed, among them Alain Resnais' *Hiroshima Mon Amour* and *L'Année Dernière à Marienbad* (Last Year in Marienbad). François Truffaut's *Les Quatre Cents Coups* (The 400 Blows) was partly based on his own rebellious adolescence. Jean-Luc Godard made such films as *À Bout de Souffle* (Breathless), *Alphaville* and *Pierrot le Fou* (1965), which showed even less concern for sequence and narrative. The new wave continued until the 1970s, by which stage it had lost its experimental edge.

Of the non-new wave directors of the 1950s and 1960s, one of the most notable was Jacques Tati, who made many comic films based around the charming, bumbling figure of Monsieur Hulot and his struggles to adapt to the modern age.

The most successful directors of the 1980s and 1990s include Jean-Jacques Beineix, who made *Diva*, and *Betty Blue*, and Luc Besson who made *Subway* and *The Big Blue*.

In 1986 Claude Berri came up with *Jean de Florette* followed by *Manon des Sources*, modern versions of writer/film-maker Marcel Pagnol's original works, which proved enormously popular both in France and abroad. Léos Carax in his *Boy Meets Girl* creates a kind of Parisian purgatory of souls lost in the eternal night.

Light social comedies like *Trois Hommes et un Couffin* (Three Men & a Cradle) and *Romuald et Juliette* by Coline Serreau and *La Vie est un Long Fleuve Tranquille* (Life is a Long Quiet River) by Étienne Chatiliez have been among the biggest hits in France in recent years.

Other well-regarded directors today include Bertrand Blier *(Trop Belle pour Toi)*, Bertrand Tavernier *(L 627)* and Jean-Marie Poiré *(Les Visiteurs)*. Matthieu Kassovitz's award-winning *La Haine* examines the prejudice and violence of the world of the 'Beurs' – young, French-born Algerians.

Theatre

Molière, an actor, became the most popular comic playwright of *le grand siècle*. Plays such as *Tartuffe* are staples of the classical repertoire. The tragic playwrights Pierre Corneille and Jean Racine, by contrast, drew their subjects from history and classical mythology. For instance, Racine's *Phèdre*, taken from Euripides, is a story of incest and suicide among the descendants of the Greek gods.

Painting

Voltaire wrote that French painting began with Nicolas Poussin (1594-1665), a baroque painter who frequently set scenes from classical mythology and the Bible in ordered landscapes bathed in golden light.

In the 18th century, Jean-Baptiste Chardin brought the humbler domesticity of the Dutch masters to French art. In 1785 the public reacted with enthusiasm to two large paintings with clear republican messages, *The Oath of the Horatii* and *Brutus Condemning His Son* by Jacques Louis David. David became one of the leaders of the Revolution, and a virtual dictator in matters of art, where he advocated a precise, severe classicism. He was made official state painter by Napoleon. He is perhaps best remembered for the famous painting of Marat lying dead in his bath.

Jean Auguste Dominique Ingres, David's most gifted pupil, continued in the neoclassical tradition. The historical pictures to which he devoted most of his life are now generally regarded as inferior to his portraits.

The gripping *Raft of the Medusa* by Théodore Géricault is on the threshold of romanticism; if Géricault had not died young, he would probably have become a leader of the movement, along with his friend Eugène Delacroix. Delacroix's most famous picture, perhaps, is *La Liberté Conduisant le Peuple* (Freedom Leading the People), which commemorates the July Revolution of 1830.

The members of the Barbizon School effected a parallel transformation of landscape painting. The school derived its name from the village of Barbizon near the forest of Fontainebleau, where Camille Corot and Jean-François Millet, amongst others, gathered to paint in the open air. Corot is best known for his landscapes, while Millet took many of his subjects from peasant life and had a strong influence on van Gogh.

Millet anticipated the realist programme of Gustave Courbet, a prominent member of the Paris Commune, whose paintings show the misery of manual labour and the cramped lives of the working class.

Édouard Manet used realism to depict the life of the Parisian middle classes, yet he included in his pictures numerous references to the old masters. His *Déjeuner sur l'Herbe* and *Olympia* were considered scandalous, largely because they broke with the traditional treatment of their subject matter.

Impressionism, initially a term of derision, was taken from the title of an 1874 experimental painting by Claude Monet, *Impression: Soleil Levant* (Impression: Sunrise). Monet was the leading figure of the school, which counted among its members Alfred Sisley, Camille Pisarro, Berthe Morisot and Pierre-Auguste Renoir. The Impressionists' main aim was to capture fleeting light effects, and light came to dominate the content of their painting.

Edgar Degas was a fellow traveller, but he preferred his studio to open-air painting. He found his favourite subjects at the racecourse and the ballet. Henri de Toulouse-Lautrec was a great admirer of Degas and chose similar subjects: people in the bars, brothels and music halls of Montmartre. He is best known for his posters and lithographs in which the distortion of the figures is both caricatural and decorative.

Paul Cézanne is celebrated for his still lifes and landscapes depicting the south of France, while the name of Paul Gauguin immediately conjures up his studies of Tahitian women. Both he and Cézanne are usually referred to as Post-Impressionists, something of a catchall term for the diverse styles which flowed from Impressionism.

In the late 19th century, Gauguin worked for a time in Arles with the Dutch artist Vincent van Gogh, who spent most of his painting life in France. A brilliant, innovative artist, van Gogh produced haunting self-portraits and landscapes in which colour assumes an expressive and emotive quality. His later technique paralleled pointillism, developed by Georges Seurat. Seurat applied paint in small dots or uniform brush strokes of unmixed colour, producing fine mosaics of warm and cool tones.

Henri Rousseau was a contemporary of the Post-Impressionists but his 'naive' art was totally unaffected by them. His dreamlike pictures of the Paris suburbs, jungle and desert scenes have had a lasting influence on 20th-century art.

Gustave Moreau was a member of the symbolist school. His eerie treatment of mythological subjects can be seen in his old studio (now the Musée Moreau) in Paris.

Fauvism took its name from the slur of a critic who compared the exhibitors at the 1906 autumn salon with *fauves* (wild beasts) because of their radical use of intensely bright colours. Among these 'wild' painters were Henri Matisse, André Derain and Maurice de Vlaminck.

Cubism was effectively launched in 1907 by the Spanish prodigy Pablo Picasso with his *Les Demoiselles d'Avignon*. Cubism, as developed by Picasso, Georges Braque and Juan Gris, deconstructed the subject into a system of intersecting planes and presented various aspects simultaneously.

After WW I, the School of Paris was formed by a group of expressionists, mostly foreign-born, like Amedeo Modigliani from Italy and the Russian Marc Chagall. Chagall's pictures combine fantasy and folklore.

Dada, a literary and artistic movement of revolt, started in Germany and Switzerland during WW I. In France, one of the principal Dadaists was Marcel Duchamp, whose *Mona Lisa* adorned with moustache and goatee epitomises the spirit of the movement.

Surrealism, an offshoot of Dada, flourished between the wars. Drawing on the theories of Freud, it attempted to reunite the conscious and unconscious realms, to permeate everyday life with fantasies and dreams.

WW II ended Paris' role as the world's artistic capital. Many artists left France, and though some returned after the war, the city never regained its old magnetism.

SOCIETY & CONDUCT

Interacting with the French

Some visitors to France conclude that it would be a lovely country if it weren't for the French. As in other countries, however, the more tourists a particular town or area attracts, the less patience the locals tend to have for them.

Avoiding Offence

By following a number of simple guidelines, you can usually avoid offending anyone.

A few don'ts:

- When buying fruit and vegetables anywhere except at supermarkets, do not touch the produce unless invited to do so. Show the shopkeeper what you want and he or she will choose the vegetables or fruit for you.
- In a restaurant, do not summon the waiter by shouting *'garçon'*, which means 'boy'. Saying *'s'il vous plaît'* (please) is the way it's done nowadays.
- When you're being served cheese (eg as the final course for dinner), remember two cardinal rules: never cut off the tip of the pie-shaped soft cheeses (eg Brie, Camembert) and cut cheeses whose middle is the best part (eg blue cheese) in such a way as to take your fair share of the crust.
- Money, particularly income, is a subject that is simply not discussed in France.
- In general, a French lawn is meant to be looked at and praised for its greenness, not sat upon. Watch out for *'pelouse interdite'* (Keep off the Grass!) signs.

A few dos:

- The easiest way to improve the quality of your relations with the French is always to say *'Bonjour, monsieur/madame/mademoiselle'* when you walk into a shop, and *'Merci, monsieur...au revoir'* when you leave. 'Monsieur' means 'sir' and can be used with any male person who isn't a child. 'Madame' is used where 'Mrs' would apply in English, whereas 'mademoiselle' is used when talking to unmarried women. When in doubt, use 'madame'.
- It is customary for people who know each other to exchange kisses *(bises)* as a greeting, though rarely men with men except in the south or if they are related. The

usual ritual is one glancing peck on each cheek, but depending on the region (and the personalities involved), some people go for three or even four kisses. People who don't kiss each other will almost always shake hands.
- If invited to someone's home or a party, always bring some sort of gift, such as good wine (not some 10FF *vin de table*). Flowers are another good standby, but chrysanthemums are only brought to cemeteries.
- Many French people seem to feel that going Dutch (ie splitting the bill) at restaurants is an uncivilised custom. In general, the person who did the inviting pays for dinner, though close friends and colleagues will sometimes share the cost.

RELIGION

Church and state were legally separated in France in 1905.

Catholics

Some 80% of French people say they are Catholic but, although most have been baptised, very few ever attend church. *'Conversion'*, such as that experienced by the poet Paul Claudel (1868-1955) and the novelist Henry de Montherlant (1896-1972), thus actually means 're-conversion' in English. The French Catholic Church is generally very progressive and ecumenically minded.

Protestants

France's Protestants (Huguenots), who were severely persecuted during much of the 16th and 17th centuries, now number about one million. They are concentrated in Alsace, the Jura, the south-eastern part of the Massif Central and along the Atlantic coast.

John Calvin (1509-64), born in Noyon in the far north of France, was educated in Paris, Orléans and Bourges but spent much of his life in Geneva.

Muslims

Islam has at least three million adherents in France, and they now make up the country's second-largest religious group. The vast majority are immigrants or their off-spring who came from North Africa during the 1950s and 1960s.

In recent years, France's Muslim community has been the object of racist agitation by right-wing parties and extremist groups. Many North Africans complain of discrimination by the police and employers. An ongoing controversy in France involves whether or not orthodox

Muslim girls should be allowed to wear their *foulards* (veils) and other such 'ostentatious' apparel to class.

Jews

There has been a Jewish community in France for most of the time since the Roman period. During the Middle Ages, the community suffered persecution and there were a number of mass expulsions. French Jews, the first in Europe to achieve emancipation, were granted full citizenship in 1790-91. Since 1808, the French Jewish community has had an umbrella organisation known as the Consistoire, whose Paris headquarters is at 17 Rue Saint Georges (9e; metro Notre Dame de Lorette).

The country's Jewish community, which now numbers some 700,000, grew substantially during the 1960s as a result of immigration from Algeria, Tunisia and Morocco.

LANGUAGE

Around 122 million people worldwide speak French as their first language; it is an official language in Belgium, Switzerland, Luxembourg, the Canadian province of Québec and over two dozen other countries, most of them former French colonies in Africa. It is also spoken in the Val d'Aosta region of north-western Italy. Various forms of Creole are used in Haiti, French Guiana and parts of Louisiana. France has a special government ministry (Ministère de la Francophonie) to deal with the country's relations with the French-speaking world.

French was *the* international language of culture and diplomacy until WW I, and the French are somewhat sensitive to this fact. Your best bet is always to approach people politely in French, even if the only words you know are *'Pardon, parlez-vous anglais?'* ('Excuse me, do you speak English?').

For more useful words and phrases than we have space for here, see Lonely Planet's *Western Europe phrasebook*.

Grammar

An important distinction is made in French between *tu* and *vous*, which both mean 'you'. *Tu* is only used when addressing children or people you know well. When addressing someone who is not a personal friend, *vous* should be used unless the person invites you to use *tu*. In this case they will say *'Tu peux me tutoyer'*. In general, younger people are less insistent on this formality, and they will usually use *tu* from the beginning of an acquaintance. In this book, however, we have used the more polite *vous* form.

All nouns in French are either masculine or feminine and adjectives must reflect the gender of the noun they modify. The feminine form of many nouns and adjectives is indicated by an *e* added to the masculine form – a male student is *un étudiant*, a female student is *une étudiante*. The gender of a noun is often indicated by a preceding article: 'the' is *le* (m) and *la* (f); 'a' is *un* (m) and *une* (f); 'some' is *du* (m) and *de la* (f). In this book, where both masculine and feminine forms of a word are given, the masculine appears first, separated from the feminine by a slash.

Pronunciation

French has a number of sounds that may be unfamiliar to Anglophones:

- The distinction between the 'u' sound (as in *tu*) and the 'oo' sound (as in *tout*). For both sounds, the lips are rounded and pushed forward, but to achieve the 'u' sound, try to say 'ee' while keeping the lips rounded and forward.
- The nasal vowels. In producing nasal vowels, the breath escapes partly through the nose and partly through the mouth. There are no nasal vowels in English. In French there are three: *bon vin blanc* ('good white wine'). These sounds mostly occur where a syllable ends in a single 'n' or 'm'; the 'n' or 'm' is silent but indicates the nasalisation of the preceding vowel.

SIMON BRACKEN

'Allez! Dépêchez-vous!' A school excursion in progress

SIMON BRACKEN

Tourists at the Trocadero

- The standard 'r' of Parisian French is produced by moving the bulk of the tongue backwards to constrict the airflow in the pharynx while the tip of the tongue rests behind the lower front teeth. It is similar to the noise made by some people before spitting, but with much less friction.
- The French 'j', as in the word *jour* ('day'), is pronounced as the 's' in 'leisure'.

Greetings & Civilities

Hello/Good morning.	*Bonjour.*
Good evening.	*Bonsoir.*
Goodbye.	*Au revoir.*
Yes.	*Oui.*
No.	*Non.*
Maybe.	*Peut-être.*
Please.	*S'il vous plaît.*
Thank you.	*Merci.*
You're welcome.	*Je vous en prie.*
Excuse me.	*Excusez-moi.*
Sorry (Excuse me/ Forgive me).	*Pardon.*
Just a moment.	*Attendez un moment.*

Language Difficulties

Do you speak English?
  Parlez-vous anglais?
I understand.
  Je comprends.

I don't understand.
Je ne comprends pas.
Could you please write that down?
Est-ce-que vous pouvez l'écrire?
How do you say...in French?
Comment dit-on...en français?

Small Talk

What is your name?
Comment vous appelez-vous?
My name is...
Je m'appelle...
Pleased to meet you.
Enchanté/ée.
How are you?
Comment allez-vous? (formal)
(Comment) ça va? (informal)
Well, thanks.
Bien, merci.
What country are you from?
De quel pays venez-vous?
I'm from...
Je viens d'/du/des...
How old are you?
Quel âge avez-vous?
I'm...years old.
J'ai...ans.
Do you like...?
Aimez-vous...?
I like...very much.
J'aime beaucoup...
I don't like...
Je n'aime pas...

Getting Around

I want to go to...
Je voudrais aller à...
I would like to book a seat to...
Je voudrais réserver une place pour...
Where is the (bus/tram) stop?
Où est l'arrêt (d'autobus/de tramway)?
What time does the next train (leave/arrive)?
À quelle heure (part/arrive) le prochain train?

aeroplane	*l'avion*
boat	*le bateau*
bus (city)	*le bus*
bus (intercity)	*le car*

| ferry | *le ferry* |
| tram | *le tramway* |

I'd like a (one-way/return) ticket.
Je voudrais un billet (aller simple/aller-retour).
How long does the trip take?
Combien de temps durera le trajet?
Do I need to change trains/platform?
Est-ce que je dois changer de train/quai?

1st class	*première classe*
2nd class	*deuxième classe*
left-luggage office	*consigne manuelle*
platform	*le quai*
ticket	*le billet*
ticket window	*le guichet*
timetable	*l'horaire*

I'd like to hire a bicycle/car.
Je voudrais louer un vélo/ une voiture.

Directions

How do I get to...?
Comment faire pour arriver à...?
Is it far from/near here?
C'est près/loin d'ici?
I want to go to...
Je veux aller à...
I'm looking for...
Je cherche...
Can you show it to me (on the map)?
Est-ce que vous pouvez me le montrer (sur la carte)?
Go straight ahead.
Continuez tout droit.
Turn left.
Tournez à gauche.
Turn right.
Tournez à droite.

at the traffic lights	*aux feux*
at the next corner	*au prochain carrefour*
behind	*derrière*
in front of	*devant*
opposite	*en face de*
north/south	*nord/sud*
east/west	*est/ouest*

Signs

CAMPING	CAMPING GROUND
ENTRÉE	ENTRANCE
SORTIE	EXIT
COMPLET	FULL/NO VACANCIES
RENSEIGNEMENTS	INFORMATION
OUVERT	OPEN
FERMÉ	CLOSED
POLICE	POLICE
INTERDIT	PROHIBITED
CHAMBRES LIBRES	ROOMS AVAILABLE
TOILETTES/WC	TOILETS
EN PANNE	OUT OF ORDER
HORS SERVICE	NOT IN SERVICE

Around Town

I'm looking for...	*Je cherche...*
a bank	*une banque*
an exchange office	*un bureau de change*
the city centre	*le centre-ville*
the...embassy	*l'ambassade de...*
my hotel	*mon hôtel*
the market	*le marché*
the police	*la police*
the post office	*le bureau de poste/la poste*
the public toilet	*les toilettes*
the railway station	*la gare*
a public telephone	*une cabine téléphonique*
the tourist information office	*l'office de tourisme/ le syndicat d'initiative*
bridge	*le pont*
castle/vineyard	*le château*
cathedral	*la cathédrale*
church	*l'église*
island	*l'île*
lake	*le lac*
the main square	*la place centrale*
the old city	*la vieille ville*
palace	*le palais*
quay/bank	*le quai/la rive*
square	*la place*
tower	*la tour*

I'd like to make a telephone call.
Je voudrais utiliser le téléphone.
I'd like to change some money/travellers' cheques
Je voudrais changer de l'argent/des chèques de voyage.

JAMES LYON

Les gendarmes will help you find your way.

Accommodation

I'm looking for...   *Je cherche...*
    a youth hostel   *une auberge de jeunesse*
    a camping ground   *un camping*
    a hotel   *un hôtel*

Do you have any rooms available?
    Est-ce que vous avez des chambres libres?

I'd like...   *Je voudrais...*
    a single room   *une chambre simple*
    a double room   *une chambre double*
    a room with shower   *une chambre avec douche*
        and toilet   *et WC ('vai-say')*

to stay in a dormitory   *coucher dans un dortoir*
a bed   *un lit*

How much is it per night per person?
    Quel est le prix par nuit par personne?
Is breakfast included?
    Est-ce que le petit déjeuner est compris?
Can I see the room?
    Je peux voir la chambre?
Where is the bathroom/shower?
    Où est la salle de bain/la douche?
I'm going to stay for one day/one week.
    Je resterai un jour/une semaine.

Paperwork

Surname   *Nom de famille*
Given name   *Prénom*
Date of birth   *Date de naissance*
Place of birth   *Lieu de naissance*
Nationality   *Nationalité*
Sex   *Sexe*
Passport   *Passeport*

Food

breakfast   *le petit déjeuner*
lunch   *le déjeuner*
dinner   *le dîner*

I'd like the set lunch.
    Je prends le menu.
I'm a vegetarian.
    Je suis végétarien/végétarienne.

Shopping

How much is it?
    C'est combien?
It's too expensive for me.
    C'est trop cher pour moi.
Can I look at it?
    Est-ce que je peux le/la voir?
Can I pay by credit card?
    Est-ce que je peux payer avec ma carte de crédit?
Do you take travellers' cheques?
    Est-ce que vous prenez des chèques de voyage?
Do you have another colour/size?
    Est-ce que vous avez d'autres couleurs/tailles?

Health

I'm...	*Je suis...*
diabetic	*diabétique*
epileptic	*épileptique*
asthmatic	*asthmatique*
anaemic	*anémique*

I'm allergic...	*Je suis allergique...*
to antibiotics	*aux antibiotiques*
to penicillin	*à la pénicilline*
to bees	*aux abeilles*

antiseptic	*antiseptique*
aspirin	*aspirine*
condoms	*préservatifs*
contraceptive	*le contraceptif*
medicine	*le médicament*
sunblock cream	*la crème solaire*
tampons	*tampons hygiéniques*

Time & Dates

What time is it?	*Quelle heure est-il?*

today	*aujourd'hui*
tonight	*ce soir*
tomorrow	*demain*
day after tomorrow	*après-demain*
yesterday	*hier*
every day	*tous les jours*
in the morning	*le matin*
in the afternoon	*l'après-midi*
in the evening	*le soir*

Monday	*lundi*
Tuesday	*mardi*
Wednesday	*mercredi*
Thursday	*jeudi*
Friday	*vendredi*
Saturday	*samedi*
Sunday	*dimanche*

Numbers

0	*zéro*
1	*un*
2	*deux*
3	*trois*
4	*quatre*

5	*cinq*
6	*six*
7	*sept*
8	*huit*
9	*neuf*
10	*dix*
11	*onze*
12	*douze*
13	*treize*
14	*quatorze*
15	*quinze*
16	*seize*
17	*dix-sept*
18	*dix-huit*
19	*dix-neuf*
20	*vingt*
21	*vingt-et-un*
22	*vingt-deux*
30	*trente*
40	*quarante*
50	*cinquante*
60	*soixante*
70	*soixante-dix*
80	*quatre-vingt*
90	*quatre-vingt-dix*
100	*cent*
1000	*mille*
one million	*un million*

Emergencies

Help!	*Au secours!*
Call a doctor!	*Appelez un médecin!*
Call the police!	*Appelez la police!*
Go away!	*Laissez-moi tranquille!*
Leave me alone!	*Fichez-moi la paix!*

Facts for the Visitor

WHEN TO GO

Paris is at its best in spring, though winter-like relapses are not unknown. Autumn is also pleasant, but the days are fairly short. In winter Paris has all sorts of cultural events going on, while in July and August the weather is warm and even hot. True Parisians leave the city in August for their annual vacation; as a result many places will be closed, although visitors will be as thick on the ground as ever. If you understand French you can find out the national weather forecast by calling ☎ 36 68 01 01.

ORIENTATION

The location of every museum, hotel, restaurant etc mentioned in this book is referenced to one of the colour maps, named M1 to M16.

Arrondissements

For more than a century Paris has been divided into 20 arrondissements (districts) that spiral out from the city centre clockwise like a conch shell. Paris addresses *always* include the arrondissement number.

In this book, arrondissement numbers follow the usual French notation: *1er* for *premier* (1st), *4e* for *quatrième* (4th), and so forth.

MAPS

The most useful map of Paris is the 1:10,000-scale *Paris Plan* published by Michelin. It comes in booklet form, large format and sheet form; the last two are particularly useful if you're driving.

Many Parisians swear by the hand-drawn, pocket-sized map books called *Paris par Arrondissement*, which have a double-page street plan of each arrondissement.

TOURIST OFFICES

Paris' main tourist office (M6; ☎ 01 49 52 53 54; fax 01 49 52 53 00; metro George V) is at 127 Ave des Champs-Élysées (8e). It's open every day of the year, except on 1 May, from 9 am to 8 pm although it may shut earlier on Sundays in winter.

There are tourist office annexes in all of Paris' train stations except the Gare Saint Lazare. They are open daily, except Sunday and holidays, from 8 am to 9 pm (8 pm from November to April); at Gare d'Austerlitz, closing time is 3 pm (1 pm on Saturday). The tourist office annexe at the base of the Eiffel Tower is open from 2 May to September daily (including holidays) from 11 am to 6 pm.

DOCUMENTS

By law, everyone in France, including tourists, must carry some sort of ID on them at all times. For foreign visitors, this means a passport or, for EU citizens, a national ID card or British Visitor's Passport.

Visas

There are no entry requirements or restrictions on nationals of the EU, and citizens of the USA, Canada, New Zealand and Israel do not need visas to visit France as tourists for up to three months. Except for people from a handful of other European countries, everyone else must have a visa.

Among those who need visas are Australians, for whom it costs an expensive A\$16.20 for a short five-day stay and an astronomical A\$54 for longer stays of up to two months.

If all the forms are in order, your visa will be issued on the spot. You can also apply for a French visa after arriving in Europe – the fee is the same, but you may not have to produce a return ticket. If you enter France overland, your visa may not be checked at the border, but major problems can arise if you don't have one later on (eg at the airport as you leave the country).

Long-Stay If you'd like to work or study in Paris or stay for over three months, apply to the French consulate nearest where you live for the appropriate sort of *long séjour* (long-stay) visa. Unless you live in the EU, it is extremely difficult to get a visa that will allow you to work in France. For any sort of long-stay visa, begin the paperwork in your home country several months before you plan to leave (applications cannot usually be made in a third country).

If you are issued a long-stay visa valid for six or more months, you'll probably have to apply for a *carte de séjour* (residence permit) within eight days of arrival in France. In Paris, students must apply to the office at 13 Rue Miollis (15e; metro Cambronne), open weekdays from 9 am to 4 pm. Most other people should apply to the Centre de Réception des Étrangers responsible for the arrondissement where they live. Details are available from the Préfecture de Police (M14; ☎ 01 53 71 51 68; metro Cité) at 1 Rue de Lutèce (4e).

Student If you'd like to study in France, you must apply for a student visa in your country of residence; tourist visas cannot be turned into student visas after you arrive in France. People with student visas can apply for permission to work part-time (enquire at your place of study).

Au Pair For details on au pair visas, which must be arranged *before* you leave home (unless you're an EU resident), see Au Pair under Work later in this chapter.

Visa Extensions

Tourist visas *cannot* be extended except in emergencies (eg medical problems). You might try going to the visa office on the ground floor of Escalier (stairway) E in the Préfecture de Police.

If you don't need a visa to visit France, you'll almost certainly qualify for another automatic three-month stay if you take the train to Geneva or Brussels and then re-enter French territory. The fewer recent French entry stamps you have in your passport the easier this is likely to be. If you needed a visa the first time around, one way to extend your stay is to go to a French consulate in a neighbouring country and apply for another one there.

Photocopies

All important documents should be photocopied before you leave home. Leave one copy at home and keep another one with you, separate from the originals.

Travel Insurance

If you require a visa to enter France you will need to provide evidence that you have travel insurance to the consulate at which you apply.

TONY WHEELER

Street of Bad Boys

TONY WHEELER

The Meeting Place of Nosey Women

TONY WHEELER

Street of Schools

Driving Licence & Permits

It's a good idea to bring along an International Driving Permit (IDP), especially when hiring cars and motorbikes. It is not valid unless accompanied by your original driver's licence. An IDP can be obtained for a small fee from your local automobile association – bring along a passport photo and a valid licence.

Hostelling International Card

A Hostelling International card is necessary only at official *auberges de jeunesse* (youth hostels), although it may get you small discounts at other hostels. If you don't pick one up before leaving home, you can buy one for about 100FF at almost any French auberge de jeunesse.

Student & Youth Cards

An International Student Identity Card (ISIC) can pay for itself through half-price admissions, discounted air and ferry tickets, and cheap meals in some student cafeterias. Many places stipulate a maximum age, usually 24 or 25. Accueil des Jeunes en France (AJF) and other student travel agencies issue ISIC cards for 60FF.

If you're under 26 but not a student, you can apply for a GO 25 Card, issued by the Federation of International Youth Travel Organisations (FIYTO) for about US$16 or 50FF. It entitles you to much the same discounts as an ISIC, and is also issued by student unions or student travel agencies.

Teachers, professional artists, museum conservators and certain categories of students are admitted to some museums free. Bring along proof of affiliation, eg an International Teacher Identity Card (ITIC).

A Carte Jeunes (120FF for one year) is available to anyone under 26 who has been in the country for at least six months. It gets you discounts on things like air tickets, car rental, sports events, concerts and movies. You can pick one up at AJF and student travel agencies.

Carte Musées et Monuments

This card is valid for entry to around 60 venues in Paris such as the Louvre. The cost for 1/3/5 days is 70/140/200FF. There is no discount rate. The carte is available from the venues or tourist offices in Paris.

Seniors' Cards

Reduced entry prices are charged for people over 65 at most cultural centres, including museums, galleries and public theatres. SNCF has a Carte Vermeil for people over 65. It gives a 20% reduction on train tickets and costs 140FF for a card valid for purchasing four tickets or 270FF for a card valid for one year.

EMBASSIES

French Embassies Abroad

Don't expect France's diplomatic and consular representatives abroad to be helpful, though you do come across the odd exception. Addresses include the following (note that BP means 'post office box'):

Australia
    Embassy: 6 Perth Ave, Yarralumla, Canberra, ACT 2600 (☎ 06-216 0100; fax 06-216 0127)
    Consulates: Level 4, 492 St Kilda Rd, Melbourne, Vic 3004 (☎ 03-9820 0944, 03-9820 0921; fax 03-9820 9363)
    31 Market St, 20th floor, Sydney, NSW 2000 (☎ 02-9261 5779; fax 02-9283 1210)
Belgium
    Consulate: 14 Place de Louvain, 1000 Brussels (☎ 02-229 8500; fax 02-229 8510)
Canada
    Embassy: 42 Sussex Drive, Ottowa, Ont K1M 2C9 (☎ 613-789 1795; fax 613-789 0279)
    Consulate: 130 Bloor St West, Suite 400, Toronto, Ont M9S 1N5 (☎ 416-925 8041; fax 416-925 3076)
Germany
    Consulates: Kurfürstendamm 211, D-10719 Berlin (☎ 030-885 90243; fax 030-882 5295)
    Johannisstrasse 2, D-66111 Saarbrücken (☎ 0681-936 750; fax 0681-31028)
    Richard Wagner Strasse 53, D-70184 Stuttgart (☎ 0711-23 7470; fax 0711-236 0537)
Hong Kong
    Admiralty Centre, Tower Two, 26th floor, 18 Harcourt Rd, Admiralty (☎ 852-2529 4350; fax 852-2866 9693)
Ireland
    36 Ailesbury Rd, Ballsbridge, Dublin 4 (☎ 01-260 1666; fax 01-283 0178)
Israel
    Consulate: Migdalor Building, 1/3 Ben Yehuda St (11th floor), 61261 Tel Aviv (☎ 03-510 1415/6/7; fax 03-510 4370)
Italy
    Consulates: Via Giulia 251, 00186 Rome (☎ 06-6880 6437; fax 06-6860 1260)
    Via della Moscova 12, 20121 Milan (☎ 02-6559 141; fax 02-6559 1344)
Japan
    11-44 4-chome, Minami Azabu, Minato-ku, Tokyo 106 (☎ 03-5420 8800; fax 03-5420 8917)

Netherlands
 Consulate: Vijzelgracht 2, Postbus 20018, 1000 HA
 Amsterdam (☎ 020-624 8346; fax 020-626 0841)
New Zealand
 Robert Jones House, 1-3 Willeston St, Wellington (☎ 04-472 0200; fax 04-472 5887); postal address: PO Box 1695,
 Wellington
Singapore
 5 Gallop Rd, Singapore 1025 (☎ 65-466 4866; fax 65-469
 0907)
South Africa
 1009 Main Tower, Cape Town Center, Heerengracht, 8001
 Cape Town (☎ 021-21 2050; fax 021-26 1996)
 807 George Ave, Arcadia, 0083 Pretoria (☎ 012-43 5564; fax
 012-43 3481)
Spain
 Consulates: Calle Marques de la Enseada 10, 28004
 Madrid (☎ 91-319 7188; fax 91-308 6273)
 11 Paseo de Gracia, 08007 Barcelona (☎ 93-317 8150; fax
 93-412 4282)
Switzerland
 Schosshaldenstrasse 46, BP 3000, 3006 Berne (☎ 031-351
 2424/9; fax 031-352 0526)
 11 Rue Imbert Galloix, BP 1200, 1205 Geneva (☎ 022-311
 3441; fax 022-310 8339)
UK
 Embassy: 58 Knightsbridge, London SW1X 7JT (☎ 0171-201 1000)
 Consulate: 21 Cromwell Rd, London SW7 ZEN (☎ 0171-838 2000; fax 0171-838 2001). The visa section is at 6A
 Cromwell Place, London SW7 2EW (☎ 0171-838 2051).
 Dial ☎ 0891-887733 for general information on visa
 requirements.
USA
 Embassy: 4104 Reservoir Rd NW, Washington, DC 20007
 (☎ 202-944 6000; fax 202-944 6166/75)
 Consulates: 934 Fifth Ave, New York, NY 10021 (☎ 212-606 3688/9; fax 202-606 3620)
 540 Bush St, San Francisco, CA 94108 (☎ 415-397 4330; fax
 415-433 8357)
 Other consulates: Atlanta, Boston, Chicago, Honolulu,
 Houston, Los Angeles, Miami, New Orleans and San Juan
 (Puerto Rico).

Foreign Embassies in Paris

Australia
 4 Rue Jean Rey, 15e (M10; ☎ 01 40 59 33 00; functions as an
 emergency number after hours; metro Bir Hakeim). The
 consular section, which handles matters concerning Australian nationals, is open Monday to Friday from 9.30 am
 to noon and 2 to 4 pm.

Belgium
> 9 Rue de Tilsitt, 17e (☎ 01 44 09 39 39; metro Charles de Gaulle-Étoile)

Canada
> 35 Ave Montaigne, 8e (M7; ☎ 01 44 43 29 00, also good for emergencies; metro Alma Marceau or Franklin D Roosevelt). Canadian citizens in need of consular services should call the embassy Monday to Friday from 9.30 to 10.30 am or 2 to 3 pm to set up a weekday appointment from 11 am to noon or 3.30 to 4.30 pm.

Czech Republic
> 15 Ave Charles Floquet, 7e (☎ 01 40 65 13 00; metro Bir Hakeim)

Germany
> 13 Ave Franklin D Roosevelt, 8e (☎ 01 53 83 45 00; metro Franklin D Roosevelt)

Ireland
> 4 Rue Rude (or François Rude), 16e (M6; ☎ 01 45 00 20 87; by Minitel: 3615 IRLANDE; metro Argentine), between Ave de la Grande Armée and Ave Foch; open Monday to Friday from 9.15 am to noon (or by appointment). The phone is staffed on weekdays from 9.30 am to 1 pm and 2.30 to 5.45 pm; an after-hours emergency number is available from the answering machine.

Israel
> 3 Rue Rabelais, 8e (☎ 01 40 76 55 00; metro Franklin D Roosevelt)

Italy
> 51 Rue de Varenne, 7e (☎ 01 49 54 03 00; metro Rue du Bac)

Japan
> 7 Ave Hoche, 8e (☎ 01 48 88 62 00; metro Courcelles)

New Zealand
> 7ter Rue Léonard de Vinci, 16e (M6; ☎ 01 45 00 24 11 for 24-hour voice mail and emergencies; metro Victor Hugo), one block south of Ave Foch across Place du Venezuela from 7 Rue Léonard de Vinci; open Monday to Friday from 9 am to 1 pm and 2 to 5.30 pm (in July and August, Friday hours are 8.30 am to 2 pm)

South Africa
> 59 Quai d'Orsay, 7e (☎ 01 45 55 92 37; metro Invalides), near the American Church

Spain
> 22 Ave Marceau, 8e (☎ 01 44 43 18 00; metro Alma Marceau)

Switzerland
> 142 Rue de Grenelle, 7e (☎ 01 49 55 67 00; metro Varenne)

UK
> Consular section (handles matters concerning UK subjects): 6 Rue d'Anjou, 8e (M7; ☎ 01 42 66 38 10 for a recording or, 24 hours a day in an emergency, ☎ 01 42 66 29 79; by Minitel: 3615 GBRETAGNE; metro Concorde); open weekdays except on bank holidays from 9.30 am to 12.30 pm and 2.30 to 5 pm.

USA
Consulate: 2 Rue Saint Florentin, 1er (M7; ☎ 01 40 20 01 99 for a recording, ☎ 01 43 12 12 12 in an emergency, 24 hours; by Minitel: 3614 ETATS-UNIS; metro Concorde). Except on French and US holidays, the American Services section is open Monday to Friday from 9 am to 4 pm.

CUSTOMS

If you are not a resident of the EU, you can get a VAT refund (TVA in French) provided that: you're over 15; you'll be spending less than six months in France; you purchase goods worth at least 2000FF at a single shop; and the shop offers *vente en détaxe* (duty-free sales).

SIMON BRACKEN

Pont d'Arcole

SIMON BRACKEN

Rooftops in the Marais

Present a passport at the time of purchase and ask for a *bordereau* (export sales invoice). Some shops may refund 14% of the purchase price rather than the full 20.6% in order to cover the time and expense involved in the refund procedure.

As you leave France or another EU country, have all three pages of the bordereau validated by the country's customs officials at the airport or at the border. Customs officials will take the two pink sheets and the stamped self-addressed envelope provided by the store; the green sheet is your receipt. One of the pink sheets will then be sent to the shop where you made your purchase, which will then send you a *virement* (transfer of funds) in the form you have requested, such as by French-franc cheque.

Instant Refunds

If you're flying out of Orly or Charles de Gaulle airports certain stores can arrange for you to receive your refund as you're leaving the country. You must make such arrangements at the time of purchase.

When you arrive at the airport you have to do three things:

- Up to three hours before your flight leaves, bring your bordereau, passport, air ticket and the things you purchased (don't put them in your checked luggage) to the *douane* (customs) office so they can stamp all three copies of the bordereau (one of which they keep).
- Go to an Aéroports de Paris (ADP) information counter, where they will check the figures and put another stamp on the documents.
- Go to the nearest CCF Change bureau (open whenever the airport is operating) to pick up your refund.

MONEY

Cash

Bringing along the equivalent of about US$100 in low-denomination notes will make it easier to change a small sum of money when an inferior rate is on offer or you need just a few francs. Keep the equivalent of about US$50 separate from the rest of your money as an emergency stash.

Travellers' Cheques

Except at exchange bureaux and the Banque de France, you have to pay to cash travellers' cheques: at banks, expect a charge of 22 to 30FF per transaction; the post office charges a minimum of 16FF. A percentage fee may apply for large sums.

The travellers' cheques offering the greatest degree of flexibility are those issued by American Express (in US dollars or French francs) and Visa (in French francs), because they can be changed at many French post offices.

Keep a record of cheque numbers, where they were purchased and which ones were cashed. Obviously, keep all such information separate from the cheques themselves.

Lost or Stolen Travellers' Cheques If your American Express travellers' cheques are lost or stolen in Paris, call ☎ 05 90 86 00, a 24-hour toll-free number. American Express' office (M7; ☎ 01 47 77 70 07; metro Auber or Opéra) is at 11 Rue Scribe (9e). Reimbursements are available Monday to Saturday from 9 am to 6.30 or 7 pm (5.30 pm on Saturday).

Other offices are at 38 Ave de Wagram (8e) (M6; ☎ 01 42 27 58 80), 5 Rue St Eleuthère (18e) (☎ 01 42 23 93 52) and 26 Ave de l'Opéra (1er) (☎ 01 53 29 40 39).

If you lose your Thomas Cook cheques, contact any Thomas Cook bureau (eg in a major train station) for replacements. The company's customer service bureau in the UK can be contacted toll-free from Paris by dialling ☎ 05 90 83 30.

Eurocheques Eurocheques, available if you have a European bank account, are guaranteed up to a certain limit. When cashing them (eg at post offices), you will be asked to show your Eurocheque card, marked with your signature and registration number, and perhaps a passport or ID card. Your Eurocheque card should be kept separately from the cheques. Many hotels and merchants refuse to accept Eurocheques because of the large commissions.

ATMs

ATMs are known in French as DABs or *distributeurs automatiques de billets, guichets automatiques de banque* or *points d'argent*. ATM cards can give you direct access to your cash reserves back home at a superior exchange rate. Most ATMs will also give you cash advances through your Visa or MasterCard although they may reject foreign PIN codes if they're feeling Gallocentric.

Some non-US ATMs won't accept PIN codes with more than four digits – ask your bank how to handle this, and while you're at it find out about daily withdrawal limits. There are plenty of ATMs in Paris linked to the international Maestro and Cirrus networks. If you normally remember your PIN code as a string of letters, translate it back into numbers, as keyboards may not have letters indicated.

All of Paris' six major train stations have ATMs that are open seven days a week until at least 7 pm (later in summer and at the Gare du Nord; the Gare d'Austerlitz bureau closes at 1.30 pm on Sunday from October to March). Unfortunately, what you gain in convenience you pay for in the less-than-optimal rates and the commissions.

Credit Cards

The cheapest way to take your money with you to France is by using a credit or debit card to get cash advances. Visa (Carte Bleue) is the most widely accepted, followed by MasterCard (Access or Eurocard). American Express cards are not very useful except at up-market establishments, but they do allow you to get cash at over a dozen American Express offices. In general, all three cards can be used to pay for travel by train and in many establishments, such as restaurants.

Exchange rates may change – to your advantage or disadvantage – between the day you use the card and the date of billing.

It may be impossible to get a lost Visa or MasterCard reissued until you get home (American Express and Diners Club offer on-the-spot replacement cards), hence, two different credit cards are safer than one; keep some spare travellers' cheques or cash on hand.

Lost or Stolen Cards If your Visa card is lost or stolen in Paris, call ☎ 01 42 77 11 90, 24 hours a day. To get a replacement card you'll have to deal with the issuer.

Report a lost MasterCard (Access or Eurocard) to ☎ 01 45 67 84 84 and, if you can, to your credit card issuer back home (for cards from the USA, call ☎ 314-275 6690). The people at the French number *may* be able to get authorisation to issue you a replacement card via Eurocard France (☎ 01 43 23 45 67; metro Sèvres Lecourbe) at 16 Rue Lecourbe, 15e, open Monday to Friday until 5.30 pm.

If your American Express card is lost or stolen, call ☎ 01 47 77 72 00 or 01 47 77 70 00, both staffed 24 hours a day. In an emergency, American Express card holders from the USA can call collect on ☎ 202-783 7474. Replacements can be arranged at any American Express office (see Lost or Stolen Travellers' Cheques earlier).

International Transfers

Telegraphic transfers are not very expensive (US$30 from the USA, A$20 from Australia) but, despite their name, can be quite slow.

Be sure to specify the name of the bank and the name and address of the branch where you'd like to pick it up.

It's quicker and easier to have money wired via American Express.

Currency

The national currency is the French franc, abbreviated in this book by the letters 'FF'. One franc is divided into 100 centimes.

French coins come in denominations of 5, 10, 20 and 50 centimes (0.5FF) and 1, 2, 5, 10 and 20FF. Banknotes are issued in denominations of 20, 50, 100, 200 and 500FF. Note that it is sometimes difficult to get change for a 500FF bill.

Currency Exchange

USA	US$1	=	5.14FF
Australia	A$1	=	4.03FF
UK	UK£1	=	8.01FF
Germany	DM1	=	3.38FF
Spain	100 pta	=	4.02FF
ECU	ECU1	=	6.40FF
Canada	C$1	=	3.78FF
New Zealand	NZ$1	=	3.52FF
Japan	¥100	=	4.70FF

Changing Money

Banks and exchange bureaux often give a better rate for travellers' cheques than for cash. Major train stations and fancy hotels have exchange facilities that operate in the evening, on weekends and during holidays.

Banque de France Banque de France, France's central bank, offers the best exchange rates in the country. It does not accept Eurocheques or provide credit card cash advances.

Post Offices Many post offices perform exchange transactions for a middling rate. The commission for travellers' cheques is 1.2% (minimum 16FF).

Post offices accept banknotes in a variety of currencies as well as travellers' cheques issued by American Express (denominated in either US dollars or French francs) or Visa (in French francs only). If you have any other kind of travellers' cheques, you're out of luck.

Commercial Banks Commercial banks usually charge between 22 and 50FF per foreign currency transaction. The rates offered vary, so it pays to compare.

Commercial banks are generally open either from Monday to Friday or Tuesday to Saturday. Hours are variable but are usually from 8 or 9 am to sometime between 11.30 and 1 pm and 1.30 or 2 to 4.30 or 5 pm. Exchange services may end half an hour before closing time.

Exchange Bureaux In Paris, *bureaux de change* are faster, easier, open longer and give better rates than the banks.

Exchange bureaux at both airports are open daily from 6 or 6.30 am until 11 or 11.30 pm. All of Paris' six major train stations have exchange bureaux run by Thomas Cook, but their rates are less than stellar. Changing money at the bureau de change chains like Chequepoint and Exact Change is only slightly less foolish than making your travellers' cheques into paper aeroplanes and launching them into the Seine; they offer about 10% less than a fair rate. When using bureaux, shop around and beware of the small print – for example Rue de Rivoli bureaux specialise in offering good rates which only apply if you're changing US$3000 or more!

Costs

If you stay in hostels or showerless, toiletless rooms in bottom-end hotels and have picnics rather than dining out, it is possible to stay in Paris for about US$45 a day per person. A couple staying in two-star hotels and eating one cheap restaurant meal each day should count on spending at least US$70 a day per person, not including car rental.

Tipping & Bargaining

French law requires that restaurant, café and hotel bills include the service charge (usually 10 to 15%), so a *pourboire* (tip) is neither necessary nor expected. However, most people leave a few francs, unless the service was bad.

In taxis, the usual tip is just a few francs no matter what the fare. People in France rarely bargain except at flea markets.

Discounts

Museums, cinemas, SNCF, ferry companies and other institutions offer all sorts of price breaks to:

- people under the age of either 25 or 26
- students with ISIC cards (age limits may apply)
- *le troisième âge* (senior citizens), ie people over 60 or, in some cases, 65

Look for the words *demi-tarif* or *tarif réduit* (half-price tariff or reduced rate) on rate charts and then ask if you qualify. Some senior-citizen discounts have been done away with recently.

Those under 18 get an even wider range of discounts, including free entry to *musées nationaux* (museums run by the French government).

Carte Musées et Monuments
The Paris Museum Pass gives you free entry to 65 of the most important museums and monuments in Paris and the surrounding region for one (70FF), three (140FF) or five (200FF) days. The pass is available at major metro stations, participating museums and monuments, FNAC ticket counters and various information offices. You can make repeat visits to any of the sites covered by the pass and it can save considerable time queueing up to buy tickets. Note, however, that entry is often free for those under 16 or 18 years of age, and reduced prices are often available for those under 25 and sometimes for those over 60. ■

Taxes & Refunds

France's VAT is 20.6% on most goods except food, medicine and books, for which it's 5.5%. Prices that include VAT are often marked TTC *(toutes taxes comprises,* ie 'all taxes included'). For details on VAT refunds available to tourists, see Customs.

DOING BUSINESS

France is not the easiest country in which to do business, as legal matters are quite complicated (the French legal system is based on the Napoleonic Code). The best advice is to find a lawyer specialised in international matters.

To rent a fully equipped office, you can expect to pay around 500FF a day. Faxes cost 15FF per page; the rate for a bilingual secretary is around 160FF an hour; an English translator charges around 400FF per page, 600FF for Japanese; and the services of an interpreter are around 5000FF a day. The major luxury hotels offer fully serviced business centres but they can be quite expensive. For example, the Euro-Disneyland Centre de Convention (☎ 01 60 45 75 00; fax 01 60 45 76 91) has a seminar package which costs between 1200 and 1400FF per person per day.

The Chambre de Commerce et d'Industrie de Paris (CCI; ☎ 01 42 89 72 18; fax 01 42 89 72 08), 27 Ave de Friedland, 75008 Paris, has lists of organisations providing translation, secretarial, fax, answering and message services. They also have a legal department (☎ 01 42 89 75 75). The American Chamber of Commerce (☎ 01 40 43 89 90; fax 01 47 20 18 62), 21 Ave George V, 75008 Paris, publishes *Commerce in France* (eight per year) and a directory called *Guide to Doing Business in France* (550FF). Once you are in Paris, you will discover that Minitel is a great tool for tracking down information.

Before you leave home, it's a good idea to contact your embassy's trade office in Paris. The major offices are:

Service de Documentation Commerciale
    (☎ 01 43 12 25 32; fax 01 43 12 21 72)
Trade Office of the American Embassy
    2 Ave Gabriel, 75008 Paris (☎ 01 43 12 22 22; fax 01 42 66 97 83)
Trade Office of the Australian Embassy
    4 Rue Jean Rey, 75017 Paris (☎ 01 40 59 33 00; fax 01 40 59 33 10; Internet: http:\\www.austgov.fr)
Trade Office of the Japanese Embassy
    7 Ave Hoche, 75008 Paris (☎ 01 48 88 62 00; fax 01 42 27 50 81)
Trade Office of the UK Embassy
    35 Rue du Faubourg Saint Honoré, 75008 Paris (☎ 01 44 51 31 00; fax 01 44 51 34 01)

POST & COMMUNICATIONS

Post

Most post offices in Paris are open Monday to Friday from 8 am to 7 pm and on Saturday from 8 am to noon.

The main post office (M8; ☎ 01 40 28 20 00; metro Sentier or Les Halles) at 52 Rue du Louvre (1er), five

blocks north of the east end of the Louvre, is open 24
hours a day, seven days a week – but only for sending
mail, telegrams and domestic faxes, picking up poste
restante mail and making calls with *télécartes* (phone
cards). Other services, including currency exchange, are
available only during regular post office hours. Be prepared for long lines after 7 pm. Poste restante mail not
specifically addressed to a particular branch post office
is delivered here.

At the post office at 71 Ave des Champs-Élysées (8e)
(M6; ☎ 01 42 56 13 71; metro George V), you can send
letters, telegrams and faxes, pick up poste restante and
make télécarte phone calls Monday to Saturday from 8
am to 10 pm and on Sunday and holidays from 10 am to
noon and 2 to 8 pm. Exchange services are available
during regular post office hours.

RACHEL BLACK

Busker at Rue de Rivoli

Postal Rates Domestic letters up to 20 grams cost 3FF. Postcards and letters up to 20 grams cost 3FF within the EU; 3.80FF to most of the rest of Europe and Africa; 4.40FF to the USA, Canada and the Middle East; and 5.20FF to Australasia. Aerograms cost 5FF to all destinations.

In Paris packages weighing over two kg are handled by the *poste principale* of each arrondissement.

Telephone

Almost all public telephones in France require a télécarte, which can be purchased at post offices, *tabacs* (tobacconists' shops), supermarket check-out counters, SNCF ticket windows, Paris metro stations and anywhere you see a blue sticker reading *'télécarte en vente ici'*. Cards worth 50 calling units cost 40.60FF; those worth 120 units are 97.50FF.

Many cafés and restaurants have privately owned and coin-operated Point Phones. To find a Point Phone, look for blue-on-white window stickers bearing the Point Phone emblem.

All public phones except Point Phones can receive both domestic and international calls.

For France Telecom's *service des renseignements* (directory enquiries or assistance), dial ☎ 12. Don't be surprised if the operator does not speak English. The call is free from public phones but costs 3.71FF from private lines.

Calling Paris To call the Paris area from outside France, dial your country's international access code, then 33 (France's country code), 1 and finally the ten digit number.

Calls Abroad To call someone outside France, dial the international access code (00), wait for the tone, and then add the country code, area code (without the initial zero) and local number. International direct dial (IDD) calls to almost anywhere in the world can be placed from public telephones.

To make a reverse-charges (collect) or person-to-person call, dial 00, wait for the tone and then dial 33 plus the country code of the place you're calling (for the USA and Canada, dial 11 instead of 1).

For directory enquiries concerning subscriber numbers outside France, dial 00, and when the tone sounds dial 3312 and finally the relevant country code (again, 11 instead of 1 for the USA and Canada).

International Rates Daytime calls to other parts of Europe cost from 3.71 to 8.41FF a minute. Reduced tariffs apply on weekends and public holidays.

Nondiscount calls to continental USA and Canada are 4.94FF a minute on weekdays from 2 to 8 pm. The price then drops to 3.96FF. The rate to Alaska, Hawaii and the Caribbean is a whopping 12.74FF a minute (no discounts).

Full-price calls to Australia, New Zealand, Japan, Hong Kong or Singapore are 9.52FF a minute. A rate of 7.67FF a minute applies daily from 9.30 pm (Saturday from 2 pm) to 8 am and all day on Sunday and public holidays.

Calls to Asia, non-Francophone Africa and Latin America are generally 12 to 14FF a minute, though to some countries a rate of 9 to 11FF will apply at certain times.

Home Direct Services Home Direct lets you phone home by billing the long-distance carrier you use at home. Home Direct numbers can be dialled from public phones without inserting a télécarte; with some models, you're meant to dial even if there's no dial tone. The numbers listed below will connect you, free of charge, with an operator in your home country, who will verify your method of payment: by credit card, reverse charges etc. Wait for the tone after dialling 00.

Australia	Telecom	00-61
	Optus	Call ☎ 008 555 555 in Australia to organise a calling card before you leave.
Canada		00-16
Hong Kong		00-852
Ireland		00-353
New Zealand		00-64
Singapore		00-65
UK		00-44
USA	AT&T	00-11
	MCI	00-19
	Sprint	00-87

Domestic Calls Local calls are quite cheap, from 0.74FF, depending on the time the call was made, the length of time taken, and the distance covered. To call the provinces from Paris, dial the area code and the local number. To call the Paris area from the provinces, dial the 10-digit number starting with 01.

Minitel Minitel is an extremely useful telephone-con-
nected, computerised information service. The most
basic Minitels, equipped with a B&W monitor and a
clumsy keyboard, are available for no charge to telephone subscribers. Newer models have colour screens,
and many people now access the system with a home
computer and a modem.

Minitel numbers consist of four digits (3613 to 3618)
and a string of letters. Home users pay a per-minute
access charge. Most of the Minitels in post offices are free
for directory enquiries, and some of them let you access
pay-as-you-go on-line services. For an explanation of
how to use a given Minitel model (each kind is a bit
different), ask a native.

Fax & Telegraph

Virtually all Parisian post offices can send and receive
domestic and international faxes, telexes and telegrams.
It costs about 80FF (20FF within France) to send a one-
page fax.

BOOKS

Most books are published in different editions by different publishers in different countries. As a result, a book
might be a hardcover rarity in one country, yet be readily
available in paperback in another. Fortunately, bookshops and libraries search by title or author, so your local
bookshop or library is best placed to advise you on the
availability of the following recommendations. See
Bookshops under Shopping for details of Parisian bookshops.

Lonely Planet

Lonely Planet's guides to France, Western Europe and
Mediterranean Europe all deal with Paris and the
country in general.

Guidebooks

Walking guides include *Walking Paris* by Gilles
Desmons, *Paris Step by Step* by Christopher Turner and
Pariswalks by Alison & Sonia Landes. *The Paris Literary
Companion* by Ian Littlewood takes you by the buildings
once inhabited by famous literary personalities. *Paris
Pas Cher*, updated annually, lists inexpensive shopping
options. Another source of information on penny-wise
living in Paris is *Paris aux Meilleurs Prix*.

History

Larry Collins & Dominique Lapierre's *Is Paris Burning?* is a dramatic account of the liberation of Paris in 1944.

Alistair Horne's *The Fall of Paris* deals with the Commune of 1870-71 and *Citizens* by Simon Schama is a highly acclaimed and truly monumental work that examines the first few years after the storming of the Bastille in 1789.

You might also want to try *A Moveable Feast* by Ernest Hemingway, which portrays bohemian life in Paris between the wars, or *Down and Out in Paris and London*, George Orwell's account of the time he spent living with tramps in Paris and London in the late 1920s.

General

The French by Theodore Zeldin is a highly acclaimed survey of French passions, peculiarities and perspectives. *France Today* by John Ardagh is a good introduction to modern-day France, its politics, its people and their idiosyncrasies.

Past Imperfect: French Intellectuals, 1944-1956 by Tony Judt is an examination of the lively intellectual life of post-war France.

The Food of France by Waverley Root is an absolutely superb introduction to French cuisine.

NEWSPAPERS & MAGAZINES

English-Language

Issued daily except Sunday, the *International Herald Tribune* (10FF) is edited in Paris and has very good coverage of French news.

The *Guardian*, the *Financial Times*, *The Times* and the colourful *USA Today* and weekly the *European* are all readily available, as are *Newsweek*, *Time* and the *Economist*.

Paris-based *France-USA Contacts*, issued every fortnight, consists of hundreds of ads placed by both companies and individuals. It is distributed free at Paris' English-language bookshops and Anglophone embassies. It can be very helpful if you're looking for au pair work, short-term accommodation etc.

French

France's main daily newspapers are *Le Figaro* (right wing; aimed at professionals, business people and the bourgeoisie), *Le Monde* (centre-left; very popular with business people, professionals and intellectuals), *Le Parisien* (centre; middle-class, easy to read if your French is basic), *France Soir* (right; working and middle-class), *Libération* (left; popular with students and intellectuals) and *L'Humanité* (communist; working-class).

RADIO & TV

You can pick up a mixture of the BBC World Service and BBC for Europe on 648 kHz AM. The Voice of America's European service is on 1197 kHz AM.

Radio France International (RFI) broadcasts the world news in English every day from 3 to about 4 pm on 738 kHz AM.

Up-market hotels often offer cable TV access to CNN, BBC Prime and other networks. Canal+ (pronounced 'ka-NAHL Pluce'), a French subscription TV station available in many mid-range hotels, sometimes screens nondubbed English movies.

A variety of weekend-to-weekend TV listings are sold at newsstands. Foreign movies that haven't been dubbed and are shown with subtitles are marked 'VO' or *version originale*.

PHOTOGRAPHY & VIDEO

Be prepared to have your camera and film run through x-ray machines at airports and the entrances to sensitive public buildings. The gadgets are ostensibly film-safe up to 1000 ASA, and laptops and computer disks appear to pass through without losing data, but there is always some degree of risk.

Photography is rarely forbidden except in museums and art galleries. When photographing people, it is a basic courtesy to ask permission. If you don't know any French, smile while pointing at your camera and they'll get the picture.

Colour-print film produced by Kodak and Fuji is widely available in supermarkets, photo shops and FNAC stores.

Unlike the rest of Western Europe and Australia, which use PAL (phase alternation line), French TV broadcasts are in SECAM *(système électronique couleur avec mémoire)*. North America and Japan use a third incompatible system, NTSC (National Television Systems Committee). Non-SECAM TVs will not work in France, and French videotapes cannot be played on videocassette recorders and TVs that lack a SECAM capability.

WEIGHTS & MEASURES

Metric System

France uses the metric system, which was invented after the Revolution by the French Academy of Sciences, at the request of the National Assembly, and adopted by the French government in 1795. Inspired by the same rationalist spirit, in whose name churches were ransacked and turned into Temples of Reason, the metric system replaced a confusing welter of traditional units

---

METRIC CONVERSION

Temperature
To convert °C to °F multiply by 1.8 and add 32.
To convert °F to °C subtract 32 and multiply by 0.55.

Length, Distance & Area

	multiply by
inches to centimetres	2.54
centimetres to inches	0.39
feet to metres	0.30
metres to feet	3.28
yards to metres	0.91
metres to yards	1.09
miles to kilometres	1.61
kilometres to miles	0.62
acres to hectares	0.40
hectares to acres	2.47
square miles to square kilometres	2.59
square kilometres to square miles	0.39

Weight

	multiply by
ounces to grams	28.35
grams to ounces	0.035
pounds to kilograms	0.45
kilograms to pounds	2.20
British tons to kilograms	1016
US tons to kilograms	907

A British ton is 2240 lbs, a US ton is 2000 lbs.

Volume

	multiply by
imperial gallons to litres	4.55
litres to imperial gallons	0.22
US gallons to litres	3.79
litres to US gallons	0.26

Five imperial gallons equal just over six US gallons.
A litre is slightly more than a US quart, slightly less than a British one.

TEMPERATURE

°C   °F

of measure, which lacked all logical basis and made conversion complicated and commerce chaotic.

Numbers

For numbers with four or more digits, the French use full stops (periods) or spaces where Anglo-Saxons would use commas: one million therefore appears as 1.000.000 or 1 000 000. For decimals, on the other hand, the French use commas, so 1.75 comes out as 1,75.

TIME

France uses the 24-hour clock, with the hours separated from the minutes by a lower-case letter 'h'. Thus, 15h30 is 3.30 pm, 21h50 is 9.50 pm and 00h30 is 12.30 am.

France is one hour ahead of, or later than, Greenwich Mean Time/Universal Time Coordinated (GMT/UTC). During daylight-saving time, which runs from the last Sunday in March to the last Sunday in September, France is two hours ahead of GMT/UTC. The UK and France are almost always one hour apart – when it's 6 pm in London, it's 7 pm in Paris.

New York is generally six hours behind Paris. This may fluctuate a bit depending on exactly when daylight-saving time begins and ends on both sides of the Atlantic.

The Australian east coast is between eight and 10 hours ahead of (later than) France.

ELECTRICITY

France runs on 220V at 50 Hz AC. Old-type wall sockets, often rated at 600 watts, take two round prongs. The new kinds of sockets take fatter prongs and a protruding earth (ground) prong. Adapters to make new plugs fit into the old sockets are said to be illegal but are available at electricians' shops. Tape recorders not equipped with built-in adapters may function poorly.

Adapters and transformers of all sorts are available at the BHP department store (☎ 01 42 74 90 00; metro Hôtel de Ville) at 52 Rue de Rivoli (4e).

There are two types of adapters; mixing them up will destroy either the transformer or your appliance. The 'heavy' kind, usually designed to handle 35 watts or less (see the tag) and often metal-clad, is designed for use with small electric devices such as radios, tape recorders and razors. The other kind, which weighs much less but is rated for up to 1500 watts, is for use only with appliances that contain heating elements, such as hair dryers and irons.

LAUNDRY

There are countless *laverie libre-service* (unstaffed, self-service laundrettes) in Paris; your hotel or hostel can suggest nearby ones. French laundrettes are not cheap – count on 20FF for a smaller seven-kg machine and 2FF for five minutes of drying. Some laundrettes have self-service *nettoyage à sec* (dry cleaning).

Change machines are often out of order, so come prepared. Two-franc pieces are especially handy for the *séchoirs* (dryers) and the *lessive* (laundry powder) dispenser.

TOILETS

French bathrooms hold a few surprises for the uninitiated.

Bidets

In many hotel rooms – even those without toilets or showers – you will find a bidet, a porcelain fixture that looks like a shallow toilet with a pop-up stopper in the base. Originally conceived to improve the personal hygiene of aristocratic women, its primary purpose is for washing the genitals and anal area, though its uses have expanded to include everything from hand-washing laundry to soaking your feet.

Public Toilets

Public toilets are signposted as *toilettes* or *WC*. In Paris, there are a number of superb public toilets from the *belle époque* (eg at Place de la Madeleine), but you're more likely to come upon one of the tan-coloured, self-disinfecting toilet pods. Get your change ready: many public toilets cost 2FF or even 2.50FF. Some café toilets have the washbasins and urinals in a common area through which you pass to get to the closed toilet stalls.

In older cafés and hotels, the amenities may consist of a *toilette à la turque* (Turkish-style toilet), a squat toilet.

HEALTH

Your main health risk in Paris is likely to be an upset stomach from eating and drinking too much. You might experience mild stomach problems if you're not used to copious amounts of rich cream and olive-oil-based sauces, but you'll get used to it after a while.

Organise a visit to your dentist before departure and arrange travel insurance with good medical cover. If you wear glasses, take along a spare pair and your prescription. If you require a particular medication, take an adequate supply. No jabs are required to travel to France.

Travel with Children by Maureen Wheeler (Lonely Planet) includes basic advice on travel health for young children.

EU residents are covered for emergency medical treatment throughout the EU. The coverage provided by most private US health insurance policies continues if you travel abroad, at least for a limited period. Canadians covered by the Régie de l'Assurance-Maladie du Québec, and who have a valid Assurance-Maladie du Québec card, can benefit from certain reimbursement agreements with France's national health-care system. Australian Medicare provides absolutely no coverage in France.

France has an extensive public health-care system. Anyone (including foreigners) who is sick, even mildly so, can receive treatment in the *service des urgences* (casualty ward or emergency room) of any public hospital.

Medical Services

There are about 50 *assistance publique* (public health service) hospitals in Paris. If you need an ambulance, call ☎ 15 or 01 45 67 50 50. For emergency treatment, call Urgences Médicales on ☎ 01 48 28 40 04 or SOS Médecin on ☎ 01 47 07 77 77. Both offer 24-hour house calls.

Some hospital, dental service and pharmacy possibilities are:

Hôtel Dieu, on the north side of Place du Parvis Notre Dame (M14; ☎ 01 42 34 82 32; metro Cité; 4e). After 10 pm use the emergency entrance on Rue de la Cité. The 24-hour emergency room can refer you to the hospital's emergency gynaecological services in case of sexual assault.
American Hospital, at 63 Blvd Victor Hugo (M1; ☎ 01 46 41 27 37; fax 01 46 41 27 00; 16e), offers emergency medical and dental care 24 hours a day.
Hôpital Franco-Britannique, at 3 Rue Barbès (M1; ☎ 01 46 39 22 22; metro Anatole France), is a less expensive English-speaking option. People from outside the EU are asked to pay up front.
La Pitié-Salpêtrière hospital, on Rue Bruand (M1; M13; metro Chevaleret; 13e), is the only dental hospital with extended hours. The after-hours entrance, open from 5.30 pm to 8.30 am, is at 47 Blvd de l'Hôpital (M13; metro Gare d'Austerlitz).
Pharmacie des Champs, inside the shopping arcade at 84 Ave des Champs-Élysées (M7; ☎ 01 45 62 02 41; metro George V; 8e), is open 24 hours a day, 365 days a year.

Pharmacie de la Huchette, 16 Rue de la Huchette (M14; ☎ 01 43 54 13 03; metro Saint Michel, 5e), is open every day of the year from 11 am to 9 pm (10 pm in July and August).

Pharmacie des Halles, at 10 Blvd de Sébastopol (M15; ☎ 01 42 72 03 23; metro Châtelet; 4e), is open daily from 9 am (noon on Sunday and holidays) to midnight.

HIV/AIDS Organisations

For information on free and anonymous HIV-testing centres (centres de dépistage) in and around Paris, ring the SIDA Info Service toll-free, 24 hours a day, on ☎ 0 800 36 66 36. In the Marais quarter of Paris, information is also available at Le Kiosque (☎ 01 44 78 00 00; metro Saint Paul) at 36 Rue Geoffroy l'Asnier (4e), open weekdays from 10 am to 7 pm and on Saturday from 2 to 8 pm.

The offices of AIDES (☎ 01 44 52 00 00; metro Télégraphe) at 247 Rue de Belleville (19e), an organisation that works for the prevention of AIDS and assists AIDS sufferers, are staffed on weekdays from 9 am to 8 pm, on Saturday from 11 am to 5 pm and on Sunday afternoon.

WOMEN TRAVELLERS

Women attract more unwanted attention than men, but female travellers need not walk around France in fear: people are rarely assaulted on the street. However, the French seem to have given relatively little thought to sexual harassment (harcèlement sexuel), and many men (and some women) still think that to stare suavely at a passing woman is to pay her a flattering compliment.

Assault

Using the metros until late at night is generally OK, as stations are rarely deserted.

France's national rape-crisis hotline (☎ 0 800 05 95 95) can be reached toll-free from any telephone without using a télécarte. Staffed by volunteers Monday to Friday from 10 am to 6 pm, it's run by a women's organisation called Viols Femmes Informations, whose Paris office is at 9 Villa d'Este (13e; metro Porte d'Ivry).

In an emergency, you can always call the police (☎ 17), who will take you to the hospital. Medical, psychological and legal services are available to people referred by the police at the 24-hour Service Médico-Judiciaire (☎ 01 42 34 84 46) of the Hôtel Dieu hospital.

Women's Movement

Women were given the right to vote in 1945 by De Gaulle's short-lived postwar government, but until 1964 a woman needed her husband's permission to open a bank account or get a passport. It was in such an environment that Simone de Beauvoir wrote *Le Deuxième Sexe* (The Second Sex) in 1949.

For reasons that have more to do with French society than anything else, few women's groups function as the kind of supportive social institutions that have been formed in the USA, UK and Australia.

Maison des Femmes

The women-only Maison des Femmes (M13; ☎ 01 43 48 24 91; metro Charonne) at 8 Cité Prost (11e) is the main meeting place for women of all ages and nationalities. For the last few years, urban-renewal plans have threatened the old building in which it's housed, but as we go to press municipal bureaucrats have yet to agree on a new location. It is staffed on Monday, Wednesday and Friday from 2 to 7 pm. On Friday nights, a cafeteria for women opens at 8 pm.

GAY & LESBIAN TRAVELLERS

France is one of Europe's most liberal countries when it comes to homosexuality, in part because of the long French tradition of public tolerance towards groups of people who choose not to live by conventional social codes. France's lesbian scene is much less public than its gay counterpart and is centred mainly around women's cafés and bars.

Organisations

Most of France's major gay organisations are based in Paris:

Act Up Paris
  45 Rue Sedaine, 11e (☎ 01 48 06 13 89 for a recording; by Minitel: 3615 ACT UP; metro Voltaire). Meetings are held every Tuesday night at 7.30 pm at the Institut Océanographique, 195 Rue Saint Jacques (5e; metro Luxembourg).
Archives Lesbiennes
  The organisation (☎ 01 43 56 11 49) that publishes *L'Annuaire* (see Lesbian Publications). Holds meetings on the ground floor of the Maison des Femmes (see under Women Travellers) every Friday from 7 to 10 pm.

Association des Médecins Gais
BP 433, 75527 Paris CEDEX 11 (☎ 01 48 05 81 71). The Association of Gay Medical Doctors, based in the Centre Gai et Lesbien, deals with health issues of special importance to gays. Staffed on Wednesday from 6 to 8 pm and on Saturday from 2 to 4 pm.

Centre Gai et Lesbien (CGL)
3 Rue Keller, 11e (M13; ☎ 01 43 57 21 47; metro Ledru Rollin). The bar, library etc are open Monday to Saturday from 2 to 8 pm; the Sunday activities (2 to 7 pm) are mainly for people who are HIV positive.

Écoute Gaie
A hotline (☎ 01 44 93 01 02) for gays and lesbians that's staffed on weekdays from 6 to 10 pm.

Gay Publications

Published monthly, *Illico* has articles (in French) and lots of ads for places that cater to gays. It is available free at gay venues or for 9FF at newsagents. *Double Face*, also published monthly, has fewer articles and more information on nightlife. *Exit* (15FF; free at gay venues) is another monthly for gay men.

Guidebooks listing pubs, restaurants, discotheques, beaches, saunas, sex shops and cruising areas include:

Guide Gai
A predominantly male, English-French guide (69FF) which is published yearly by Les Éditions du Triangle Rose (☎ 01 43 57 52 05).

Guide Gay Paris
A French-English guide to Paris by Vincent Vichit-Vadakan with information of particular interest to gays and lesbians.

Spartacus International Gay Guide
A male-only guide to the world with 100 pages devoted to France.

All three works are available from Les Mots à la Bouche (see Bookshops in the Shopping chapter).

Lesbian Publications

The monthly national magazine *Lesbia* (25FF; ☎ 01 43 48 89 54) gives a rundown of what's happening around the country. Some of the journals listed under Gay Publications also have information for lesbians.

Guidebooks include:

L'Annuaire des Lieux, Groupes et Activités Lesbiennes, Feministes et Homosexuelle
A guide (70FF) to 350 places of lesbian and feminist interest all over France. Issued every two years, it is available from some French bookshops, including Paris' Librairie des Femmes at 74 Rue de Seine, 6e (metro Mabillon) and at the Maison des Femmes.

DISABLED TRAVELLERS

France is not particularly well equipped for the *handicapés* (disabled people): kerb ramps are few and far between, older public facilities and bottom-end hotels often lack lifts, and the Paris metro, most of it built decades ago, is hopeless. But physically disabled people who would like to visit Paris can overcome these problems. Most hotels with two or more stars are equipped with lifts, and Michelin's *Guide Rouge* indicates hotels with lifts and facilities for disabled people. Both the Foyer International d'Accueil de Paris Jean Monnet and the Centre International de Séjour de Paris Kellermann have facilities for disabled travellers (see Hostels & Foyers in the Places to Stay chapter).

Publications you might look for include:

Holidays and Travel Abroad: A Guide for Disabled People
An annual publication (UK£5) that gives a good overview of facilities available to disabled travellers in Europe (published in even-numbered years). Published by the Royal Association for Disability & Rehabilitation (RADAR; ☎ 0171-250 3222), based at 12 City Forum, 250 City Rd, London EC1V 8AF.
Paris Pour Tous
Available from the Paris tourist office for 60FF.
Guide Pratique du Voyageur à Mobilité Réduite
(Practical Guide for the Traveller with Reduced Mobility). An SNCF pamphlet which details services available to train travellers in wheelchairs. One page is in English.

PARIS FOR CHILDREN

Paris abounds in places that will delight children of all ages. Family visits to many areas of the city can be designed around a rest stop (or picnic) at the following attractions (see the Things to See & Do chapter for further details):

- 6e arrondissement (M14): Jardin du Luxembourg
- 19e arrondissement (M1): Parc de la Villette, Cité des Enfants in the Cité des Sciences et de l'Industrie

- Bastille Area (M13; 4e, 11e & 12e): playground at the Port de Plaisance de Paris-Arsenal
- Bois de Boulogne (M1): Jardin d'Acclimatation
- Bois de Vincennes (M1): zoo
- Champs-Élysées Area (M7; 8e): Palais de la Découverte
- Eiffel Tower Area (M10; 7e): Champ de Mars
- Jardin des Plantes Area (M12; eastern 5e): Grande Galerie de l'Évolution, zoo, playground
- Montmartre (M8; 18e): playground

USEFUL ORGANISATIONS

French Cultural Service

The offices of the Service Culturel, many of them attached to embassies or consulates, provide information to people who would like to study in France.

Australia
6 Perth Ave, Yarralumla, Canberra, ACT 2600 (☎ 06-216 0100)
Canada
175 Bloor St East, Suite 606, Toronto, Ont M8W 3R8 (☎ 416-925 0025)
Hong Kong
Admiralty Centre, Tower Two, 25th floor, 18 Harcourt Rd, Admiralty (☎ 02-529 4358)
Ireland
1 Kildare St, Dublin 2 (☎ 01-676 2197)
New Zealand
Robert Jones House, 1-3 Willeston St, Wellington (☎ 04-494 1320); postal address: PO Box 53, Wellington
Singapore
5 Gallop Rd, Singapore 1025 (☎ 65-468 4663)
South Africa
795 George Ave, Arcadia, 0083 Pretoria (☎ 012-43 5658, 43 3845)
UK
23 Cromwell Rd, London SW7 2EL (☎ 0171-838 2055)
USA
972 Fifth Ave, New York, NY 10021 (☎ 212-439 1400)

Centres Régionaux Information Jeunesse

CRIJ offices have much information on housing, jobs, professional training and educational options. The Paris headquarters (☎ 01 44 49 12 00; fax 01 40 65 02 61; metro Champ de Mars-Tour Eiffel) is at 101 Quai Branly (15e).

LIBRARIES

The free, three-storey Bibliothèque Publique d'Information (BPI; ☎ 01 44 78 12 33) is a huge, non-circulating library in the Centre Pompidou. The 2300 periodicals include quite a few English-language newspapers and magazines from around the world. It is open the same days and hours as the rest of the Centre Pompidou (see Centre Pompidou in the Things to See & Do chapter). It's so popular that, from 2 to 4 pm, you sometimes have to wait in line to get in.

The British Council (M11; ☎ 01 49 55 73 00; metro Invalides), on the eastern side of Esplanade des Invalides at 11 Rue de Constantine (7e), has a lending library (250FF a year for membership, 200FF with a student card) and a free reference library open weekdays from 11 am to 6 pm (to 7 pm on Wednesday). See Cultural Centres for more information.

CULTURAL CENTRES

The brand-new American Center at Bercy closed down in early 1996 when it ran out of money; cost over-runs on its construction ate up all the operating funds.

The British Council (M11; ☎ 01 49 55 73 00; metro Invalides) at 11 Rue de Constantine (7e), whose mission is 'to promote British culture and civilisation', has reference and lending libraries (see above), and also runs language courses through the British Institute. The café in the basement is open weekdays from 9.30 am to 6.45 pm.

The British Institute's bulletin board (in the basement) has a few job and accommodation offers. The British Council's bulletin board (outside the main door) has information on cultural activities.

The American Church (M11; ☎ 01 47 05 07 99; metro Pont de l'Alma) at 65 Quai d'Orsay (7e) functions as a community centre for English speakers and is an excellent source of information on flats, jobs etc. Reception is staffed daily from 9 am to 1 pm and 2 to 10.30 pm (7.30 pm on Sunday). The church has three bulletin boards: an informal board downstairs on which people post all sorts of announcements (for no charge), and two identical official bulletin boards – one near reception, the other outside – listing flats, things for sale and jobs, especially work for au pairs, babysitters and English-language teachers. The American Church sponsors a variety of classes, workshops, concerts and other cultural activities.

The English-speaking Saint Joseph's Church (M6; ☎ 01 42 27 28 56; metro Charles de Gaulle-Étoile) is two blocks north-east of the Arc de Triomphe at 50 Ave Hoche (8e). It also has a bulletin board with information on work, apartments, cultural events etc.

DANGERS & ANNOYANCES

In general, Paris is a safe city and occurrences of random street assaults are rare. The City of Lights is generally well lit, and there's no reason not to use the metro until it stops running (around 12.45 am). As you'll notice, women *do* travel alone on the metro late at night in most areas, though not all who do so report feeling 100% comfortable. The Bois de Boulogne and Bois de Vincennes are best avoided after dark.

Nonviolent crime (such as pickpocketing and thefts from handbags or packs) is a problem wherever there are crowds, especially crowds of tourists. Places to be especially careful include Montmartre, Pigalle, the area around Forum des Halles, on the metro at rush hour and even the Latin Quarter. Be especially wary of children: kids who jostle up against you in the crowds may be diving into your bag with professional aplomb at the same instant.

Metro stations that are probably best avoided late at night include: Châtelet-Les Halles and its many, seemingly endless tunnels; Château Rouge in Montmartre; Gare du Nord; Strasbourg Saint Denis; Réaumur Sébastopol; and Montparnasse Bienvenüe. *Bornes d'alarme* (alarm boxes) are located in the centre of each metro/RER platform and in some station corridors.

The Paris municipality spends vast sums of money to keep the city's pavements relatively passable, and the technology they employ is undeniably impressive. But it would seem that a recent campaign to get people to clean up after their pooches – the latest in a long series of such noble civic efforts – has been less than a howling success.

Paris tests out its air-raid and all-clear sirens on the first Wednesday of each month at noon and 12.10 pm.

LEGAL MATTERS

Police

Thanks to the Napoleonic Code, the police can pretty much search anyone they want to at any time, whether or not there seems to be probable cause. They have been known to stop and search charter buses solely because they are coming from Amsterdam.

France has two separate police forces. The Police Nationale, under the command of departmental prefects (and, in Paris, the Préfet de Police), includes the Police de l'Air et des Frontières (PAF), the border police. The Gendarmerie Nationale, a paramilitary force under the control of the defence minister, handles airports, borders etc. During times of crisis (eg a wave of terrorist attacks), the army may be called in to patrol public places.

The dreaded Compagnies Républicaines de Sécurité (CRS), riot police heavies, are part of the Police Nationale. You often see hundreds of them, equipped with the latest riot gear, at strikes or demonstrations.

Police with shoulder patches reading 'Police Municipale' are under the control of the local mayor.

If asked a question, cops are likely to be correct and helpful but no more than that (though you may get a salute).

If stopped by the police for any reason, your best course of action is to be polite and to remain calm. The French police have wide powers of search and seizure, and if they take a dislike to you may opt to use them. The police can, without any particular reason, decide to examine your passport, visa etc, which is, at the very least, a hassle.

The French police are very strict about security, especially at airports. Do not leave baggage unattended: they're serious when they warn that suspicious objects will be summarily blown up.

Drinking & Driving

The laws are very tough when it comes to drinking and driving, and for many years the slogan has been: *'Boire ou conduire, il faut choisir'* (to drink or to drive, you have to choose). The acceptable blood-alcohol limit is 0.05%, and drivers exceeding this amount face fines of up to 30,000FF (two years in jail maximum). Licences can also be immediately suspended.

Drugs

Importing or exporting drugs can lead to a 10 to 30-year jail sentence. The fine for possession of drugs for personal use can be as high as 500,000FF.

Littering

The fine for littering is about 1000FF.

Smoking

Laws banning smoking in public places do exist, but no-one pays much attention to them. If a restaurant has a nonsmoking section, customers will still smoke!

BUSINESS HOURS

Most museums are closed on either Monday or Tuesday, though in summer some are open daily. A few places (eg the Louvre) stay open until 8 pm or later one or two nights a week.

Small businesses are open daily except Sunday and perhaps Monday. Hours are usually 9 or 10 am to 6.30 or 7 pm, with a midday break from noon or 1 pm to 2 or 3 pm.

Supermarkets and hypermarkets are open Monday to Saturday; a few open on Sunday morning in July and August. Small food shops are mostly closed on Sunday morning or afternoon and Monday, so Saturday afternoon may be your last chance to stock up on provisions until Tuesday, unless you come across a supermarket, seven-day grocery or a boulangerie on duty by rotational agreement. Many restaurants are closed on Sunday.

In Paris, local laws require that most business establishments close for one day a week. Exceptions include family-run businesses, such as grocery stores and small restaurants, and places large enough to rotate staff so everyone has a day off. Since you can never tell what day of the week an individual merchant or restaurateur has chosen to take off, this book includes, where possible, details on weekly closures.

In August, lots of establishments shut down so owners and employees alike can head for the hills or the beaches.

PUBLIC HOLIDAYS

The following holidays are observed in Paris:

1 January	
New Year's Day	*Jour de l'an*
late March or April	
Easter Sunday	*Pâques*
late March or April	
Easter Monday	*lundi de Pâques*
1 May	
May Day	*Fête du Travail*
8 May	
Victory Day for WW II	*Victoire 1945*
May (40th day after Easter)	
Ascension Day	*l'Ascension*

mid-May to mid-June (7th Sunday after Easter)	
Pentecost or Whit Sunday	*Pentecôte*
mid-May to mid-June	
Whit Monday	*lundi de Pentecôte*
14 July	
Bastille Day (National Day)	*Fête Nationale*
15 August	
Assumption Day	*l'Assomption*
1 November	
All Saints' Day	*La Toussaint*
11 November	
Armistice Day 1918 or Remembrance Day	*le onze novembre*
25 December	
Christmas	*Noël*

Note: Shrove Tuesday (Mardi Gras; the first day of Lent), Maundy Thursday (jeudi saint), Good Friday (vendredi saint; the Friday before Easter) and Boxing Day (26 December) are *not* public holidays.

SPECIAL EVENTS

France's *vacances scolaires* (school holidays), during which millions of families take domestic vacations, generally fall as follows:

Christmas & New Year
    Schools all over the country are closed from 20 December to 4 January.
February/March
    The 'February' holidays last from about 11 February to 11 March; pupils in each of three zones are off for overlapping 15-day periods.
Easter
    The month-long spring break, which begins a week before Easter, also means pupils have overlapping 15-day holidays.
Summer
    The nationwide summer recess lasts from the tail end of June until very early September.

WORK

Despite France's 12% unemployment rate and laws that forbid people who aren't EU nationals from working in France, working 'in the black' (ie without documents) is still possible. Au pair work is popular and can be done legally even by non-EU citizens.

For practical information on employment in France, you might want to pick up *Working in France* (US$12.95) by Carol Pineau & Maureen Kelly.

To work legally in France you must have a residence permit known as a carte de séjour. Getting one is almost automatic for EU nationals and almost impossible for anyone else except full-time students (see Visas).

Non-EU nationals cannot work legally unless they obtain a work permit *(autorisation de travail)* before arriving in France. This is no easy matter, as a prospective employer has to convince the authorities that there is no French person who can do the job being offered to you.

The Agence Nationale pour l'Emploi (ANPE), France's national employment service, has lists of job openings. The Centres Régionals Information Jeunesse (CRIJ) sometimes have noticeboards with work possibilities. Both these bodies are useless if you don't have a carte de séjour.

If you play an instrument or have some other talent you could try busking. Busking is a common sight in front of the Centre Pompidou, around Sacré Cœur and on the metro, where the RATP police are in charge. To avoid hassles, talk to other street artists.

Au Pair Work

Under the au pair system, single young people who are studying in France live with a French family and receive lodging, full board and a bit of pocket money in exchange for taking care of the kids, doing light housework and perhaps teaching English to the children. Most families prefer young women, but a few positions are also available for young men.

For practical information, pick up *The Au Pair and Nanny's Guide to Working Abroad* by Susan Griffith & Sharon Legg.

By law, au pairs must have one full day off a week. In Paris, some families also provide weekly or monthly metro passes. The family must also pay for French social security, which covers about 70% of medical expenses (it's a good idea to get supplementary insurance).

Residents of the EU can easily arrange for an au pair job and a carte de séjour after arriving in France. Non-EU nationals who decide to try to find an au pair position after entering the country cannot to do so legally and won't be covered by the protections provided for under French law.

Check the bulletin boards at the American Church and Saint Joseph's Church (see Cultural Centres) for job ads. The Paris tourist office has a list of au pair placement agencies.

Getting There & Away

For information on transport options between the city and the airports, see the Getting Around chapter.

AIR

Paris has two airports: Aéroport d'Orly, which is 16 km south of central Paris, and Aéroport Charles de Gaulle, which is 27 km north of the city centre. Air Inter, TAT and other domestic airlines have flights from Paris to other parts of France, although the high-speed TGV train services make it easy to reach most parts of the country by rail.

England

A straightforward London-Paris ticket with British Airways, British Midland or Air France will cost £138 one-way, although an excursion ticket taking in a weekend can often be less than £100 – sometimes a lot less. The fare war between trains via the Channel Tunnel, cross-channel ferry operators and the airlines means there are often good deals going. Sometimes you can find return fares for as low as £60 with carriers like Air Liberté and Air UK, or with more exotic Asian carriers tagging on London-Paris at the start or end of a longer flight.

From Paris, tickets are occasionally available for as little as 400/500FF one-way/return, but you have a much better chance of finding something in the 700FF range (return).

Continental Europe

Return discount charter fares from Paris include: Athens (1600 to 1800FF), Berlin (1400 to 1800FF), Budapest (around 1900FF), Dublin (1100 to 1200FF), Istanbul (1200 to 1800FF), Madrid (1200 to 1400FF) and Rome (1000 to 1300FF). The cheapest fares are available in early spring and late autumn.

North America

You should be able to fly New York-Paris return for US$360 to US$450 in the low season and US$550 to US$650 in the high season. Equivalent fares from the west coast would be around US$500 in the low season and US$600 in the high. Check the travel pages of major city Sunday newspapers like the *New York Times*, *Los Angeles Times* or *San Francisco Chronicle-Examiner* for cheap flight ads or try travel agents like STA or Council Travel if all you're looking for is the lowest priced fare.

From Paris, one-way charter flights on the Paris-New York route usually cost about 1250 to 1500FF. Return fares of 2000FF or less are sometimes available, but a more usual fare is 2500FF. Return fares to the west coast are about 500 to 1000FF higher.

Another option is a courier flight. A New York-London return ticket can be had from about US$450 in the low season and from $680 in the high season (about $100 more from the west coast). You can also fly one-way. The drawbacks are that your stay in Europe may be limited to one or two weeks; your luggage is usually restricted to hand luggage (the courier company uses your checked luggage allowance to send its parcel) and you may have to be a local resident and apply for an interview before they'll take you on.

You can find out more about courier flights from Council Travel in New York (☎ 212-822 2700) and Los Angeles (☎ 310-208 3551), and Discount Travel International in New York (☎ 212-362 3636). It is a good idea to call two or three months in advance, at the very beginning of the calendar month.

If you are travelling from Canada, Travel CUTS has offices in all major cities. You might also scan the budget travel agents' ads in the *Toronto Globe & Mail*, the *Toronto Star* and the *Vancouver Province*.

For courier flights from Canada contact FB On Board Courier Services (☎ 514-631 7925) in Montreal or Vancouver (☎ 604-278 1266). A return courier flight to Paris will set you back about C$350 from Toronto or Montreal, and C$425 from Vancouver.

From Paris, you may find that flights are a bit cheaper to Montreal than to Toronto, with one-way/return fares as low as 1200/2000FF, depending on the time of the year you travel.

Australia & New Zealand

Discounted return fares on mainstream airlines through a reputable budget ticket agency like STA or Flight

Centre cost between A$1700 (October to mid-November and mid-January to late February) and A$2500 (mid-May to late August, and mid-December). Flights to/from Perth are a couple of hundred dollars cheaper.

From Paris, return trips to Melbourne or Sydney start at about 6000 or 7000FF. Nouvelles Frontières and the student travel companies have some of the best fares.

The cheapest fares to Paris from New Zealand are routed through the USA. A Round the World (RTW) ticket could be cheaper than a return ticket.

Asia

Many of the cheapest fares from Asia to Europe are offered by Eastern European or Middle Eastern carriers. STA has branches in Hong Kong, Tokyo, Singapore, Bangkok and Kuala Lumpur.

In Paris, sample discount return prices include: Bangkok (3600 to 4000FF), Bombay (3700 to 4300FF), Hong Kong (around 4000FF), Jakarta (4600FF), Kathmandu (4500FF) and Singapore (around 4200FF).

Airline Offices

Airline offices can also be found in the Paris Yellow Pages under *Transports Aériens*. British Airways is listed below but note that it is not in the Paris phone directories or on Minitel.

Air France
 ☎ 01 44 08 24 24 (for information), ☎ 01 44 08 22 22 (for reservations), ☎ 08 36 68 10 48 (for recorded information on arrivals and departures). By Minitel, dial 3615 AF. Offices (generally open Monday to Saturday from 9 am to 6 pm) include 40 Ave George V, 8e (M6; metro George V), just off the Champs-Élysées.
Air Inter
 ☎ 01 45 46 90 00 (for information and reservations), ☎ 08 36 68 34 24 (for flight information). By Minitel, dial 3615 AIRINTER. Offices include 119 Ave des Champs-Élysées, 8e (M6; metro George V).
Air Liberté
 38 Rue du Sentier, 2e (☎ 01 40 28 47 31; metro Sentier)
Air Littoral
 100 Blvd Montparnasse, 14e (☎ 01 40 64 76 76; metro Vavin)
Air UK
 3 Rue de Choiseul, 2e (☎ 01 44 56 18 08; metro Quatre Septembre)

American Airlines
    109 Rue du Faubourg Saint Honoré, 8e (☎ 01 42 89 05 22
    or, toll free from outside Paris, 05 23 00 35; metro Saint
    Philippe du Roule)
British Airways
    13 Blvd de la Madeleine, 1er (☎ 01 47 78 14 14; metro
    Madeleine)
Canadian Airlines International
    109 Rue du Faubourg Saint Honoré, 8e (☎ 01 49 53 07 07;
    metro Miromesnil)
Continental
    92 Ave des Champs-Élysées, 8e (☎ 01 42 99 09 09 or, toll
    free from outside Paris, 05 25 31 81; metro George V)
Corsair
    ☎ 01 49 79 49 79 or 42 73 10 64
El Al
    35 Blvd des Capucines, 9e (☎ 01 44 55 00 00; metro Madeleine)
Northwest Airlines
    16 Rue Chauveau Lagarde, just north of Église la Made-
    leine, 8e (☎ 01 42 66 90 00; metro Madeleine)
Qantas
    13 Blvd de la Madeleine, 1er (☎ 01 44 55 52 00; metro
    Madeleine)
SAS
    18 Blvd Malesherbes, 8e (☎ 53 43 25 25; metro St Augustin)
Singapore Airlines
    43 Rue Boissière, 16e (☎ 01 45 53 90 90; metro Boissière)
South African Airways (SAA)
    350 Rue Saint Honoré, 1er (☎ 01 49 27 05 50; metro Tuile-
    ries)
TAT
    17 Rue de la Paix, 2e (☎ 01 42 61 82 10 or 05 05 50 05; metro
    Opéra)
Thai
    23 Ave des Champs-Élysées, 8e (☎ 01 44 20 70 80; metro
    Franklin D Roosevelt)
Tower Air
    4 Rue de La Michodière, 2e (☎ 01 44 51 56 56; metro Quatre
    Septembre)
United
    34 Ave de l'Opéra, 2e (☎ 01 48 97 82 82; metro Opéra)

BUS

Eurolines runs buses from Paris to cities all over Europe.
The company's Gare Routière Internationale Paris-
Galiéni (international bus terminal; M1; ☎ 01 49 72 51 51;
metro Galiéni) is on the eastern edge of the 20e in the
inner suburb of Bagnolet.
    Eurolines's ticket office (M14; ☎ 01 43 54 11 99, 49 72
51 51; by Minitel: 3615 EUROLINES; metro Cluny-La
Sorbonne) at 55 Rue Saint Jacques (5e) is open from 9.30
am to 1 pm and 2.30 to 7 pm (6 pm on Monday and

Saturday, closed Sunday); from late June to August, there's no midday closure. In summer, it's not a bad idea to make a reservation a few days in advance.

England

Eurolines' London booking office (☎ 0171-730 8235) is at 52 Grosvenor Gardens (SW1W 0AU), with bus services from London's Victoria Coach Station (as low as £30 one-way or £40 return, eight hours). It's even less if there's a fare war underway. Bookings can be made through any office of National Express.

Hoverspeed (☎ 01304-240 241 in Dover, 21 46 14 14 in Calais) runs City Sprint bus-boat-bus from London's Victoria Coach Station (☎ 0171-730 3499) to 165 Ave de Clichy (17e) (☎ 01 40 25 22 00; metro Brochant) in Paris. The trip takes nine hours, and the regular fare is £36/44 one-way/return.

Continental Europe

Eurolines has representatives across Europe, including: Eurolines (☎ 020-694 56 31), Amstel Station, Amsterdam; Deutsche Touring (☎ 089-54 58 70 15), Train Station Munich; and Lazzi Express (☎ 06-88 40 840), Via Tagliamento 27R, Rome.

From Paris, Eurolines has direct overnight buses to Amsterdam, Athens, Berlin, Budapest, Istanbul, Madrid, Prague and Rome.

TRAIN

Paris has six major train stations (Gare d'Austerlitz, Gare de l'Est, Gare de Lyon, Gare du Nord, Gare Mont-parnasse and Gare St Lazare), each of which handles passenger traffic to different parts of France and Europe. SNCF train information is available on ☎ 36 35 35 35 (for mainline services) and ☎ 01 45 65 60 00 (for suburban services). By Minitel, key in 3615 SNCF.

England

After many delays, cost over-runs and false starts, trains now zip back and forth under the Channel via the Channel Tunnel, but there are two distinctly different services. Eurostar operates between London and Paris carrying passengers. Le Shuttle goes only between Folkestone and just beyond Calais carrying cars, motor-cycles and (from mid 1996) bicycles with their passengers or riders. Train-boat-train connections are possible but scarcely worth considering.

London-Paris Fares & Travel Times
The arrival of the Channel Tunnel has unleashed periodic all-out fare wars between the airlines, the Eurostar and Le Shuttle Channel Tunnel train services, the bus services and the channel ferry operators. Fares London-Paris or simply across the Channel are very variable and it's definitely worth shopping around to see what special deals are available. The costs we've indicated are strictly guidelines, as the situation is currently highly volatile.

Flying London-Paris takes about an hour, while Eurostar takes about three hours, but there's not much in it, city centre to city centre, when getting to and from the airport, check-in times and waiting for baggage (sometimes a mysteriously long operation at Paris Charles de Gaulle airport) are taken into account. ■

Eurostar The highly civilised Eurostar passenger train service through the Channel Tunnel takes only three hours (not including the one-hour time change) to get from London's Waterloo Station to Paris' Gare du Nord. Passport and customs checks take place on board or very cursorily on arrival.

The regular 2nd-class fare is £77.50/155 one-way/return or £110/220 if you want to travel 1st class. A 2nd-class Leisure Return ticket costs £125 return and requires that you stay either three nights or Saturday night. You can get a 90% refund if you want to change the return booking. A 2nd-class advance purchase ticket must be bought at least 14 days ahead of departure; it costs £47.50/95 and although there's a 50% refund before you start you're locked into the return booking. An excursion fare costs just £79 return, requires a three-night or Saturday-night stay and can be 50% refunded before departure, but once you've started there is no refund if you want to change the return time.

Those under 26 pay £39.50/79 one-way/return at all times and do not have to book ahead. Cheaper fares are available for children aged four to 11 years. There are often special deals on offer, so it pays to phone Eurostar or its agents for the latest information.

Eurostar tickets are available from some travel agents, at Waterloo Station, from Victoria Station's International Rail Centre and the international ticket offices at many of the UK's mainline train stations, and from SNCF's French Railways House (☎ 0171-493 9731; tube Piccadilly Circus) at 179 Piccadilly, London (W1V 0BA), which also sells all other SNCF tickets. To book by phone you can ring Eurostar on ☎ 0990-300 003. Tickets, for which you pay by credit card, can be either sent to you by post or picked up at Waterloo Station.

Bicycles can only be taken on Eurostar as registered baggage; phone ☎ 0990-850 850 for more details.

Le Shuttle Le Shuttle, the train service through the Channel Tunnel between Folkestone and Coquelles (five km south-west of Calais), takes cars, motorcycles and, on some services, bicycles with their passengers or riders. Fares on Le Shuttle vary with the time of year, the day of the week, the time of the day and a variety of competitive pressures! You can get a car, with driver and passengers, across for as little as £60 one-way or £100 return, but at peak periods the cost can nearly double. Price wars can drop those costs considerably. A motorcycle and riders start from £35 and £60.

Bicycles can be taken on Le Shuttle but only on two trips per day and they must be booked 24 hours in advance on ☎ 01303-270 111. The cost is £15 for bicycle and rider.

For information and reservations, contact a travel agent or call Le Shuttle (☎ 0990-353 535 in the UK; in France by Minitel: 3615 LE SHUTTLE).

Le Shuttle runs 24 hours a day, every day of the year, with up to four departures an hour during peak periods. During the 35-minute crossing, passengers can sit in their cars or walk around the air-conditioned, soundproofed rail carriage. The entire process, including loading and unloading, should take about an hour.

Train-Boat-Train British Rail International (☎ 0171-834 2345) has train-boat-train combos (with Hoverspeed or others) from London's Charing Cross Station to Paris' Gare du Nord which take about nine hours and cost £45 one-way or £59 return. You've got to mess around transferring by bus between the train station and the ferry terminal on both sides and all in all it is no bargain compared to the three-hour Eurostar trip at often similar prices.

Continental Europe

Rail services link France with every country in Europe; schedules and tickets are available from major SNCF train stations. Because of different track gauges, you often have to change trains at the border (eg to Spain). There are TGV services to Brussels and in mid-1996 TGVs started operating to Amsterdam. The SNCF and the Spanish national railways are planning a high-speed rail link between Narbonne and Barcelona.

CAR & MOTORCYCLE

Taking a car or motorcycle to Paris is quick and convenient if you want to brave the traffic. From the UK to France you can cross under the channel via Le Shuttle (see Train) or sail over via a variety of ferry routes (see Boat). Once in France, modern autoroutes will get you to Paris quickly if rather expensively since tolls are charged. The Périphérique ring road encircles central Paris and it's often quicker to skirt around Paris to the closest point on the Périphérique before diving into the city traffic.

HITCHING

Hitching is never entirely safe in any country in the world, and we don't recommend it. Travellers who decide to hitch should understand that they are taking a small but potentially serious risk. People who do choose to hitch will be safer if they travel in pairs and let someone know where they are planning to go.

Le Shuttle car drivers can take a car full of passengers through the Channel Tunnel free so you can hitch to France for nothing and at no cost to the driver. Channel ferry services also often include a number of passengers free with each car carried.

Two organisations link up travellers and drivers going to the same destination: Allostop Provoya and Auto-Partage. Allostop Provoya is at 84 Passage Brady, 10e (M8; ☎ 01 42 46 00 66 or, from outside Paris or abroad, 01 47 70 02 01; metro Château d'Eau). It is open Monday to Friday from 9 am to 7.30 pm and on Saturday from 9 am to 1 pm and 2 to 6 pm. Auto-Partage is at 189 Ave de Choisy, 13e (M1; ☎ 01 45 85 52 53; metro Place d'Italie). It is open from 10 am to 1 pm and 2 to 7 pm (closed all day Sunday and on Monday morning).

BOAT

Tickets and reservations for ferry services across the Channel are available from the ferry operators and from travel agencies.

England

Fares vary widely according to seasonal demand and competitive pressures. Three or five-day excursion return fares cost about the same as regular one-way tickets.

The shortest Channel crossings are between Kent and the far-northern tip of France. The fastest way to cross the English Channel is to take one of Hoverspeed's (☎ 01304-240 241) hovercraft or the Stena Line's (☎ 0990-70 70 70) high-speed catamarans which ply the waters between Dover and Calais in less than an hour. Conventional car ferries are operated on the Dover-Calais route by P&O (☎ 0990-980 980) and Sea France (☎ 01304-212 696) and by the Stena Line. They take around 1½ hours. Note that the hovercrafts cannot operate in really rough weather.

Return passage for passengers on the Dover-Calais route is typically £50 (£26 for children). For a small car, the return cost starts at around £180 to £200, including passengers on some services but with additional charges on others. These fares are very changeable at present. It's typically £20 to £30 cheaper on the longer Folkestone-Boulogne route.

Other routes across the channel include Folkestone-Boulogne, Ramsgate-Dunkerque, Newhaven-Dieppe, Poole-Cherbourg, Portsmouth-Cherbourg, Portsmouth-Le Havre, Southampton-Cherbourg, Plymouth-Roscoff, Poole-Saint Malo, Portsmouth-Saint Malo and Weymouth-Saint Malo. There are also services via the Channel Islands to Saint Malo with Condor and Émeraude Lines.

Passengers can take bicycles free on hovercraft and ferry services. Although it's often more expensive than Le Shuttle train services, departures and routes may be more convenient.

Ireland

Eurail passes are valid for ferry crossings between Ireland and France. There is a charge to take along a bicycle.

Irish Ferries has runs to Rosslare (and, from May to September, to Cork) from Le Havre and Cherbourg (17 to 21 hours). There are three ferries a week from September to May; sailings are almost daily during the rest of the year. Pedestrians pay 400 to 600FF one-way; fares for students and people over 65 start at 320FF. From France, the cheapest couchette will cost an extra 50FF. A car with up to four passengers costs 1800 to 3000FF, depending on the season. Bicycles cost 120 to 180FF.

From mid-March to October, Brittany Ferries has weekly car ferries linking Cork (Ringaskiddy) with Roscoff (14 hours) and Cork with Saint Malo (18 hours). Foot passengers pay from 450 to 670FF one-way; a car plus driver costs 1250 to 2000FF.

WARNING

The information in this chapter is particularly vulnerable to change: prices for international travel are volatile, routes are introduced and cancelled, schedules change, special deals come and go, and rules and visa requirements are amended. Airlines and governments seem to take a perverse pleasure in making price structures and regulations as complicated as possible. You should check directly with the airline or a travel agent to make sure you understand how a fare (and ticket you may buy) works. In addition, the travel industry is highly competitive and there are many lurks and perks.

The upshot of this is that you should get opinions, quotes and advice from as many airlines and travel agents as possible before you part with your hard-earned cash. The details given in this chapter should be regarded as pointers and are not a substitute for your own careful, up-to-date research.

Getting Around

Driving in Paris may be a bad dream but the public transit system is one of the most efficient in the world.

ORLY AIRPORT

All six public transport options linking Orly with the city run daily every 15 minutes or so (less frequently late at night) from sometime between 5.30 and 6.30 am to 11 or 11.30 pm. Tickets are sold on board the buses.

Orlyval
Links the airport with the city centre in 30 minutes flat, no matter what the traffic situation is like (52FF; 22FF for kids aged four to 10). A completely automated (ie driverless) shuttle train connects both Orly terminals with the Antony RER station on RER line B; to get to Antony from the city, take line B4 toward Saint Rémy-lès-Chevreuse. Tickets are valid for 1st-class passage on the RER and metro travel within the city. Orlyval runs Monday to Saturday from 6 am to 10.30 pm and on Sunday from 7 am to 10.55 pm.

Orlyrail
Links the airport with RER line C (28FF; 40 minutes to the city centre). An ADP shuttle bus takes you to/from the Pont de Rungis-Aéroport d'Orly RER station; to get there from the city, take a C2 train codenamed ROMI or MONA toward Massy-Palaiseau. Tickets are valid for onward metro travel.

Orlybus
An RATP-run bus to/from the Denfert Rochereau metro station, in the heart of the 14e, near Place Denfert Rochereau (M1; 30FF; 25 minutes). In both directions, it makes several stops in the eastern 14e.

Jetbus
The cheapest way to get into the city (22FF; 20 minutes; ☎ 01 60 48 00 98). A bus links both terminals with the Villejuif-Louis Aragon metro stop, which is a bit south of the 13e on the city's southern fringe. From there a metro ticket will get you into the city.

Air France bus
Bus transport (☎ 01 41 56 78 00) to/from Gare Montparnasse in the 15e (M11; metro Montparnasse Bienvenüe) and Aérogare des Invalides in the 7e (M11; metro Invalides). The trip costs 40FF and takes 30 to 50 minutes. On your way into the city, you can request to get off at the Porte d'Orléans or Duroc metro stops.

RATP bus No 183
Ａ slow public bus that links Orly-Sud with the Porte de
Choisy metro station (M1), at the southern edge of the 13e
arrondissement. The cost is 30FF or three bus/metro tickets.
It runs daily from 5.35 am to 12.40 am every 35 minutes. Not
all buses with this number go all the way to Orly.

Taxi rides
Taxis to/from central Paris cost only about 130FF (plus
6FF per piece of luggage over five kg) and take 15 or 20
minutes if there's no traffic.

CHARLES DE GAULLE AIRPORT

The airport now has two train stations: Aéroport Charles
de Gaulle 1, linked to other parts of the airport complex
by the free SK mini-metro, and the shiny, new, TGV-
friendly Aéroport Charles de Gaulle 2, at Aérogare 2.
Both are served by commuter trains on RER line B3 (ie
Roissyrail); the latter is on the new TGV link that connects the TGV Nord line with the TGV Sud-Est line. It
will soon be connected with the TGV Atlantique as well.

There are six public transport options for travel
between Aéroport Charles de Gaulle and Paris. Unless
otherwise indicated, they run from sometime between 5
and 6.30 am until 11 or 11.30 pm. Tickets are sold on
board the buses.

Roissyrail
Links the city with both of the airport's train stations
(45FF; 35 minutes). To get to the airport, take any line B
train whose four-letter destination code begins with E.
Regular metro ticket windows can't always sell tickets, so
you may have to buy one at the RER station where you
board. The last train in both directions is sometime
around midnight.

Roissybus
An RATP-run bus (40FF; 45 minutes) that links all three
aérogares with Place de l'Opéra, 9e (M7 & M8; ☎ 01 48 04
18 24; metro Opéra).

Air France bus to the Arc de Triomphe
Links the airport with two locations on the Right Bank:
the end of Ave Carnot nearest the Arc de Triomphe (M6;
metro Charles de Gaulle-Étoile) and the Palais des
Congrès at Porte Maillot (17e; M6; metro Porte Maillot).
For information, ring ☎ 01 49 38 57 57. The cost is 55FF
and the trip takes 40 minutes.

Air France bus to Gare Montparnasse
Links the airport with Gare Montparnasse (15e; M11; metro
Montparnasse Bienvenüe). The ride costs 65FF and takes
about 60 minutes. Buses leave the airport every hour on the
half-hour from 7.30 am to 7.30 pm; there are departures from
the city every hour on the hour from 7 am to 9 pm.

RATP Bus No 350
Links both aérogares with Porte de la Chapelle (18e) and stops at Gare du Nord (at 184 Rue du Faubourg Saint Denis, 10e; M8) and Gare de l'Est (on Rue du 8 Mai 1945,10e; M8). The trip takes 50 minutes (60 or 70 minutes during rush hour) and costs 45FF or six bus/metro tickets (five tickets or 37.50FF if you have a two-zone Carte Orange).

RATP Bus No 351
Goes to Ave du Trôtelne (11e & 12e), on the eastern side of Place de la Nation (M1; metro Nation), and runs every half-hour or so until 8.20 pm (9.30 pm from the airport to the city). The trip costs 45FF or six bus/metro tickets (five tickets or 37.50FF if you have a two-zone Carte Orange).

Taxi rides
Taxis to the city centre should cost 200 to 230FF in the daytime (seven days a week) and 180 to 250FF at night (7 pm to 7 am), depending on the traffic. Luggage costs 6FF per bag over five kg.

From Airport to Airport

Air France bus No 3 (☎ 01 49 38 57 57) runs between the two airports every 20 minutes from 6 am to 11 pm (70FF; free for Air France passengers with connecting flights). When traffic is not heavy, the ride takes 50 minutes.

Taking a combination of Roissyrail and Orlyval costs 97FF and takes about an hour. A taxi from one airport to the other should cost around 300FF.

BUS

Regular bus services operate Monday to Saturday from about 6 am to 8.30 pm. Bus service is drastically reduced on Sundays, holidays and after 8.30 pm. As your bus approaches, signal the driver by waving.

Bus Fares

Short bus rides (ie rides in one or two bus zones) cost one bus/metro ticket; longer rides within the city require two. Transfers to other buses or the metro are not allowed. Travel to the suburbs costs two to six tickets, depending on the distance. Special tickets valid only on the bus can be purchased from the driver.

Whatever kind of single-journey ticket you have, you must cancel (oblitérer) it in the composteur (cancelling machine) next to the driver. If you have a Carte Orange, Formule 1 or Paris Visite pass, just flash it at the driver when you board. Do not cancel your magnetic coupon.

Noctambus

After the metro shuts down at around 12.45 am, the Noctambus network links the area just west of the Hôtel de Ville, 4e (M15), with lots of places on the Right Bank (served by lines A to H) and a few destinations on the Left Bank (served by lines J and R). Look for the symbol of a little black owl silhouetted against a yellow moon. All 10 lines depart every hour on the half-hour from 1.30 to 5.30 am; line R also leaves at 1, 2, 3, 4 and 5 am.

Noctambus service is free if you have a Carte Orange or a Paris Visite or Formule 1 pass. Otherwise, a ride costs 22.50FF (30FF if your journey involves a transfer).

METRO

There is almost always a metro station within 500 metres of wherever you want to go in Paris. Metro stations often have a *plan du quartier* (map of nearby streets) hung on the wall near the exits.

Paris' underground network consists of two separate but linked systems: the Métropolitain, known as the *métro*, which has 13 lines and over 300 stations, and the RER, a network of suburban services that pass through the city centre. The term 'metro' is used in this book to refer to the Métropolitain as well as any part of the RER system within Paris proper.

For a list of the metro stations many Parisians try to avoid late at night, see Dangers & Annoyances in the Facts for the Visitor chapter.

Information

Metro maps are available for free at metro ticket windows. For information on the metro, RER and bus system, call the RATP's 24-hour enquiries number, ☎ 08 36 68 41 14 (2.23FF a minute). By Minitel, key in 3615 RATP.

Information on SNCF's suburban services (including certain RER lines) is available on ☎ 01 45 65 60 00. By Minitel, type 3615 SNCF.

Metro Lines

Each Métropolitain train is known by the name of its end-of-the-line stop, which means that trains on the same line have different names depending on which direction they are travelling in.

Each line is also officially known by a number from one to 13, but Parisians don't often use the numbers.

Art in the Metro

There are more modern subway systems than the Paris metro but few as convenient or, at the better stations, more elegant. Which is not to say that it can't be very tedious when the metro workers have one of their periodic *grèves* (strikes), or very sleazy at some of the more down and dirty stations late at night.

There are stations not to be missed, like the Louvre-Rivoli (a small taste of the nearby Musée du Louvre; M12), Cluny-La Sorbonne (decorated with ceramic replicas of the signatures of intellectuals, artists and scientists from the quarter; M14) or, best of all, Arts et Métier (looking like a brass-plated Jules Verne submarine; M15). Metro entrances are proclaimed by a variety of elegant sign-posts, and from Place de la Bastille (M13) you can spot all three standard signs. There are modern yellow big-Ms beside the Opéra, standard red Art Nouveau signs on the Marais side of Place de la Bastille and, best of all, at the nearby Bréguet Sabin station, the writhing pale green metalwork of one of Hector Guimard's Art Nouveau metro signs, looking like an escapee from War of the Worlds. ∎

RICHARD NEBESKY

Louvre–Rivoli metro entrance

In the stations, blue-on-white *direction* signs indicate how to get to the right platform. On metro lines that split into several branches the terminus served by each train is indicated on the cars with backlit panels.

Black-on-orange *correspondance* signs show how to get to connecting trains. In general, the more lines that stop at a station, the longer the *correspondances* will be.

White-on-blue *sortie* signs indicate the station exits you have to choose from.

The last metro train on each line begins its final run of the night sometime between 12.25 and 12.45 am. After about midnight, metro travel is free. The metro resumes functioning around 5.30 am.

RER

The RER is faster than the Métropolitain but the stops are more widely spaced. Some parts of the city, such as the Musée d'Orsay and the Eiffel Tower, can be reached far more conveniently by RER than by Métropolitain.

RER lines are known by an alphanumeric combination – the letter (A, B, C or D) refers to the line, the number to the spur it will follow somewhere out in the suburbs. Even-numbered lines head to Paris' southern or eastern suburbs, odd-numbered ones go north or west. All trains whose code begins with the same letter have the same end-of-run stop.

Stations served are usually indicated on electric destination boards above the platform.

1st-class cars, which are located in the middle of the train, can be identified by the yellow stripe across the upper part of the car and the numeral '1'.

Suburban Services

The RER and the SNCF's commuter lines serve destinations outside the city, ie in zones 2 to 8. Purchase a special ticket *before* you board the train or you won't be able to get out of the station when you arrive at your destination (you can't simply pay the additional fare when you get there).

If you are issued a full-sized SNCF ticket for travel to the suburbs, validate it in one of the orange time-stamp pillars before boarding the train. You may also be given a *contremarque magnétique* (magnetic ticket) to get through any metro/RER-type turnstiles you'll have to cross on the way to/from the platform. If you are travelling on a multizone Carte Orange, Paris Visite or Formule 1, do *not* punch the magnetic coupon in SNCF's orange time-stamp machines. By the way, some RER/SNCF tickets purchased in the suburbs for travel to the city allow you to continue your journey by metro – if in doubt, ask the person selling you the ticket.

For some destinations, tickets can be purchased at any metro ticket window, but for others you'll have to get to an RER station on the line you need in order to buy a ticket. If you're trying to save every franc and have a

Carte Orange, Paris Visite or Formule 1, you could get off the train at the last station covered by your coupon and then purchase a separate ticket for the rest of your trip.

Bus & Metro Tickets

The same 2nd-class tickets are valid on buses, trams, the Montmartre *funiculaire*, the metro and – for travel within the Paris city limits – the RER. They cost 8FF if bought individually and 46FF for a *carnet* of 10. Children under four travel free; children under 10 for half fare. Tickets are sold at every metro station, though not always at each and every entrance. At some stations, you can pay by credit card if the bill comes to at least 100FF.

One bus/metro ticket lets you travel between any two metro stations for a period of two hours, no matter how many transfers are required. You can also use it on the RER commuter rail system for travel within Paris (that is, within zone 1). However, it cannot be used to transfer from the metro to a bus, from a bus to the metro or between buses.

Always keep your ticket until you arrive at your destination and exit the station.

Weekly & Monthly Tickets
The cheapest and easiest way to travel the metro is to get a Carte Orange, a bus/metro/RER pass whose accompanying magnetic coupon comes in weekly and monthly versions. You can get tickets for travel in from two to eight urban and suburban zones, but unless you'll be using the suburban commuter lines an awful lot, the basic ticket – valid for zones 1 and 2 – is probably enough.

The weekly ticket costs 70FF for zones 1 and 2 and is valid from Monday to Sunday. Even if you'll be in Paris for only three or four days, it may very well work out cheaper than purchasing single-ride tickets (break even at 15 rides), and it will certainly cost less than buying three days travel on a Formule 1 or Paris Visite tourist pass. The monthly ticket (243FF for zones 1 and 2) begins on the first day of each calendar month. Both are on sale in metro & RER stations from 6.30 am to 10 pm and at certain bus terminals.

To get a Carte Orange, bring a small photograph of yourself to any metro or RER ticket counter (four photos for 20 to 30FF are available from automatic booths in the train stations and certain metro stations). Request a Carte Orange (which is free) and the kind of coupon you'd like. To prevent tickets from being used by more than one person, you must write your surname and given name (*nom* and *prénom*) on the Carte Orange, and the number of your Carte Orange on each weekly or monthly coupon you buy (next to the words *Carte No*).

Tourist Passes The rather pricey Formule 1 and Paris Visite passes allow unlimited 1st-class travel on the metro, the RER, SNCF's suburban lines, buses, the Noctambus system, trams and the Montmartre funicular railway. They do not require a passport photo, though you should write your card number on the ticket.

The Formule 1 card and its attendant coupon allow unlimited travel for one day in three or five zones (40FF or 100FF). It is on sale at all metro and RER ticket windows as well as SNCF stations in the Paris region, but you have to make nine metro trips in a day to break even on this pass.

Paris Visite passes are valid for two/three/five consecutive days of travel in either three or five zones; the one to three-zone version costs 70/105/165FF. They can be purchased at larger metro and RER stations, at SNCF bureaux in Paris and at the airports.

CAR

Driving in Paris is nerve-wracking but not impossible by any means – except for the insecure, faint-hearted or indecisive. The fastest way to get across Paris is usually the Blvd Périphérique (M1), the ring road (beltway) that encircles the city.

In many parts of Paris you have to pay 5 to 10FF (or more) an hour to park your car. Large municipal parking garages usually charge about 12FF an hour or, for periods of 12 to 24 hours, 90FF. Parking fines are usually 75 or 200FF. Parking attendants dispense them with great abandon but Parisians appear to simply ignore them.

Rental

The easiest (if not cheapest) way to turn a stay in Paris into an uninterrupted series of hassles is to take upon yourself the responsibility of a rental car. If driving the car doesn't destroy your holiday-induced sense of carefree spontaneity, parking the damn thing (or trying to) just may. A small car (Peugeot 106) for one day with 400 km, plus insurance and taxes, costs about 340FF.

Most of the larger companies below have offices at the airports, and several are also represented at Aérogare des Invalides (7e; M11; metro Invalides). Higher rates may apply for airport rental, and you may have to return the car to the airport. Avis has offices at all six train stations.

To contact the major companies, ring their reservations centres:

Avis	☎ 01 46 10 60 60
Citer (Euro Dollar)	☎ 01 42 06 06 06
Europcar	☎ 01 30 43 82 82
Hertz	☎ 01 39 38 38 38

For other rental operators check the Yellow Pages under 'Location d'automobiles: tourisme et utilitaires'. One of the larger local rental operators is:

ADA
    271 Blvd Pereire, 17e (M6; ☎ 01 45 72 36 36; metro Porte Maillot); 74 Rue de Rome, 8e (M7; ☎ 01 42 93 65 13; metro Rome); 11 Rue de la Gaîté, 14e (M11; ☎ 01 43 27 67 67; metro Edgar Quinet); and 49 Ave de Versailles, 16e (☎ 01 42 15 06 06; metro Mirabeau).

TAXI

Parisian taxi drivers have a reputation for arrogance but, within reason, it's all part of the fun. They're often hair-raisingly bad drivers and not all of them know their way around Paris.

The flagfall *(prise en charge)* fee is 13FF. Within the city, it costs 3.56FF per km for travel undertaken Monday to Saturday from 7 am to 7 pm (tariff A). At night and on Sundays and holidays (tariff B) it's 5.45FF per km. It costs 120FF an hour to have a taxi sit and wait for you (or when the taxi is doing less than 23 km/h).

There's an extra 9FF charge for taking a fourth passenger but you must always ask first, as many drivers are reluctant to take four. Each piece of baggage costs 6FF and from certain train stations there's a 5FF supplement. A full list of surcharges is posted on the side window behind the driver.

Radio-dispatched taxi companies, on call 24 hours, include:

Alpha Taxis	☎ 01 45 85 85 85
Artaxi	☎ 01 42 41 50 50
G7 Radio	☎ 01 47 39 47 39
Taxis Bleus	☎ 01 49 36 10 10
Taxis-Radio Étoile	☎ 01 41 27 27 27

BICYCLE

There's plenty of space for cyclists in the Bois de Boulogne (16e), the Bois de Vincennes (12e), along the Canal Saint Martin (10e) to Parc de la Villette (19e) and then along the south bank of the 108-km-long Canal de l'Ourcq. For information on bicycle tours, see Organised Tours.

Bike rental is possible in the Bois de Boulogne, and at a number of RER/SNCF stations.

Bikes are not allowed on the metro. You can take your bicycle for free on some RER lines out to the Paris suburbs on weekends and holidays (all day), and on weekdays before 6.30 am, between 9.30 am and 4.30 pm, and after 7.30 pm. More lenient rules apply to SNCF commuter services. For details, call the SNCF or the RATP or stop by one of their information offices.

WALKING

Paris is a surprisingly pedestrian-friendly city, in part because it's relatively compact. Metro stations are often so close you can see down the tunnel from one station to the next, so it can be as fast to walk as to wait the minute or two for the next metro to turn up. Furthermore, it's a relatively level city, so apart from toiling up to Montmartre there's no hill climbing involved. Traffic is, of course, a problem. Cars will only stop for pedestrians if they absolutely assert their rights on pedestrian crossings. And then there's those damned dogs.

BOAT

For information on the Batobus river shuttle, see Organised Tours.

TONY WHEELER

Batobus

ORGANISED TOURS

Sight-seeing boats run by a number of companies ply the Seine between the Eiffel Tower and the Île Saint Louis.

Boat

From March to October, Canauxrama (M13; ☎ 01 42 39 15 00) barges travel between Port de Plaisance de Paris-Arsenal (12e) and Parc de la Villette (19e) along charming Canal Saint Martin and Canal de l'Ourcq. Departures are around 9.30 am and 2.45 pm. The cost is 75FF (60FF for students, 45FF for kids under 12).

From about mid-April to October, the Bateaux Parisiens Batobus river shuttle (☎ 01 44 11 33 44) docks at the following stops:

- Eiffel Tower (Port de la Bourdonnais; M10)
- Musée d'Orsay (Port de Solférino; M11)
- opposite the Louvre (Quai Malaquais; M12)
- Notre Dame (Quai Montebello; M12 & M15)
- Hôtel de Ville (Quai de l'Hôtel de Ville; M15)

The boats come by every 35 minutes from about 10 am to 7 pm and cost 12FF per journey between dockings. Unlimited travel for the whole day costs 60FF (25FF for children under 12). Note that if you're travelling west (Hôtel de Ville to Eiffel Tower) you can travel the whole length of the trip for just 12FF (one stop); in the opposite direction it's three stops and will cost 36FF.

From their base just north of the Eiffel Tower (M10) at Port de la Bourdonnais (7e) Batobus also runs one-hour river circuits (45FF, 20FF for under 12s) and lunch/dinner cruises (300/560FF). From May to October, boats also depart from the dock (M15; ☎ 01 43 26 92 55; metro Maubert Mutualité) opposite Notre Dame, on Quai de Montebello (5e).

The Bateaux Mouches company (M6 & M7; ☎ 01 42 25 96 10 or 01 40 76 99 99 for an English recording; metro Alma Marceau), based on the right (north) bank of the Seine just east of Pont de l'Alma (8e), runs 1000-seat tour boats, the biggest on the Seine. From mid-November to mid-March, there are sailings daily at 11 am, 2.30 pm, 4 pm and 9 pm, and, depending on demand, at other times as well. The rest of the year, boats depart every half-hour from 10 am to 12.30 pm and 1.30 to 11 pm. A one-hour cruise with commentary costs 40FF (20FF for those under 14). Lunch cruises are 300 to 350FF, dinner cruises 500 to 650FF.

Vedettes du Pont Neuf (M14; ☎ 01 46 33 98 38; metro Pont Neuf), whose home dock is at the far western tip of the Île de la Cité (1er), offers one-hour boat excursions. Boats generally leave every half-hour between 10 am and noon and 1.30 to 6.30 pm. Night cruises depart every 30 minutes from 9 to 10.30 pm (service stops earlier from Monday to Thursday during the November to February period). A ticket costs 45FF (20FF for children under 10).

Bus

On Sunday afternoons from mid-April to mid-September, RATP's Balabus follows a 50-minute route from Gare de Lyon to La Défense that passes by many of central Paris' most famous sights. Details should be available at metro counters.

PariBus (☎ 01 42 30 55 50) runs red, London-style double-decker buses in a 2¼-hour circuit that takes in Notre Dame and the usual list of Right Bank tourist sights. For 125FF (60FF for children aged four to 13) you can, over a period of two days, get on and off the company's buses wherever you like; their progress through the city is accompanied by commentary in English and French. Brochures showing the exact locations of PariBus's stops are available at many hotels.

Cityrama (M7; ☎ 01 44 55 61 00) runs two-hour tours of the city daily (150FF), accompanied by taped commentary in a dozen or so languages. The company also has trips to Chartres, Versailles and other places around Paris, and is based near the western end of the Louvre at 4 Place des Pyramides (1er; metro Tuileries).

Bicycle

Mountain Bike Trip (☎ 01 09 21 14 59 for their voice mail account) runs well-reviewed bicycle tours of Paris and its major monuments. Unless there's heavy rain, tours take place every day, all year round, and last from 11 am to about 6 pm. The accompanying commentary is in English. The cost, including rental, is 120FF. To reserve a place, phone a day ahead. They also rent bicycles for 90FF a day.

Slightly more expensive bilingual bicycle tours are offered by Paris-Vélo (M12; ☎ 01 43 37 59 22; metro Censier Daubenton) at 2 Rue du Fer à Moulin (5e).

Things to See & Do

HIGHLIGHTS

Paris has a wealth of wonderful places to visit, but some features are so outstanding they deserve special mention. Here are the places not to miss in Paris:

- Churches – La Madeleine, Notre Dame, Sainte Chapelle & Saint Eustache
- Monuments – Arc de Triomphe, Eiffel Tower, Panthéon & Place de la Concorde
- Museums & Art Galleries – Centre Pompidou, Musée du Louvre, Musée d'Orsay, Musée Picasso & Musée Rodin
- Neighbourhoods – Bastille, Île Saint Louis, Latin Quarter, the Marais & Montmartre
- Odd Attractions – Catacombes & Musée des Égouts de Paris
- Parks, Gardens & Cemeteries – Bois de Boulogne, Cimetière du Père Lachaise, Jardin du Luxembourg & Jardin des Tuileries
- Shopping – Blvd Montmartre arcades, the Marais, Rue du Faubourg Saint Honoré, Saint Germain des Prés & Triangle d'Or
- Tourist Traps – Champs-Élysées, Montmartre & Jim Morrison's grave
- Views – Eiffel Tower, Parc des Buttes-Chaumont, Sacré Cœur & Tour Montparnasse.

LOUVRE AREA (western 1er)

From the enormous Palais du Louvre, you can walk in literally any direction and come upon some well-known sights, including many of Paris' most famous public spaces. The Louvre area has long been a chic residential area for people of means.

Musée du Louvre

The vast Louvre (M12; ☎ 01 40 20 53 17 or 01 40 20 51 51 for a recording; metro Palais Royal), constructed around 1200 as a fortress and rebuilt in the mid-16th century for use as a royal palace, began its career as a public museum in 1793. The paintings, sculptures and artefacts on display have been assembled by French governments over the past five centuries. Among them are works of art and artisanship from all over Europe and important

Places & Squares

Postcard visions of Paris are often constructed around pretty little squares, arrayed with café tables where happy imbibers quaff wine in the spring sunshine. Try the Place du Marché Sainte Catherine (M15; metro Saint Paul) in the colourful Marais district for a perfect vision of exactly that sort of square. Place des Vosges (M15; metro Bastille) is only a few minutes' stroll away if you want a more formal version of the Paris *place*. And while you're in the Marais, search out the intricate courtyards of the Village Saint Paul, just off antique-shop-studded Rue Saint Paul (M15; metro Saint Paul).

On the Left Bank, Place de la Contrescarpe, 5e (M12; metro Cardinal Lemoine) is a lively and picturesque little traffic roundabout surrounded by cafés, shops and students. James Joyce and Ernest Hemingway were once locals (there's a 'Hemingway lived here' sign just a few steps away), and Lonely Planet's Paris office is nearby. Once upon a time this area was just outside the city walls, and there are large chunks of medieval city walls off Rue du Cardinal Lemoine and Rue Clovis. ∎

collections of Assyrian, Etruscan, Greek, Coptic, Roman and Islamic art and antiquities.

The Louvre may be the most actively avoided museum in Paris. Tourists and residents alike, daunted by the richness of the place and its sheer size (the side facing the Seine is almost 0.75 km long), often find the prospect of an afternoon at a smaller museum far more inviting. Eventually, most people do their duty and

TONY WHEELER

The Louvre – Pavillon Richelieu

come, but many leave overwhelmed, unfulfilled, exhausted and frustrated at having gotten lost on their way to the *Mona Lisa*.

The Louvre was one of former President François Mitterrand's most ambitious and boldly conceived *grands projets*, and the French government has invested over US$1 billion in restoring, renovating and upgrading its exhibition halls and public spaces. The whole project is slated to be completed around the turn of the century. If you haven't visited the Louvre for a few years, you'll hardly recognise the place: hundreds of masterpieces have come out of storage, old favourites have been moved, and grand new halls have been opened.

Orientation The Louvre's main entrance and ticket windows are covered by a 21-metre-high **glass pyramid** (M12) designed by Chinese-born American architect I M Pei. Commissioned by Mitterrand and completed in 1990, the design generated bitter controversy in the mid-1980s but is now generally acknowledged to be a brilliant success. You can avoid the queues outside the pyramid by entering the Louvre complex via the Carrousel du Louvre shopping area – there's an entrance opposite 174 Rue de Rivoli (M12).

The Louvre is divided into four sections. **Sully** forms the four sides of the Cour Carrée (Square Courtyard) at the eastern end of the building. **Denon** stretches for 500 metres along the Seine. **Richelieu**, the wing along the Rue de Rivoli, was occupied by the Ministry of Finance until the late 1980s and has some superb new halls. The new, underground **Carrousel du Louvre** shopping mall, where you'll find museum shops, a Virgin Megastore and a bunch of up-market boutiques, stretches from the pyramid to the Arc de Triomphe du Carrousel (see below). Its centrepiece is an *inverted* glass pyramid (M12), also by Pei.

The split-level public area under the pyramid is known as **Hall Napoléon**. It has an exhibit on the history of the Louvre, a bookshop, a restaurant, a café and auditoriums for concerts, lectures and films. Rudimentary maps of the Louvre are available at the round Information desk.

Hours & Tickets The Louvre is open daily except Tuesday and certain holidays. From Thursday to Sunday, hours are 9 am to 6 pm. On Monday and Wednesday, hours are 9 am to 10 pm, but on Monday only the Richelieu wing is open after 5.30 pm. Ticket sales end 45 minutes before closing time, and the guards begin clearing the halls 30 minutes before closing.

Entry to the permanent collections (but not temporary exhibitions) costs 45FF (26FF after 3 pm and all day Sunday). There are no discounts for students or senior citizens, but under 18s get in free. Tickets are valid all day long, so you can leave and re-enter as you please.

Except from January to Easter, be prepared for queues. The best times to come if you want to avoid the crowds are on Wednesday night and on Thursday and Friday afternoons. If possible, it's best to avoid the place entirely during the Christmas and Easter school holidays.

Guided Tours English-language guided tours (☎ 01 40 20 51 77) lasting 1½ hours are held three to five times a day except on Sunday, when the museum is too crowded. They depart from the Accueil des Groupes area under the pyramid. Tickets cost 33FF (20FF for 13 to 18-year-olds, free for children under 13), in addition to the regular entry fee. Groups are limited to 25 people, so it's a good idea to sign up at least 30 minutes before departure time.

Cassette tours *(acoustiguides)* in six languages, available until 4.30 pm, can be rented for 30FF under the pyramid, at the entrances to each wing. The recording lasts 1½ hours as well.

Detailed explanations in a variety of languages, printed on heavy, plastic-coated *feuillets* (sheets), are stored on racks in each display room.

Église Saint Germain L'Auxerrois

Built between the 13th and 16th centuries in a mixture of Gothic and Renaissance styles, this parish church (M12; metro Louvre) stands on a site – facing the eastern side of the Louvre – that has been used for Christian worship since about 500 AD. After being mutilated by 18th-century churchmen intent on 'modernisation' and vandals during the Revolution, it was restored by Viollet-le-Duc in the mid-1800s. It is open daily from 8 am to 8 pm.

The square, Romanesque **belfry** that rises from next to the south transept arm contains the bell whose tolling served as a signal to begin the Saint Bartholomew's Day Massacre in August 1572, in which 3000 Protestants were slaughtered according to a plan devised by Catherine de' Medici and approved by her son, the French King Charles IX.

Jardin du Palais Royal

The **Palais Royal** (M12; metro Palais Royal), which briefly housed young Louis XIV in the 1640s, is opposite Place du Palais Royal, north of the Louvre. Construction was begun in the 17th century by Cardinal Richelieu, though most of the present neoclassical complex dates from the latter part of the 18th century. The interior is closed to the public. The colonnaded building facing Place André Malraux is the **Comédie Française** (M12), founded in 1680 and the world's oldest national theatre.

Just north of the main part of the palace is the Jardin du Palais Royal (M8), a lovely park surrounded by arcades. During the late 1700s there was something of a permanent carnival here, and all sorts of things hard to find elsewhere in Paris (for example incendiary political tracts) were openly available since this was the private domain of the Duc d'Orléans and the police were unable to interfere. On 12 July 1789, the revolutionary Camille Desmoulins came to the gardens and made a fiery speech that helped push Paris toward open revolt.

The arcades on the eastern side of the garden, **Galerie de Valois**, shelter antiquarian bookshops; on the other side, in **Galerie de Montpensier**, you'll find art galleries, places that make colourful Legion-of-Honour-type medals (at Nos 3 and 7) and a place that specialises in toy soldiers (at No 38). Le Grand Véfour (M8), one of Paris' oldest and most illustrious restaurants, is at the northern end. At the southern end there's a controversial **sculpture** of black-and-white striped columns by Daniel Buren, installed in 1986.

The park is open daily until sometime between 8.30 pm in winter and 11 pm in summer.

Le Louvre des Antiquaires

This impressive building on the eastern side of Place du Palais Royal (M12; metro Palais Royal) houses about 250 elegant antique shops. Each is filled with precious objects from the past (objets d'art, furniture, clocks, classical antiquities). It is open Tuesday to Sunday from 11 am to 7 pm. In July and August it closes on Sunday.

Galerie Véro Dodat

For a quick taste of 19th-century Paris, it's hard to beat this shopping arcade (M12) between 19 Rue Jean-Jacques Rousseau and 2 Rue du Bouloi, which opened in 1826 and retains its 19th-century skylights, ceiling murals and store fronts. The shops specialise in antiques, objets d'art, art books and fashion accessories. Café de l'Époque at No 37 has drinks and light meals (closed, like the Galerie, on Sunday).

Musée des Arts Décoratifs

The Museum of Decorative Arts (M11; ☎ 01 44 55 57 50; metro Tuileries) at 107 Rue de Rivoli occupies the western tip of the Louvre's north wing. Displays include furniture, jewellery and objets d'art (such as ceramics and glassware) from the Middle Ages and the Renaissance through to the Art Nouveau and Art Deco periods. It's open Wednesday to Sunday from 12.30 pm (noon on Sunday) to 6 pm. Entrance costs 25FF (16FF reduced price).

In the same part of the Louvre you'll find the **Musée des Arts de la Mode** (Museum of Costume & Fashion; ☎ 01 44 55 57 50) and the **Musée de la Publicité** (Museum of Advertising), both of which are set to reopen in 1997 after being completely redesigned.

Place des Pyramides

The brightly gilded, 19th-century statue of Joan of Arc at Place des Pyramides (next to 192 Rue de Rivoli; M7) is a favourite rallying point for royalists and parties of the extreme right.

Arc de Triomphe du Carrousel

Constructed by Napoleon to celebrate his battlefield triumphs of 1805, this triumphal arch (M11) set in the Jardin du Carrousel, at the eastern end of the Jardin des

RICHARD NEBESKY

Arc de Triomphe du Carrousel

Tuileries, was once crowned by the Horses of Saint Mark's, stolen from Venice by Napoleon and taken back after Waterloo. The group of statues on top, added in 1828, celebrates the return of the Bourbons to the French throne after Napoleon's downfall. The sides are adorned with depictions of Napoleonic victories and eight pink marble columns, atop each of which stands a soldier of the emperor's Grande Armée.

Jardin des Tuileries

The formal Tuileries Gardens (M7 & M11), which begin just west of the Louvre, were laid out in their present form (more or less) in the mid-1600s by André Le Nôtre, who also created the gardens at Versailles. The Tuileries soon became the most fashionable spot in Paris for parading about in one's finery. On 10 August 1792, after Louis XVI and his family had fled from the Louvre via the Tuileries, enraged revolutionaries attacked the Swiss Guards (responsible for palace security) and butchered 600 of them in the gardens. Over the past few years, the gardens have been cleaned up and replanted.

The Voie Triomphale (also known as the **Grande Axe** or 'Great Axis'), the western continuation of the Tuileries' east-west axis, follows the Champs-Élysées to the Arc de Triomphe and, eventually, to the Grande Arche in the modern skyscraper district of La Défense.

Musée de l'Orangerie

The Orangerie Museum (M7; ☎ 01 42 97 48 16; metro Concorde), in the south-west corner of the Jardin des Tuileries at Place de la Concorde, has important Impressionist works, including a series of Monet's *Décorations des Nymphéas* (Water Lilies) and paintings by Cézanne, Matisse, Picasso, Renoir and Soutine. It's open daily except Tuesday from 9.45 am to 5 pm. Entrance costs 28FF (18FF reduced price); everyone pays 18FF on Sunday.

Jeu de Paume

The Galerie Nationale du Jeu de Paume (M7; ☎ 01 47 03 12 50; metro Concorde) is housed in a one-time *jeu de paume* (a court for playing real – ie royal – tennis) built in 1861 during the reign of Napoleon III in the north-west corner of the Jardin des Tuileries. Once the home of a good part of France's national collection of Impressionist works (now in the Musée d'Orsay), it reopened in 1992 as a gallery for innovative, two or three-month exhibitions of contemporary art (ie art from the last 20 or 30 years).

It's open Tuesday to Friday from noon to 7 pm (9.30 pm on Tuesday) and on weekends from 10 am to 7 pm. Admission is 35FF (25FF for young people aged 13 to 18, students under 26 and people over 60). The Carte Musées is not valid here.

Place Vendôme

Eight-sided Place Vendôme (M7) and the arcaded and colonnaded buildings around it were built between 1687 and 1721. In March 1796, Napoleon married Josephine in the building at No 3 (formerly the city hall of the 2e arrondissement). The Ministry of Justice has been at Nos 11-13 since 1815.

Today, the buildings around the square house the posh Hôtel Ritz (M7) and some of Paris' most fashionable and expensive boutiques, more of which can be found along nearby Rue de Castiglione, Rue Saint Honoré and Rue de la Paix.

Originally, Place Vendôme was built to showcase a giant statue of Louis XIV, which was destroyed during the Revolution. The 43.5-metre column now in the centre of the square, **Colonne Vendôme**, consists of a stone core wrapped in a 160-metre-long bronze spiral made from 1250 Austrian and Russian cannons captured by Napoleon at the Battle of Austerlitz (1805). The bas-reliefs on the spiral depict Napoleon's victories of 1805-07. The statue on top, placed there in 1873, depicts Napoleon as a Roman emperor.

Walking in the Louvre Area

Strolling options to/from the Louvre are countless.

The Voie Triomphale (Triumphal Way; M7), the axis of Ave des Champs-Élysées as it heads north-westward from the Louvre, has been a favourite venue for elegant promenades since its construction began in the 16th century. A stroll from the Louvre through the Jardin des Tuileries to the Arc de Triomphe involves about 3.5 km of walking.

Opéra Garnier is one km north of the Louvre along the prestigious Ave de l'Opéra, home to numerous airline offices and luxury goods shops.

Since Jardin des Tuileries is right across the Seine from the Musée d'Orsay, you can easily pop over to see the sights covered in the 7e Arrondissement section.

The eastern end of the Louvre is only half a km north-west of Île de la Cité and about the same distance south-west of the lively streets around Les Halles. It is linked with the area around Saint Germain des Prés (6e) by one of Paris' most romantic bridges, the pedestrians-only Pont des Arts (M14).

LES HALLES AREA (1er & 4e)

The huge pedestrian zone between the Centre Pompidou and the Forum des Halles is always filled with people, just as it was for the 850-odd years during which the area served as Paris' main marketplace. During the day, the main attractions are museums, art galleries, shops and places to eat, while at night – and into the wee hours of the morning – restaurants, theatres and discos draw Parisians out for a night on the town.

Forum des Halles

Les Halles, Paris' main wholesale food market, occupied the area just south of Église Saint Eustache from around 1110 until 1969, when it was moved out to the suburb of Rungis. In its place, Forum des Halles (M12; metro Les Halles or Châtelet-Les Halles) – a huge and aesthetically controversial underground shopping mall – was constructed in the high-tech, glass-and-chrome style which was in vogue in the early 1970s. The complex's four levels of shops, built around an open courtyard, have proved highly popular with Parisian shoppers, especially those in search of reasonable prices.

Around Forum des Halles

Atop Forum des Halles is a popular **park** where you can picnic, people-watch and sunbathe on the lawn while gazing at the flying buttresses of Église Saint Eustache. During the warm months, street musicians, fire eaters and other performers display their talents throughout the area, especially at **Square des Innocents**, whose centre is adorned by a multitiered Renaissance fountain, **Fontaine des Innocents** (1549; M12). The square and the fountain are named after the Cimetière des Innocents, a cemetery on this site from which two million skeletons were transferred to the Catacombes (14e; M1) in the 1780s. One block south of the fountain is **Rue de la Ferronnerie**, where in 1610 Henri IV was assassinated by Ravaillac while passing house No 11 in his carriage.

Église Saint Eustache

This majestic church (M12; metro Les Halles), one of the most attractive in Paris, is just north of the grassy area on top of Forum des Halles. Constructed between 1532

RICHARD NEBESKY

Roofs of Les Halles

RICHARD NEBESKY

Les Halles with Église Saint Eustache in the background

and 1637, its general design is Gothic. The classical west façade was added in the mid-18th century.

Inside, there's some exceptional Flamboyant archwork holding up the ceiling of the chancel, though most of the interior ornamentation is Renaissance and classical, as you can see from the cornices and Corinthian columns. The gargantuan, 101-stop, 8000-pipe organ above the west entrance is used for concerts, a long tradition here. The nave and choir are lined with chapels, some containing tombs, including that of Louis XIV's finance minister, Jean-Baptise Colbert (1619-83). It is open Monday to Saturday from 9 am to 7 pm (8 pm in summer); Sunday from 8.15 am to 12.30 pm and 2.30 to 7 pm (8 pm in summer).

La Samaritaine Rooftop Terrace

For an amazing 360° panoramic view of central Paris, head to the roof of La Samaritaine department store (M12; ☎ 01 40 41 20 20; metro Pont Neuf) on Rue de la Monnaie (1er), just north of Pont Neuf. The 11th-floor lookout and its viewpoint indicator, open Monday to Saturday from 9.30 am to 7 pm (10 pm on Thursday), are atop the Art Nouveau-style Building 2. You can have something to drink at the outdoor café on the 10th floor, reached by taking the lift to the 9th floor and then climbing a flight of stairs.

Centre Pompidou

The Centre Georges Pompidou (M12 & M15; ☎ 01 44 78 12 33; metro Rambuteau), also known as the Centre Beaubourg, is dedicated to displaying and promoting modern and contemporary art. Thanks in part to its vigorous schedule of outstanding temporary exhibitions, it is by far the most visited cultural sight in Paris.

The design of the Centre Pompidou has not ceased to draw wide-eyed gazes and critical comment since its construction between 1972 and 1977. In order to keep the exhibition halls as spacious and uncluttered as possible, the architects – one Italian, the other British – put the building's 'insides' on the outside. The purpose of each of the ducts, pipes and vents that enclose the centre's glass walls can be divined from the paint job: escalators and lifts are red, electrical circuitry is yellow, the plumbing is green and the air-conditioning system is blue. Alas, the innovative structure has aged poorly, and parts of it will be closed for renovation – section by section – until 1999.

The Centre Pompidou complex is open daily except Tuesday from noon (10 am on weekends and public holidays) to 10 pm. Ticket sales end at 9 pm.

Orientation & Tickets The Centre Pompidou consists of several distinct parts, each of which has its own entrance fees. Tickets for all sections are sold at the ticket windows on the ground floor.

The **Musée National d'Art Moderne (MNAM)**, which displays France's national collection of modern and contemporary (ie 20th-century) art, costs 35FF (24FF for people aged 16 to 24, and on Sunday and holidays for everyone; free for under 16s).

The **Galeries Contemporaines**, which form part of the MNAM, host temporary shows with separate admission fees.

The 5th-floor **Grande Galerie**, which is used for major exhibitions lasting about three months (with a one to 1½-month break between shows), also has its own, usually steep, admission fees.

For information on the Bibliothèque Publique d'Information (BPI), which occupies the Centre Pompidou's 2nd floor, see Libraries in the Facts for the Visitor chapter.

If you'll be visiting several parts of the complex on the same day, the Forfait 1 Jour (One-Day Pass), which costs 70FF (45FF if you're aged 16 to 24; free for kids under 16), is a good deal.

Tours Free, English-language tours (☎ 01 44 78 40 36) of various parts of the centre take place in the warm months, especially on weekends, often at 2.30 or 3.30 pm. You must have a ticket valid for the exhibit the tour covers.

Around the Centre Pompidou

The **square** on the west side of the Centre Pompidou and nearby pedestrianised streets attract buskers, street artists, musicians, jugglers, mime artists and, so Parisians complain, pickpockets and drug dealers. The fanciful, colourful **fountains** (M15) at Place Igor Stravinsky, on the centre's south side, were created by Jean Tinguely and Niki de Saint-Phalle.

Le Défenseur du Temps (the Defender of Time; M15), a mechanical clock whose protagonist does hourly battle with the elements (air, water and earth in the form of vicious beasts), is a block north of the Centre Pompidou along Rue Brantôme (3e), in a modern development known as Quartier de l'Horloge. Particularly lively combat takes place at 2 and 6 pm.

RICHARD NEBESKY

Centre Pompidou

Hôtel de Ville

Paris' city hall (M12 & M15; ☎ 01 42 76 40 40; metro Hôtel de Ville) was rebuilt in the neo-Renaissance style between 1874 and 1882 after having been gutted during the Paris Commune (1871). The ornate façade is decorated with 108 statues of noteworthy Parisians. Free guided tours (☎ 01 42 76 59 46) of the interior are held in French every Monday at 10.30 am, except on public holidays and during official functions. The visitors' entrance is at 29 Rue de Rivoli (4e), where there's a hall used for temporary exhibitions (open Monday to Saturday from 9.30 am to 6 pm).

The Hôtel de Ville faces majestic, fountain-and-lamp-adorned **Place de l'Hôtel de Ville**, used since the Middle Ages to stage many of Paris' celebrations, rebellions, book burnings and public executions. Known as Place de Grève (Strand Square) until 1830, it was in centuries past a favourite gathering place of the unemployed, which is why a strike is, to this day, called a *grève* in French.

Walking in Les Halles Area

Rue Quincampoix (4e; metro Rambuteau or Châtelet), two blocks west of the Centre Pompidou, is home to quite a few art galleries, including **Galerie Zabriskie** (M15; ☎ 01 42 72 35 47) at No 37.

The Centre Pompidou is within easy walking distance of the Louvre (one km to the west) and Notre Dame (800 metres due south). The Marais, with its many museums, is only a few blocks to the east. Place de l'Hôtel de Ville

BETHUNE CARMICHAEL

Hôtel de Ville

(M12) is the perfect place to enjoy an ice cream on a sunny day.

MARAIS (southern 3e & 4e)

The Marais (literally, marsh), the area of the Right Bank directly north of Île Saint Louis, was in fact a swamp until the 13th century, when it was converted to agricultural use. In the early 1600s, Henri IV built Place des Vosges, turning the area into Paris' most fashionable residential district and attracting wealthy aristocrats, who erected luxurious but discreet **hôtels particuliers** (private mansions). When the aristocracy moved to Versailles and Faubourg Saint Germain (7e) during the late

17th and 18th centuries, the Marais and its townhouses passed into the hands of ordinary Parisians.

Today, the Marais is one of the few neighbourhoods of Paris that still has almost all of its pre-Revolutionary architecture extant. In recent years the area has become trendy, but it's still home to a long-established Jewish community and is a major centre of Paris' gay life. On Friday and Saturday nights, the Marais is crowded with people out dining or bar-hopping with friends.

A number of the 16th and 17th-century hôtels particuliers, many built around enclosed garden courtyards, have been turned into museums.

Place des Vosges

Place des Vosges (4e; M15; metro Bastille or Chemin Vert), inaugurated in 1612 as Place Royale, is a square ensemble of 36 symmetrical houses with ground-floor arcades, steep slate roofs and large dormer windows. Only the earliest houses were built of brick: to save time, the rest were given timber frames and faced with plaster, later painted to resemble brick. Duels were once fought in the elegant park in the middle. The square received its present name in 1800 to honour the Vosges department, the first in France to pay its taxes. Today, the arcades around Place des Vosges are occupied by up-market art galleries, pricey antique shops and elegant places to sip tea.

Victor Hugo lived at 6 Place des Vosges from 1832 to 1848. **Maison de Victor Hugo** (M15; ☎ 01 42 72 10 16) is now a municipal museum, and is open from 10 am to 5.40 pm (closed Monday and holidays). The entry fee is 17.50FF (9FF for students, free for under 18s).

Hôtel de Sully

While in the vicinity of Place des Vosges it's well worth ducking into the Hôtel de Sully (M15; metro Saint Paul), a superb, early 17th-century aristocratic mansion at 62 Rue Saint Antoine (4e) that is now home to the Caisse Nationale des Monuments Historiques et des Sites (a body responsible for many of France's historical monuments). The two beautifully decorated late Renaissance-style courtyards are adorned with bas-reliefs of the seasons and the elements.

Musée Carnavalet

Also known as the Musée de l'Histoire de Paris (M15; ☎ 01 42 72 21 13; metro Saint Paul or Chemin Vert), at 23

Rue de Sévigné (3e), this museum of Parisian history is housed in two hôtels particuliers: the mid-16th-century, Renaissance-style Hôtel Carnavalet, once home to the late 17th-century writer Madame de Sévigné, and the late 17th-century Hôtel Le Peletier de Saint Fargeau. The artefacts on display chart the history of Paris from the Gallo-Roman period to the 20th century. The museum has the country's most important collection of documents, paintings and other objects from the French Revolution.

The Musée Carnavalet is open daily (except on Monday and public holidays) from 10 am to 5.40 pm; from 1.10 pm for some areas. Entrance costs 27FF (14.50FF reduced price); the price goes up a bit during temporary exhibitions.

Musée Picasso

The Picasso Museum (M15; ☎ 01 42 71 25 21; metro Saint Paul or Chemin Vert) at 5 Rue de Thorigny (3e), housed in the mid-17th-century Hôtel Salé, is one of Paris' best loved art museums. Displays include engravings, paintings, ceramic works, drawings and an unparalleled collection of sculptures that the heirs of Pablo Picasso (1881-1973) donated to the French government in lieu of inheritance taxes. You can also see part of Picasso's personal art collection, which includes works by Braque, Cézanne, Matisse and Degas. Inaugurated in 1985, the museum is open daily except Tuesday from 9.30 am to 6 pm (5.30 pm from October to March); ticket sales end 45 minutes earlier. The entry fee is 36FF (26FF reduced price and, on Sunday, for everyone).

Musée de la Serrure

The Lock Museum (M15; ☎ 01 42 77 79 62; metro Saint Paul or Chemin Vert) at 1 Rue de la Perle (3e), also known as the Musée Bricard, showcases a fine collection of locks, keys and door knockers. One lock, made around 1780, traps your hand in the jaws of a bronze lion if you try to use the wrong key. Another one, created in the 19th century, shoots anyone who inserts an incorrect key! The museum is open from 10 am to noon and 2 to 5 pm (closed on weekends, holidays, Monday mornings and in August). Entrance costs 30FF (15FF for students and seniors; free for under 18s).

Musée Cognacq-Jay

The Musée Cognacq-Jay (M15; ☎ 01 40 27 07 21; metro Saint Paul) at 8 Rue Élzévir (3e) brings together oil

SIMON BRACKEN

Place des Vosges

paintings, pastels, sculpture, objets d'art, jewellery, porcelain and furniture from the 18th century. The objects on display, assembled by the founders of La Samaritaine department store, give a pretty good idea of upper-class tastes during the Age of Enlightenment. It is open from 10 am to 5.40 pm (closed Monday and holidays). Entry costs 17FF (9FF if you're aged 18 to 25; free for under 18s).

Maison Européenne de la Photographie

The Maison Européenne de la Photographie (M15; ☎ 01 44 78 75 00; metro Saint Paul) at 5/7 Rue de Fourcy (4e) is a recent addition to the Marais museum collection and has permanent and temporary exhibits on the history of photography with particular connection to France. The museum is open Wednesday to Sunday, 11 am to 8 pm, and entry is 30FF (15FF for those under 26 or over 60).

Archives Nationales

France's national archives are headquartered in the impressive, early 18th-century **Hôtel de Soubise** (M15; metro Rambuteau) at 60 Rue des Francs Bourgeois (3e). The complex also contains the **Musée de l'Histoire de France** (☎ 01 40 27 62 18), where you can see documents dating from the Middle Ages. The ceiling and walls of the early 18th-century interior are extravagantly painted and gilded in the rococo style. The museum is open from 1.45 to 5.45 pm (closed Tuesday and holidays). Entrance costs 15FF (10FF for teachers and people under 25 or over 60).

Jewish Neighbourhood

The area around **Rue des Rosiers** and **Rue des Écouffes**, known as the Pletzl (M15; metro Saint Paul), is one of Paris' liveliest Jewish neighbourhoods. Jewish cuisines from North Africa, Central Europe and Israel are served at a variety of eating establishments.

When renovation of the Marais was begun in the 1960s, the area – long home to a poor but vibrant Jewish community – was pretty run-down. Now trendy and expensive boutiques coexist side-by-side with Jewish bookshops and *cacher* (kosher) grocery shops, butcher shops and restaurants. The area is very quiet on Saturday.

The so-called **Guimard synagogue** (M15) at 10 Rue Pavée, built in 1913, is renowned for its Art Nouveau architecture, which is the work of Hector Guimard, designer of the famous noodle-like metro entrances. The interior is closed to the public.

There are Jewish neighbourhoods with a distinctly North African flair in Belleville and in the 9e along Rue Richer and Rue Cadet (metro Cadet; M8).

SIMON BRACKEN

Metro Saint Paul, the Marais

Mémorial du Martyr Juif Inconnu

The Memorial to the Unknown Jewish Martyr (M15;
☎ 01 42 77 44 72; metro Pont Marie or Saint Paul) at 17
Rue Geoffroy l'Asnier (4e), established in 1956, includes
a memorial to the victims of the Holocaust, various
temporary exhibits and small permanent exhibits on the
1st, 2nd and 3rd floors. It is open daily except Saturday
from 10 am to 1 pm and 2 to 6 pm (5 pm on Friday). Entry
to the crypt and museum is 15FF.

Walking in the Marais

Super streets for strolling include Rue des Rosiers, Rue
des Francs Bourgeois and Place des Vosges. Some of
Paris' most interesting shops for cute little decorative
items – the kind of expensive things with which a *branché*
(trendy) young Parisian might enliven a *chi-chi* flat – can
be found along Rue du Bourg Tibourg, Rue Sainte Croix
de la Bretonnerie, Rue Saint Merri, Rue du Roi de Sicile
and Rue François Miron (all metro Saint Paul or Hôtel
de Ville). The area also has quite a few small art galleries,
for example along Rue Sainte Croix de la Bretonnerie.

The Marais is within easy walking distance of much
of central Paris, including the Centre Pompidou, Place
de la Bastille, Île Saint Louis, Notre Dame and – a bit over
a km to the west – the Louvre.

BASTILLE AREA (4e, 11e & 12e)

After years as a run-down immigrant neighbourhood
notorious for its high crime rate, the Bastille area has
undergone a fair degree of gentrification in recent years,
in large part because of the new opera house. But the
area east of Place de la Bastille still retains its lively
atmosphere and ethnic flair.

Bastille

The Bastille, built during the 14th century as a fortified
royal residence, is the most famous monument in Paris
that doesn't exist: the notorious prison – the quintessential symbol of monarchic despotism – was demolished
shortly after a mob stormed it on 14 July 1789 and freed
all seven prisoners. The site where it once stood, Place
de la Bastille, is now a very busy traffic roundabout.

In the centre of Place de la Bastille is the 52-metre
Colonne de Juillet (July Column; M13), whose shaft of
greenish bronze is topped by a gilded and winged figure
of Liberty. It was erected in 1833 as a memorial to the

people killed in the street battles that accompanied the July Revolution of 1830; they are buried in vaults under the column. It was later consecrated as a memorial to the victims of the February Revolution of 1848.

Opéra Bastille

Paris' giant new opera house (M13; ☎ 01 44 73 13 00; metro Bastille) at 2-6 Place de la Bastille (12e), designed by the Canadian Carlos Ott, was inaugurated on 14 July 1989, the 200th anniversary of the storming of the Bastille. Conceived by the Socialist François Mitterrand as an opera house for the people, it was built in a resolutely working-class part of the city, but huge cost overruns have kept ticket prices out of the reach of the average Parisian. For details on the building's almost-daily guided tours (50FF, 30FF for children, students and seniors), call ☎ 01 40 01 19 70. See the Entertainment chapter for information on tickets.

Walking in the Bastille Area

There are a number of attractive **art galleries** along Rue de Charonne, just north of Rue du Faubourg Saint Antoine.

On its south side, Place de la Bastille abuts the **Port de Plaisance de Paris-Arsenal** (M13), the city's main pleasure-boat port. There's a **children's playground** (M13) just north of the footbridge over the port.

The Bastille area is a few blocks east of the Marais. Blvd Henri IV links Place de la Bastille with Île Saint Louis.

ÎLE DE LA CITÉ (4e & 1er)

The site of the first settlement around the 3rd century BC and later the centre of the Roman town of Lutèce, the Île de la Cité remained the centre of royal and ecclesiastical power even after the city spread to both banks of the Seine during the Middle Ages. The middle part of the island was demolished and rebuilt during Baron Haussmann's great urban renewal work of the late 19th century.

The Île de la Cité is well endowed with great spots for a picnic. They include: **Square Jean XXIII** (M15), the park that runs along the south side of Notre Dame; the shaded, triangular **Place Dauphine** (M14), created in 1607 near the island's western end; and **Square du Vert Galant** (M14), the little park next to Pont Neuf at the prow-shaped western tip of the island. You can picnic, walk or sunbathe on the stone walkways along the riverbanks.

Notre Dame

Notre Dame (M15; ☎ 01 42 34 56 10; metro Cité), Paris'
cathedral, is one of the most magnificent achievements
of Gothic architecture. Built on a site occupied by earlier
churches – and, some two millennia ago, a Gallo-Roman
temple – it was begun in 1163 and completed around
1345. The interior is 130 metres long, 48 metres wide and
35 metres high, and can accommodate over 6000 wor-
shippers. Some 12 million people visit it each year.

Notre Dame is known for its sublime balance,
although if you look closely you'll see all sorts of minor
asymmetrical elements introduced, in accordance with
Gothic practice, to avoid monotony. These include the

BETHUNE CARMICHAEL

Rose window of Notre Dame Cathedral

SIMON BRACKEN

SIMON BRACKEN

Details of the façades of Notre Dome

slightly different shapes of each of the three main entrances, whose statues were once brightly coloured to make them more effective as a *Biblia pauperum* (Bible lessons for the illiterate and poor masses). One of the best views of Notre Dame is from Square Jean XXIII, the lovely little park behind the cathedral, where you can see the mass of ornate **flying buttresses** that encircle the chancel and hold up its walls and roof.

Inside, exceptional features include three spectacular **rose windows**, the most renowned of which are the window over the west façade, which is a full 10 metres across, and the window on the north side of the transept, which has remained virtually unchanged since the 13th century. The 7800-pipe organ was restored in 1990-92 at a cost of US$2 million but has not been working properly since.

Notre Dame is open daily from 8 am to 6.45 pm (7.45 pm on weekends); on Saturday it's closed for upkeep from 12.30 to 2 pm. The **trésor** (treasury) at the back of the cathedral, which costs 15FF (10FF for students), is open Monday to Saturday from 9.30 am to 5.45 pm. There are **guided tours** of the cathedral in English on Wednesday and Thursday at noon (daily in August).

Distances from Paris throughout France are measured from **Place du Parvis Notre Dame**, the square in front of Notre Dame. A bronze star, set in the pavement across the street from the cathedral's main entrance, marks the exact location of *point zéro des routes de France* (M14).

Climbing the North Tower Notre Dame's north tower (M15; ☎ 01 43 29 50 40) is to the right and around the corner as you walk out of the main doorway. From the base, a long, spiral climb up 238 steps gets you to the top of the **west façade**, from where you can view many of the cathedral's most ferocious-looking gargoyles, not to mention a good part of Paris. Tickets are on sale daily from 9.30 am (10 am from November to March) to 4.30 pm (November to March), 5 pm (mid-September to October) or 6 pm (April to mid-September). Tickets cost 28FF (18FF for people aged 18 to 25; 15FF for children aged 12 to 17).

Crypte Archéologique

Under the square in front of Notre Dame, the Archaeological Crypt (M14; ☎ 01 43 29 83 51), also known as the Crypte du Parvis, displays *in situ* the remains of structures from the Gallo-Roman and later periods. It is open daily from 10 am to 5 pm (6 pm from April to September); ticket sales end 30 minutes earlier. Fees are the same as those for the cathedral's north tower. A *billet jumelé* (combination ticket) valid for both the crypt and the tower costs 40FF.

Sainte Chapelle

The gem-like Sainte Chapelle (M14; ☎ 01 43 54 30 09; metro Cité), whose upper chapel is illuminated by a veritable curtain of luminous 13th-century **stained glass** (the oldest and finest in Paris), is inside the **Palais de Justice** (law courts), which is on the west side of Blvd du Palais (1er). Consecrated in 1248, Sainte Chapelle was built in only 33 months to house what was believed to be Jesus' crown of thorns and other relics purchased by King Louis IX (Saint Louis) earlier in the 13th century. The chapel's exterior can be viewed from across the street from the law courts' magnificently gilded 18th-century gate, which faces Rue de Lutèce.

Sainte Chapelle is open daily from 9.30 or 10 am to 5 pm (6.30 pm from April to September); ticket sales end 30 minutes before. Entry costs 32FF (21FF for people aged 18 to 25; 15FF for children aged 12 to 17). A ticket valid for both Sainte Chapelle and the nearby Conciergerie costs 45FF. The visitors' entrance (M14) is directly opposite 7 Blvd du Palais. Be prepared for airport-type security.

Conciergerie

The Conciergerie (M14; ☎ 01 43 54 30 06; metro Cité), whose entrance is at 1 Quai de l'Horloge, was a luxurious royal palace when it was built in the 14th century, but it later lost favour with the kings of France and was turned into a prison and place of torture. During the Reign of Terror (1793-94), the Conciergerie was used to incarcerate presumed enemies of the Revolution before they were brought before the Revolutionary Tribunal, which met next door in the Palais de Justice. Among the 2600 prisoners held here before being sent in tumbrils to the guillotine were Queen Marie-Antoinette and, as the Revolution began to devour its children, the Revolutionary radicals Danton and Robespierre and, finally, judges of the Tribunal themselves.

The huge Gothic **Salle des Gens d'Armes** (Cavalrymen's Hall) dates from the 14th century and is the largest surviving medieval hall in Europe. **Tour de l'Horloge**, the tower on the corner, has held aloft a public clock since 1370. Hours are the same as those for Sainte Chapelle; entry fees are 28FF (18FF for people aged 18 to 25 and 15FF for those aged 12 to 17).

Flower Market

The Île de la Cité's famous **marché aux fleurs** (M14; metro Cité), Paris' oldest, has been at Place Louis Lépine – the area just north of the Préfecture de Police – since 1808. It is open Monday to Saturday (and when holidays fall on Sunday) from 8 or 9 am to about 7 pm.

On Sunday, the marché aux fleurs is transformed into a **marché aux oiseaux** (bird market). Small house pets are also on sale.

Mémorial des Martyrs de la Déportation

At the south-eastern tip of the Île de la Cité, behind Notre Dame, is the Deportation Memorial (1962; M15), a stark, haunting monument to the 200,000 residents of France – including 76,000 Jews – killed in Nazi concentration camps. A single barred window divides the bleak concrete courtyard from the Seine. The Tomb of the Unknown Deportee is flanked by 200,000 bits of backlit glass.

Unless the Seine is at flood stage, the memorial is open daily from 10 am to noon and 2 to 5 pm (7 pm from April to September).

Pont Neuf

The stone spans of Paris' oldest bridge, Pont Neuf (literally, New Bridge; M14), link the western end of the Île de la Cité with both banks of the Seine. Built between 1578 and 1607, it is adorned with an equestrian **statue of Henri IV**. The arches are decorated with humorous and grotesque figures of street dentists, pickpockets, loiterers and the like.

ÎLE SAINT LOUIS (4e)

The smaller of Paris' two islands, the Île Saint Louis is just upstream from the Île de la Cité. It consisted of two uninhabited islands – sometimes used for duels – until the early 1600s, when three entrepreneurs (a building contractor and two financiers) worked out a deal with Louis XIII: they would create one island out of the two and build two stone bridges to the mainland. In exchange they would receive the right to subdivide and sell the newly created real estate. This they did with great success, and between 1613 and 1664 the entire island was covered with fine new houses. Little has changed since then except that many of the buildings are now marked

TONY WHEELER

Apartment windows, Île Saint Louis

with plaques detailing when some person of note lived there.

The area around **Pont Saint Louis** (the bridge linking the island with the Île de la Cité) and **Pont Louis-Philippe** (the bridge to the Marais) is one of the most romantic spots in all of Paris. On warm summer days, lovestruck couples mingle with cello-equipped buskers and teenage skateboarding virtuosos. After nightfall, the Seine dances with the watery reflections of streetlights, headlamps, stop signals and the dim glow of curtained, apartment windows. Occasionally, tourist boats with super bright floodlamps cruise by.

The island's 17th-century, grey-stone houses and the small-town shops that line the streets and quays impart a village-like, provincial calm. Rue Saint Louis en l'Île is home to a number of up-market art galleries.

Église Saint Louis en l'Île

This French baroque-style church at 19bis Rue Saint Louis en l'Île (M15; metro Pont Marie) was built between 1656 and 1725 and is open Tuesday to Sunday from 9 am to noon and 3 to 7 pm. It often has concerts of classical music.

JARDIN DES PLANTES AREA (eastern 5e)

This area is just east of the Latin Quarter.

Jardin des Plantes

Paris' botanical gardens (M12; metro Gare d'Austerlitz
or Jussieu), founded in 1626 as a medicinal herb garden
for Louis XIII, are endearingly informal and even
decrepit, as if a group of dedicated but conservative,
underfunded and slightly absent-minded professors
had been running the place for a couple of centuries. The
first greenhouse, constructed in 1714, was home to a
coffee tree whose offspring helped establish coffee production in South America. The gardens are open daily
from 7.30 am until sometime between 5.30 pm (in the
dead of winter) and 8 pm (in summer).

The **Serres Tropicales** (Tropical Greenhouses; M12),
also known as the Jardin d'Hiver (Winter Garden), are
open on weekdays except Tuesday from 1 to 5 pm;
weekend hours are 10 am to 5 pm (6 pm from April to
September). Admission costs 15FF (10FF reduced price).
The **Jardin Alpin** (Alpine Garden; M12) and the gardens
of the **École de Botanique** (Botanical School; M12), both
of which are free, are open from April to September on
Monday, Wednesday, Thursday and Friday.

Zoo The northern section of the Jardin des Plantes is
taken up by the **Ménagerie** (M12; ☎ 01 40 79 37 94; metro
Jussieu), a medium-sized zoo founded in 1794. During
the Prussian siege of Paris in 1870, most of the animals
were eaten by starving Parisians. It is open daily from 9
am to 5 or 5.30 pm (6 pm from April to September, when
closing time is 6.30 pm on Sunday and holidays).
Entrance costs 30FF (20FF for children, students aged 16
to 25 and people over 60).

There's a **children's playground** near the Ménagerie's
western entrance.

Musée National d'Histoire Naturelle

The
National Museum of Natural History (M12; ☎ 01 40 79
30 00; metro Censier Daubenton or Gare d'Austerlitz),
created by a decree of the Convention in 1793, was the
site of important scientific research in the 19th century.
It is housed in four buildings along the southern edge of
the Jardin des Plantes.

The five-level **Grande Galerie de l'Évolution** (M12;
☎ 01 40 79 39 39) has some imaginative exhibits on
evolution and humankind's effect on the world's ecosys-
tem, but unless you can read French it's pretty much a
traditional natural history museum, with lots of
imaginatively displayed stuffed animals and mounted
insects. The African parade, as if Noah had lined up his
cargo for the ark, is quite something. The Salle des

Espèces Menacées et des Espèces Disparues, on Niveau 2, displays extremely rare specimens of 'endangered and extinct species' of animals. The Salles de Découverte (Discovery Rooms) house interactive exhibits for kids. They are all open daily except Tuesday from 10 am to 6 pm (10 pm on Thursday). Entry costs 40FF (30FF and 10FF reduced price).

The **Galerie de Minéralogie et Paléobotanie** (M12; 30FF, 20FF reduced price), which covers mineralogy and paleobotany (ie fossilised plants), has an amazing exhibit of giant natural crystals and a basement display of precious objects made from minerals. Out the front there's a rose garden. The **Galerie d'Anatomie Comparée et de Paléontologie** (M12; 30FF, 20FF reduced price) has displays on comparative anatomy and paleontology. Both are open daily except Tuesday and holidays from 10 am to 5 pm (6 pm on weekends from April to September). The **Galerie d'Entomologie** (M12; 15FF, 10FF reduced price) specialises in the study of insects. It's open Monday and Wednesday to Friday, 1 to 5 pm; Saturday and Sunday, 10 am to 5 pm.

Musée de Sculpture en Plein Air

The Open-Air Sculpture Museum (M12) is an imaginatively landscaped riverside promenade, stretching for about 600 metres along the Seine from the Jardin des Plantes to the Institut du Monde Arabe, which is right across the river from the Île Saint Louis. Colourful riverboats are often moored along the pedestrian quay.

Mosquée de Paris

Paris' central mosque (M12; ☎ 01 45 35 97 33; metro Place Monge), whose entrance is at Place du Puits de l'Ermite (next to the square minaret), was built between 1922 and 1926 in an ornate Hispano-Moorish style. Islam forbids images of people or animals, so the two serene courtyards are elaborately decorated with verses from the Koran in Arabic calligraphy and coloured tiles in geometrical designs. Shoes must be removed at the entrance to the prayer hall. Guided tours (15FF, 10FF for children and students) take place from 9 am to noon and 2 to 6 pm except on Friday; tickets are sold through the arch to the right as you enter. Visitors must be modestly and respectfully dressed (women should not wear shorts or sleeveless blouses).

The mosque complex includes a North African-style *salon de thé*, a restaurant and a *hammam* (bathhouse; M12; ☎ 01 43 31 18 14), both of whose entrances are at 39 Rue

Geoffroy Saint Hilaire (across from the Grande Galerie de l'Évolution). The hammam has separate opening hours for men and women.

Institut du Monde Arabe

The Arab World Institute (M12; ☎ 01 40 51 38 38; metro Cardinal Lemoine) at 1 Rue des Fossés Saint Bernard, set up by France and 20 Arab countries to promote cultural contacts between the Arab world and the West, is housed in a highly praised building (opened in 1987) that successfully mixes modern and traditional Arab and Western elements. The 1600 **mushrabiyah** (incredibly costly aperture-like mechanisms built into the glass walls), inspired by the traditional latticed wooden windows that let you see out without being seen, are opened and closed by electric motors in order to regulate the amount of light and heat that reach the interior of the building.

The 7th-floor **museum** displays 9th to 19th-century art and artisanship from all over the Muslim world as well as astrolabes and instruments from other fields of scientific endeavour in which Arab technology once led the world. It is open Tuesday to Sunday from 10 am to 6 pm. Tickets cost 25FF (20FF for students, people under 25 and seniors); temporary exhibitions involve a separate fee.

Arènes de Lutèce

This heavily reconstructed, 2nd-century Roman amphitheatre (M12; metro Place Monge), discovered in 1869, could once seat around 10,000 people for gladiatorial combats and other events. Today, it is used by neighbourhood youth to play football and *boules*

TONY WHEELER

Institut du Monde Arabe

(bowls). There are entrances at 49 Rue Monge and opposite 7 Rue de Navarre. Entry is free.

LATIN QUARTER (western 5e)

Known as the Quartier Latin because all communication
between students and professors took place in Latin until
the Revolution, this area has been the centre of Parisian
higher education since the Middle Ages. It has become
increasingly touristy in recent years, however, and its near
monopoly on the city's academic life has waned as students have moved to other campuses, especially since
1968. The Latin Quarter does have a large population of
students and academics affiliated with the Sorbonne
(M14), which is now part of the University of Paris system,
the Collège de France (M14), the École Normale
Supérieure (M14) and other institutions of higher learning.

Musée National du Moyen Âge

The Museum of the Middle Ages (M14; ☎ 01 43 25 62 00;
metro Cluny-La Sorbonne), also known as the Musée de
Cluny, is housed in two structures: the frigidarium and
other remains of **Gallo-Roman baths** from around the
year 200 AD, and the late 15th-century **Hôtel de Cluny**,
considered the finest example of medieval civil architecture in Paris. The spectacular displays include statuary,
illuminated manuscripts, arms, furnishings and objects
made of gold, ivory and enamel. A series of six late
15th-century tapestries from the southern Netherlands
known as **La Dame à la Licorne** (the Lady and the
Unicorn) is hung in a round room on the 1st floor.

The museum, whose entrance is opposite the park
next to 31 Rue du Sommerard, is open from 9.15 am to
5.45 pm (closed Tuesday). The entrance fee is 36FF (26FF
for people aged 18 to 25 and on Sunday for everyone
over 18).

Sorbonne

Paris' most renowned university, the Sorbonne (M14),
was founded in 1253 by Robert de Sorbon, confessor of
King Louis IX, as a college for 16 poor theology students.
Closed in 1792 by the Revolutionary government after
operating for centuries as France's premier theological
centre, it was reopened under Napoleon. Today, the
Sorbonne's main complex (bounded by Rue de la Sorbonne, Rue des Écoles, Rue Saint Jacques and Rue Cujas)
and other buildings in the vicinity house several of the
13 autonomous universities created when the Université

de Paris was reorganised following the violent student protests of 1968.

Place de la Sorbonne links Blvd Saint Michel with **Chapelle de la Sorbonne** (M14), the university's domed church, which was built between 1635 and 1642. The interior is closed except when there are special exhibitions.

Panthéon

The domed landmark now known as the Panthéon (M14; ☎ 01 43 54 34 51; metro Luxembourg) was commissioned around 1750 as an abbey church, but because of financial problems wasn't completed until 1789. Two years later, the Constituent Assembly converted it into a secular mausoleum for the *'grands hommes de l'époque de la liberté française'* (great men of the era of French liberty), removing all Christian symbols and references. After a further stint as a church, the Panthéon once again became a secular necropolis. The Panthéon's ornate marble interior is gloomy in the extreme and much of it will be closed for some time during intense renovation, but you get a great view of the city from around the colonnaded dome (261 steps).

Permanent guests of the Panthéon include Voltaire, Jean-Jacques Rousseau, Louis Braille, Victor Hugo, Émile Zola and Jean Moulin. Personages removed for reburial elsewhere after a re-evaluation of their greatness include Mirabeau and Marat. The first woman to be interred in the Panthéon in recognition of her own achievements was the double Nobel Prize-winner Marie Curie, who was reburied here (along with her husband Pierre) in 1995.

The Panthéon is open daily, April to September from 10 am to 6 pm, and October to March from 10 am to 5 pm. Ticket sales end 45 minutes before closing time. Tickets cost 32FF (21FF for people aged 18 to 25, 15FF for 12 to 17, free for under 12).

Église Saint Étienne du Mont

This lovely church (M14; metro Cardinal Lemoine) at Place de l'Abbé Basset (behind the Panthéon) was built between 1492 and 1626. The most exceptional feature of the Gothic interior is its graceful **rood screen** (1535) separating the chancel from the nave. During the late Renaissance, all of Paris' rood screens except this one were removed because they prevented the faithful assembled in the nave from seeing the priest celebrate mass. Also of interest is the carved **wooden pulpit** of 1650, held aloft by a figure of Samson, and the 16th and 17th-century **stained glass**. Just inside the entrance, a plaque in the floor marks the spot where a defrocked priest, armed with a knife, murdered an archbishop in 1857.

Walking in the Latin Quarter

Almost every street in the Latin Quarter proper – the area bordered by Blvd Saint Germain, Rue Monge, Rue Claude Bernard and Blvd Saint Michel – has something unique to offer. Among the liveliest is **Rue Mouffetard** (M12; see Latin Quarter under Places to Eat and Self-Catering), one of the oldest streets in the city. The intense urbanness of the area is softened by the green expanses and pools of the Jardin du Luxembourg (see 6e Arrondissement).

The shop-lined **Blvd Saint Michel**, popularly known as the 'Boul Mich' (pronounced 'bool mish'), runs along the border between the 5e and the 6e arrondissements. Bustling **Blvd Saint Germain** stretches over three km from the Île Saint Louis westward past Saint Germain des Prés all the way to the Assemblée Nationale.

Right across the Seine from Notre Dame, along Rue Frédéric Sauton (M15), there's a cluster of small galleries with art objects from around the world. The area east of the Latin Quarter is covered in the section entitled Jardin des Plantes Area (eastern 5e).

6e ARRONDISSEMENT

Centuries ago, Église Saint Germain des Prés (M14) and its affiliated abbey, founded by King Childebert in 542 AD, owned most of the 6e and 7e arrondissements. The neighbourhood around the church began to be built up in the late 1600s, and these days – under the name Saint Germain des Prés – is famous for its 19th-century charm. Cafés such as Les Deux Magots and Café de Flore (see Pubs/Bars – 6e Arrondissement in the Entertainment chapter), favourite hangouts of postwar, Left Bank intellectuals, are where existentialism was born.

These days, though, only very *wealthy* intellectuals can afford to buy flats in this area. The 6e arrondissement becomes increasingly hard-core bourgeois as you move west and north-west from the Jardin du Luxembourg, one of Paris' loveliest green spaces.

Jardin du Luxembourg

When the weather is warm – or even just slightly sunny – Parisians of all ages flock to the French-style formal terraces and chestnut groves of the 25-hectare Luxembourg Gardens (M14; metro Luxembourg) to read, write, relax and sunbathe. Ernest Hemingway claimed that as an impoverished young writer he would come to the gardens and, when the police were distracted with other matters, catch pigeons for his supper.

Activities for Children The Jardin du Luxembourg offers all of the delights of a Parisian childhood a century ago and is one of the best places in Paris to take kids. The atmosphere of bygone days is enhanced by the kepi-topped Senate guards.

At the Grand Bassin (the octagonal pond; M14), **model sailboats** – many of them old enough to have been sailed by today's grandparents back when they were in grammar school – can be rented for 15FF an hour on Wednesday, Saturday and Sunday (daily during school holiday periods, including July and August) from 2 pm until sometime between 4.30 pm (in winter) and 7 pm (in summer).

About 200 metres south-west of the pond, at the pint-sized **Théâtre du Luxembourg** (M14; ☎ 01 43 26 46 47), visitors are treated to a complete theatre experience in miniature: in a hall filled with child-sized seats, **Guignol puppets** put on Punch-and-Judy-type shows whose antics can be enjoyed even if you don't understand French. The puppets put on one to five performances (22FF), at least one of which starts around 3 pm, on Wednesday, Saturday, Sunday and holidays and during

SIMON BRACKEN

Model sailboats in the Jardin du Luxemburg

school vacation periods. Spectators are admitted by ticket number in ascending order.

Next to the Théâtre du Luxembourg, the modern **playground** – one half for kids up to age seven, the other half for children aged seven to 12 – costs 11FF per child (6FF for adults). Not far away, the vintage **swings** cost 6FF per child, as does the old-time **carousel** (merry-go-round).

A hundred metres north of the theatre, kids up to 35 kg can ride Shetland ponies daily (unless it's raining) starting at 11 am (2 pm on Monday, Tuesday, Thursday and Saturday).

In the gardens' south-west corner, you can visit the **beehives** (*ruches*; M14), established here in 1856, where Parisians can take beekeeping courses (☎ 01 45 42 29 08). They are staffed all day on Wednesday and, often, on other days. There's a **fruit tree orchard** just south of the beehives.

Activities for Adults In the north-west corner of the Jardin du Luxembourg, just north of the tennis courts, **chess & card games** (M14) – often a dozen at a time – are held every afternoon of the year, rain or shine. BYOB (bring your own board).

On the north side of the Théâtre du Luxembourg, there are **basketball and volleyball courts** – you could try to join in a game. **Boules courts** are located just north of the beehives.

RACHEL BLACK

Men playing chess, Jardin du Luxembourg

Statues & Sculptures
Paris is dotted with outdoor statuary and beautiful fountains, such as the romantic Fontaine des Médicis (M14; metro Luxembourg) which combines fountain, pond and statuary in one elegant group in the Jardin du Luxembourg. Like the Tuileries on the Right Bank, the Jardin du Luxembourg is dotted with sculptures and statuary. The Fontaine de l'Observatoire, at the southern point of the gardens (M14; metro Port Royal), is a favourite.
    Not far away by foot, but on the other side of the universe in concept, is the very modern *Statue of Centaur* at the junction of Rue du Cherche Midi and Rue du Sèvres (M11; metro Saint Sulpice). A much-loved modern piece of sculpture is the giant head, looking like it's just rolled away from an equally gigantic guillotine, beside Église Saint Eustache at the Forum des Halles (M12; metro Les Halles). Equally striking is Claes Oldenburg's huge Buried Bicycle, protruding from the grass in the Parc de la Villette (M1; metro Porte de la Villette).
    It was the French who gave New York City its *Statue of Liberty*, so it's fitting that they kept a smaller one for Paris. It's right in the middle of the Seine, a short distance downstream from the Eiffel Tower (M10; metro Ave du President Kennedy, Maison de Radio France). ∎

Palais du Luxembourg The Luxembourg Palace (M14), at the northern end of the Jardin du Luxembourg along Rue de Vaugirard, was built for Marie de' Medici (queen of France from 1600 to 1610) to assuage her longing for the Pitti Palace in Florence, where she spent her childhood. Just east of the palace is the baroque **Fontaine des Médicis**, a long, ornate goldfish pond built in 1624.

During WW II, the palace served as Luftwaffe headquarters, and fortified shelters were built under the gardens. It has housed the Sénat, the upper house of the French parliament, since 1958. There are tours of the interior (☎ 01 42 34 20 60 for information, 01 44 61 21 69 for reservations) on the first Sunday of each month at 10 am.

Église Saint Sulpice

This chapel-lined church (M14; metro Saint Sulpice), a block north of the Jardin du Luxembourg at Place Saint Sulpice, was built between 1646 and 1780 on the site of earlier churches dedicated to Saint Sulpicius, a 6th-century Archbishop of Bourges. The Italianate façade, designed by a Florentine architect, has two rows of superimposed columns and is topped by two towers. The neoclassical décor of the vast interior reflects the influence of the Counter-Reformation. The first **chapel** to the right as you enter was decorated by Eugène Delacroix. The monumental **organ loft** dates from 1781. Every Sunday, the 10.15 am Mass is accompanied by music and there are regular recitals.

Place Saint Sulpice is adorned by a very energetic fountain, **Fontaine des Quatre Évêques** (1844; M14). Nearby streets are known for their couture houses – see Clothes & Fashion Accessories in the Shopping chapter.

Église Saint Germain des Prés

The Romanesque-style Church of Saint Germanus of the Fields (M14), the oldest (though hardly the most interesting) church in Paris, was built in the 11th century on the site of a 6th-century abbey. It has since been altered many times, but the bell tower over the west entrance has changed little since 1000 apart from the spire, added in the 19th century.

France's Merovingian kings were buried here during the 6th and 7th centuries, but their tombs disappeared during the Revolution. The interior is disfigured by truly appalling polychrome paintings and frescoes from the 19th century. The church, which is often used for concerts, is open daily from 8 am to 7 pm.

In early September 1792, a group of priests were hacked to death by a Revolutionary mob in what is now **Square Félix Desruelles**, the park between the church and Blvd Saint Germain. The glazed arch at the park's west end was created for the World Fair of 1900 by Sèvres.

Musée Eugène Delacroix

The Eugène Delacroix Museum (M14; ☎ 01 44 41 86 50; metro Mabillon or Saint Germain des Prés) is just east of Église Saint Germain des Prés at 6 Place de Furstemberg. Also known as the Atelier Delacroix, this was the artist's home and studio at the time of his death in 1863. It is open daily except Tuesday from 10 am to 5.30 pm (last entry at 4.30 pm). Tickets cost 15FF (10FF reduced price).

Institut de France

The Institut de France was created in 1795 by bringing together France's various academies of arts and sciences. The most famous of these is the **Académie Française**,

TONY WHEELER

Fontaine des Quatre Évêques & Église Saint Sulpice

founded in 1635, whose 40 members (known as the Immortels, ie Immortals) are charged with the Herculean task of safeguarding the purity of the French language. Over the centuries, many of France's greatest writers and philosophers have been denied membership in favour of now-forgotten personages fawned over by the establishment of their day. The first woman Immortel (Marguerite Yourcenar) was not admitted until 1980.

The domed building housing the Institut de France (M14; ☎ 01 44 41 44 41; metro Mabillon or Louvre-Rivoli), a masterpiece of French neoclassical architecture from the mid-17th century, is at 23 Quai de Conti, right across the Seine from the eastern end of the Louvre.

The only part of the complex that can be visited without joining a tour is the **Bibliothèque Mazarine** (Mazarine Library; ☎ 01 44 41 44 06), the oldest public library in France (it dates from 1689). You can visit the bust-lined, late 17th-century reading room or consult the library's collection of 500,000 items on weekdays from 10 am to 6 pm (closed during the first half of August). Entry is free but you must leave your ID at the office on the left-hand side of the entryway; a second piece of ID is needed to gain access to the books.

For information on tours (about 40FF), usually held on weekends, look under 'Conférences' in *Pariscope* or *L'Officiel des Spectacles* (see Entertainment Guides in the Entertainment chapter).

Musée de la Monnaie

The Museum of Coins & Medals (M14; ☎ 01 40 46 55 33; metro Pont Neuf) at 11 Quai de Conti – just across Pont Neuf from the Île de la Cité – traces the history of French coinage from antiquity to the present and includes coins and medals as well as presses and other minting equipment. It is open daily, except Monday, from 1 to 6 pm (9 pm on Wednesday). The entry fee is 20FF (15FF for students and people over 60, free for those under 16 and everybody on Sunday).

The Hôtel des Monnaies, which houses the museum, became a royal mint during the 18th century and is still used by the Ministry of Finance to produce commemorative medals. Except in July and August, tours in French of the mint's workshops are held on Sunday at 3 pm and cost 18FF.

Walking in the 6e Arrondissement

A stroll along the streets between Église Saint Germain des Prés and the Institut de France is a good way to get a feel for the area. **Place de Furstemberg**, a lovely, shaded square near the Église Saint Germain des Prés, is named after an ex-bishop of Strasbourg who laid out the area in 1699.

The most enjoyable way to walk from Saint Germain des Prés to the Latin Quarter is go via Église Saint Sulpice and the Jardin du Luxembourg.

If you walk to the northern end of Rue Bonaparte, you'll find yourself at the Seine, from where it's a short stroll via the lovely, pedestrians-only **Pont des Arts** to the Louvre and the Forum des Halles. The Musée d'Orsay is 800 metres to the west along the river.

MONTPARNASSE (6e, 14e & 15e)

Around WW I, writers, poets and artists of the avant-garde abandoned Montmartre and crossed the Seine, shifting the centre of Paris' artistic ferment to the area around Blvd du Montparnasse. Chagall, Modigliani, Léger, Soutine, Miró, Kandinsky, Picasso, Stravinsky, Hemingway, Henry Miller and Cocteau, as well as political exiles such as Lenin and Trotsky, all used to hang out here, talking endlessly in the cafés and restaurants for which the quarter is still famous. Montparnasse remained a creative centre until the mid-1930s. Today, especially since the construction of the new Gare Montparnasse complex, there is little to remind visitors of the area's bohemian past.

Although the trendy Latin Quarter crowd considers the area hopelessly nondescript, **Blvd du Montparnasse** (on the southern border of the 6e) and its many fashionable restaurants, cafés and cinemas attract large numbers of Parisians in the evening. Rue d'Odessa and Rue de Montparnasse are famous for their crêperies, founded by Bretons who, after arriving in Paris by train, ventured no farther than the area around the station.

Tour Montparnasse

The 209-metre-high Montparnasse Tower (M11; ☎ 01 45 38 52 56; metro Montparnasse Bienvenüe) at 33 Ave du Maine (15e), built in the early 1970s of steel and smoked glass, affords spectacular views of the city, especially around sunset, when, if you stay long enough (the sun sets pretty slowly at this latitude), you can also see the city at night. The elevator to the 56th-floor indoor observatory followed by steps to the 59th-floor open-air terrace costs 42FF for adults, 26FF for under 14 years, 17FF for under three years, 33FF for students under 20 and 36FF for seniors. From April to September, the tower is open daily from 9.30 am to 11 pm. The rest of the year, hours are 9.30 am to 10 pm (10.30 pm on Friday, Saturday and holidays).

Musée de la Poste

The Postal Museum (M11; ☎ 01 42 79 23 45; metro Montparnasse Bienvenüe, Gare Montparnasse exit), a few hundred metres south-west of Tour Montparnasse at 34 Blvd de Vaugirard (5th floor; 15e), illustrates the history of postal service – a matter of particular importance in a highly centralised state like France – from Roman times to the present. The 15 rooms showcase the original designs of French stamps, antique postal and telecommunications equipment and models of postal conveyances.

Redeveloped in 1996, the museum is open Monday to Saturday, 10 am to 6 pm, and entry is about 28FF (1FF reduced price). There's a philatelic sales counter in the ground-floor lobby.

Cimetière du Montparnasse

Montparnasse Cemetery (M2; ☎ 01 43 20 68 52; metro Edgar Quinet or Raspail), accessible from Blvd Edgar Quinet and Rue Froidevaux (both 14e), was opened in 1824. It contains the tombs of such illustrious personages as Charles Baudelaire, Samuel Beckett, Guy de Maupassant, François Rude, Frédéric August Bartholdi, Constantin Brancusi, Chaim Soutine, Man Ray, Camille Saint-Saëns, André Citroën, Alfred Dreyfus, Jean Seberg, Simone de Beauvoir and Jean-Paul Sartre. If Père Lachaise has Jim Morrison, the equivalent here is French singer Serge Gainsbourg; fans leave metro tickets with their names. Maps showing the location of famous tombs are posted near most entrances and are available free from the Conservation office. The cemetery is open daily from 8 or 9 am to 6 pm (5.30 pm from early November to mid-March).

7e ARRRONDISSEMENT

The 7e arrondissement stretches along the Left Bank from Saint Germain des Prés (6e) to the Eiffel Tower (see Eiffel Tower Area) and includes the Musée d'Orsay and the Invalides.

Musée d'Orsay

The Musée d'Orsay (M11; ☎ 01 40 49 48 84 or, for a recording, 01 40 49 48 14; metro Musée d'Orsay or Solférino), along the Seine at 1 Rue de Bellechasse, displays France's national collection of paintings, sculptures, objets d'art and other works produced between 1848 and 1914, including the fruits of the Impressionist, Post-Impressionist and Art Nouveau movements. It thus fills the chronological gap between the Louvre and the Musée National d'Art Moderne at the Centre Pompidou. The Musée d'Orsay is spectacularly housed in a former railway station built in 1900 and reinaugurated in its present form in 1986.

Many visitors head straight to the upper level lit by skylight to see the famous **Impressionists** (Monet,

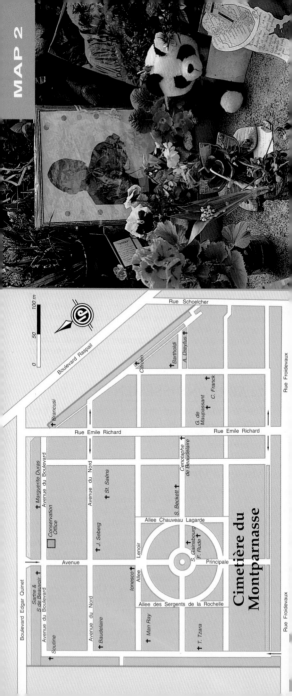

MAP 2

Rue Schoelcher

Boulevard Raspail

0   50   100 m

† Brancusi

† Barthold
A. Dreyfus †

Citroën

G. de Maupassant †
C. Franck †

Rue Emile Richard

Rue Emile Richard

† Marguerite Duras

Avenue du Boulevard

Avenue du Nord

† St. Saëns

Conservation
Office

Cénotaphe
de Baudelaire

S. Beckett †

Rue Froidevaux

† J. Seberg

Allee Chauveau Lagarde

Lenoir

Avenue

Sartre &
S. de Beauvoir †

Ionesco †
Allee

S. Gainsbourg †
F. Rude †

Principale

Boulevard Edgar Quinet

† Soutine

Avenue du Boulevard

Avenue du Nord

Allee des Sergents de la Rochelle

† Baudelaire

† Man Ray

† T. Tzara

Rue Froidevaux

Cimetière du
Montparnasse

BETHUNE CARMICHAEL

Original gilded railway clock in the central gallery of the
Musée d'Orsay

BETHUNE CARMICHAEL

Sculpture in the Musée d'Orsay

Renoir, Pissarro, Sisley, Degas, Manet, Van Gogh, Cézanne) and **Post-Impressionists** (Seurat, Matisse), but there's also a great deal to see on the ground floor, including some early works by Manet, Monet, Renoir and Pissarro. The middle level has some magnificent **Art Nouveau rooms**.

The Musée d'Orsay is open daily except Monday from 10 am (9 am on Sunday and from mid-June to August) to 6 pm (9.45 pm on Thursday). Ticket sales stop 30 minutes before closing time. Tickets for the permanent exhibits cost 36FF (24FF for people aged 18 to 25 or over 60; free for under 18s) and are valid all day long (ie you can leave and re-enter the museum as you please). There are separate fees for temporary exhibitions.

English-language **tours** begin daily, except Sunday and Monday, at 11 am and on Thursday at 7 pm; tickets (36FF in addition to the entry fee; no discounts) are sold at the information desk to the left as you enter the building. **Audioguides** (1½-hour Walkman tours), available in a variety of languages, point out 30 major works – many of which had a revolutionary impact on 19th-century art – that the uninitiated might easily miss. They can be rented for 30FF (no discounts; ID deposit) on the right just past the ticket windows. An excellent full-colour museum guide, *Guide to the Musée d'Orsay*, is available in English.

Faubourg Saint Germain

Faubourg Saint Germain, the area between the Musée d'Orsay and, a km to the south, Rue de Babylone, was Paris' most fashionable neighbourhood in the 18th century. Its luxurious homes, enclosed by high walls and ornate gates, were built by aristocrats and financiers, many of whom were later beheaded or exiled during the Revolution. Some of the most interesting mansions, many of which now serve as embassies or government ministries, are along three east-west oriented streets: Rue de Lille, Rue de Grenelle and Rue de Varenne. The **Hôtel Matignon** (M11), since 1958 the official residence of France's prime minister, is at 57 Rue de Varenne.

Assemblée Nationale

The National Assembly, the lower house of the French parliament, meets in the 18th-century Palais Bourbon (M11; ☎ 01 40 63 60 00 or 01 40 63 77 77 for a recording; metro Assemblée Nationale) at 33 Quai d'Orsay, right across the Seine from Place de la Concorde (eastern 8e). There are free guided tours (in French) every Saturday at 10 am and 2 and 3 pm. Admission is on a first-come, first-served basis (each tour has only 30 places), so join the queue early; the 10 am tour is not usually oversubscribed. National ID card or a passport is required.

The Second Empire-style **Ministère des Affaires Étrangères** (Ministry of Foreign Affairs; M11), built from 1845 to 1855 and popularly referred to as the Quai d'Orsay, is next door at 37 Quai d'Orsay. The folks who work here have a tough job: they're the ones who did the PR work for France's nuclear tests in the South Pacific, amongst other things.

Musée Rodin

The Musée Auguste Rodin (M11; ☎ 01 44 18 61 10; metro Varenne) at 77 Rue de Varenne, one of the most relaxing spots in the whole of Paris, is some people's favourite Paris museum. Rooms on two floors display extraordinarily vital bronze and marble sculptures by Rodin and Camille Claudel, including casts of some of Rodin's most celebrated works: *The Hand of God*, *The Burghers of Calais*, *The Kiss*, *Cathedral* and, of course, *The Thinker*. There's a delightful rear **garden** filled with sculptures and shade trees. The museum is housed in the Hôtel Biron, a private residence built in 1728 and bearing the name of a general who lived here before being guillotined in 1793.

The Musée Rodin is open daily except Monday from 9.30 am to 4.45 pm (5.45 pm from April to September). Entrance costs 28FF (18FF if you're 18 to 25 or over 60 and, on Sunday, for everyone; free for under 18s). The gardens are open until later and cost 5FF.

Hôtel des Invalides

The Hôtel des Invalides (M11; metro Varenne or La Tour Maubourg) was built in the 1670s by Louis XIV to provide housing for 4000 disabled veterans *(invalides)*. On 14 July 1789, the Paris mob forced its way into the building and, after fierce fighting, seized 28,000 rifles before heading on to the Bastille prison. The 500-metre-long **Esplanade des Invalides** (M11; metro Invalides), which stretches from the main building to the Seine, was laid out between 1704 and 1720.

The **Église du Dôme** (M11), whose dome sparkles again after a 1989 regilding, was built between 1677 and 1735 and is considered one of the finest religious edifices erected under Louis XIV. The church's career as a mausoleum for military leaders began in 1800, and in 1861 it received the remains of Napoleon, encased in six concentric coffins. The buildings on either side of the **Cour d'Honneur** (M11), the main courtyard, house the **Musée de l'Armée** (☎ 01 44 42 37 68 or, for a recording, 01 44 42 37 70), a huge military museum. The Musée de l'Armée and the extravagant **Tombeau de Napoléon 1er** (Napoleon's Tomb) in the Église du Dôme are open daily from 10 am to 5 pm (6 pm from April to September). Entrance to the whole show costs 35FF (25FF for children, students and seniors).

Musée des Égouts de Paris

A city cannot grow, prosper and become truly great unless some way is found to deal with the important question of sewerage. You can learn all about this aspect of Paris' greatness, if you so desire, by visiting the Paris Sewers Museum (M10; ☎ 01 47 05 10 29; metro Pont de l'Alma), a unique working museum whose entrance – a rectangular maintenance hole – is across the street from 93 Quai d'Orsay (7e). Raw sewage with all sorts of vaguely familiar objects floating in it flows beneath your feet as you walk through 480 metres of odoriferous tunnels, passing artefacts illustrating the development of Paris' wastewater disposal system. Signs are in English, German and Spanish.

The sewers are open Saturday to Wednesday (except, God forbid, when rain threatens to flood the tunnels) from 11 am to 5 pm (6 pm from May to September); the last entry is an hour earlier. Tickets cost 25FF (20FF for children, students and seniors).

EIFFEL TOWER AREA (7e & 16e)

Paris' most prominent landmark, the Eiffel Tower is surrounded by open areas on both banks of the Seine. Nearby parts of the Right Bank have several outstanding museums.

Eiffel Tower

The Tour Eiffel (M10; ☎ 01 44 11 23 45; metro Champ de Mars-Tour Eiffel) faced massive opposition from Paris' artistic and literary élite when it was built for the Exposition Universelle (World Fair) of 1889, held to commemorate the centenary of the Revolution. It was almost torn down in 1909 but was spared for purely practical reasons: it proved an ideal platform for the transmitting antennas needed for the new science of radiotelegraphy. It was the world's tallest structure until Manhattan's Chrysler Building was completed in 1930.

The Eiffel Tower, named after its designer, Gustave Eiffel, is 320 metres high, including the television antenna at the very tip. This figure can vary by as much as 15 cm, as the tower's 7000 tonnes of iron, held together by 2.5 million rivets, expand in warm weather and contract when it's cold.

When you're done peering upwards through the girders, you can choose to visit any of the three levels open to the public. The lift (west and north pillars), which follows a curved trajectory, costs 20FF for the 1st platform (57 metres above the ground), 40FF for the 2nd (115 metres) and 56FF for the 3rd (276 metres). Children aged four to 12 pay 10/20/26FF respectively; there are no youth or student rates. You can avoid the lift queues by walking up the stairs in the south pillar to the 1st or 2nd platforms (12FF).

The tower is open every day from 9.30 am (9 am from late March to early September) to 11 pm (midnight from early July to early September). The stairs are open from 9 am to 6.30 pm (9 pm in the late spring, approximately May and June; 11 pm in July and August).

Champ de Mars

The grassy area south-east of the Eiffel Tower, whose name means Field of Mars (Mars was the Roman god of war), was originally a parade ground for the cadets of the 18th-century **École Militaire** (Military Academy; M10), the vast, French classical-style building at the south-eastern end of the lawns whose graduates include Napoleon (class of 1785).

SIMON BRACKEN

Champ de Mars with the Eiffel Tower in the background

In 1783 the Champ de Mars (M10; metro École Militaire or Champ de Mars-Tour Eiffel) was the site of one of the world's first balloon flights. During the Revolutionary period, two important mass ceremonies were held here: the Fête de la Fédération (Festival of Federation), held on 14 July 1790 to celebrate the first anniversary of the storming of the Bastille, and the Fête de l'Être Suprême (Festival of the Supreme Being) of 1794, at which Robespierre presided over a ceremony that established a Revolutionary state religion.

When the weather is good, young Parisians flock to the Champ de Mars to skateboard or roller-skate. For the young at heart, there are **marionette shows** (☎ 01 48 56 01 44; metro École Militaire; 15FF) on Wednesday, Saturday, Sunday and holidays and during school holiday periods (including July and August) at 3.15 and 4.15 pm.

Jardins du Trocadéro

The Trocadéro Gardens (M10; metro Trocadéro), whose fountains and statue garden are grandly illuminated at night, are across Pont d'Iéna from the Eiffel Tower. They are named after the Trocadéro, a Spanish stronghold near Cadiz captured by the French in 1823.

Palais de Chaillot

The two curved, colonnaded wings of the Palais de Chaillot (M10; metro Trocadéro) – built for the World Exhibition of 1937 – and the terrace between them afford an exceptional panorama of the Jardins du Trocadéro, the Seine and the Eiffel Tower.

The vast complex houses four museums – all are reached from the gap between the two wings and all are closed on Tuesday (the Musée du Cinéma Henri Langlois is also closed on Monday). The **Musée de l'Homme** (Museum of Man; ☎ 01 44 05 72 72; 30FF for adults), has anthropological and ethnographic exhibits from Africa, Asia, Europe, the Arctic, the South Pacific and the Americas. The **Musée de la Marine** (Maritime Museum; ☎ 01 45 53 31 70; 38FF for adults) is known for its beautiful ship models. The eclectic film memorabilia at the **Musée du Cinéma Henri Langlois** (Cinema Museum; ☎ 01 45 53 74 39; 30FF for adults) illustrates the history of what the French call 'the seventh art'. The **Musée des Monuments Français** (French Monuments Museum; ☎ 01 44 05 39 10; 21FF for adults) traces the history of French monumental art through the use of plaster casts and reproductions.

In the far eastern tip of the Palais de Chaillot, the **Cinémathèque Française** (M10; ☎ 01 45 53 21 86 or, for a recording, 47 04 24 24) screens several nondubbed films almost every day – see Cinema under Entertainment for details.

Musée Guimet

The Guimet Museum (M6; ☎ 01 47 23 61 65; metro Iéna) at 6 Place d'Iéna (16e), which is about midway between the Eiffel Tower and the Arc de Triomphe, displays antiquities and works of art from Afghanistan, India, Nepal, Pakistan, Tibet, Cambodia, China, Japan and Korea. It is open daily except Tuesday from 9.45 am to 6 pm. Entrance costs 15FF (10FF reduced price, free for under 18).

Musée d'Art Moderne de la Ville de Paris

The **Palais de Tokyo** at 11 Ave du Président Wilson (16e), like the Palais de Chaillot built for the World Exhibition of 1937, houses the Modern Art Museum of the City of Paris (M6; ☎ 01 53 67 40 00; metro Iéna). Its collections include representatives of just about every major artistic movement of the 20th century: fauvism, cubism, the School of Paris, surrealism and expressionism. Artists with works on display include Matisse, Picasso, Braque, Soutine, Modigliani, Chagall and Dufy. Part of the museum is being rebuilt as the Palais du Cinema.

The museum is open daily, except Monday and holidays, from 10 am to at least 5 pm. Tickets cost 27FF (19FF reduced price) but more if there's a temporary exhibit.

Walking in the 7e Arrondissement & Eiffel Tower Area

The Musée d'Orsay is right across the river from the Jardin des Tuileries and the Louvre (western 1er), but don't even *think* of visiting both museums in the same day. The Assemblée Nationale is linked to Place de la Concorde (eastern 8e) by Pont de la Concorde. The grassy expanse north of the Invalides, Esplanade des Invalides, is connected to the lovely eastern end of Ave des Champs-Élysées (8e) by **Pont Alexandre III** (M11), a richly ornamented bridge completed in 1900 and named for Tsar Alexandre III of Russia.

An excellent way to approach the Eiffel Tower is from the north-west, starting at Place du Trocadéro et du 11

Novembre (M10; metro Trocadéro), known for its classy cafés. After checking out the view from the terrace of the Palais de Chaillot, walk through the Jardins du Trocadéro and across Pont d'Iéna. After visiting the tower, you can continue south-eastward across the Champ de Mars to the École Militaire.

The Eiffel Tower and nearby sights are about two km south of the Arc de Triomphe (8e), along some of the most fashionable avenues (including Ave Kléber) of the well-to-do 16e arrondissement.

PLACE DE LA CONCORDE AREA
(eastern 8e)

The cobblestone expanses of Place de la Concorde are sandwiched between the Jardin des Tuileries and the parks at the eastern end of Ave des Champs-Élysées.

Place de la Concorde

Place de la Concorde was laid out between 1755 and 1775. The 3300-year-old, pink granite **obelisk** (M7) in the middle was given to France in 1831 by Muhammad Ali, viceroy and pasha of Egypt; weighing 230 tonnes and towering 23 metres over the cobblestones, it once stood in the Temple of Ramses at Thebes (modern-day Luxor). The eight statues of feminine forms adorning the four corners of the square represent France's largest cities.

In 1793, Louis XVI's head was chopped off by a guillotine set up in the north-west corner of the square near

RICHARD NEBESKY

Place de la Concorde

the statue representing the city of Brest. During the next two years, another guillotine – this one near the entrance to the Jardin des Tuileries – was used to behead 1343 more people, including Marie-Antoinette and, six months later, the Revolutionary leader Danton. Shortly thereafter, Robespierre lost his head here, too. The square was given its present name after the Reign of Terror in the hope that it would be a place of peace and harmony.

The two imposing buildings on the north side of Place de la Concorde are the **Hôtel de la Marine** (M7), headquarters of the French Navy, and the **Hôtel de Crillon** (M7), one of Paris' most luxurious and exclusive hotels. In 1778, the treaty by which France recognised the independence of the USA was signed in the Hôtel de Crillon by Louis XVI and Benjamin Franklin.

Église de la Madeleine

The neoclassical Church of Saint Mary Magdalen (M7; metro Madeleine), known as La Madeleine, is 350 metres north of Place de la Concorde along Rue Royale. Built in the style of a Greek temple, it was consecrated in 1842 after almost a century of design changes and construction delays. It is surrounded, Parthenon-like, by 52 Corinthian columns standing 20 metres tall. The marble and gilt interior, topped by three skylighted cupolas, is open Monday to Saturday from 7 am to 7 pm, and on Sunday from 7.30 am to 1 or 1.30 pm and 3.30 to 7 pm.

The **monumental staircase** on the south side affords one of the city's most quintessential Parisian panoramas: down Rue Royale to Place de la Concorde (and the obelisk) and on across the Seine to the Assemblée Nationale (see 7e Arrondissement). The gold dome of the Invalides appears in the background, a bit to the right of the Assemblée Nationale.

Place de la Madeleine

For details on taking a gastronomic tour of Place de la Madeleine, with stops at **Fauchon** and other luxury food shops, see Places to Eat: Champs-Élysées area.

Paris' cheapest *belle époque* attraction is the **public toilet** (M7) on the east side of La Madeleine, which dates from 1905 (2.20FF to sit down, 2FF for the urinals). There has been a **flower market** (M7) on the east side of the church since 1832; it's open daily except Sunday until 8.30 or 9 pm.

Walking in the Place de la Concorde Area

From Place de la Concorde, it's a short and elegant walk up Rue Royale – home to some of the most elegant boutiques in Paris – to La Madeleine. From there, you could continue on to the Opéra Garnier (M7) and the Grands Boulevards, and then loop back to the Louvre via Ave de l'Opéra.

CHAMPS-ÉLYSÉES AREA
(8e & northern 16e)

Ave des Champs-Élysées, whose name means Elysian Fields (Elysium was where happy souls dwelt after death, according to Greek and Roman mythology), links Place de la Concorde (eastern 8e) with the Arc de Triomphe. Since the Second Empire (1852-70), it has come to symbolise the style and *joie de vivre* of life in Paris.

Ave des Champs-Élysées

Popular with the aristocracy of the mid-19th century as a stage on which to parade their wealth, the two-km-long Ave des Champs-Élysées has, since WW II, been taken over by airline offices, cinemas, car showrooms and fast-food restaurants. The wealthy denizens of the Triangle d'Or (see below) consider the Champs-Élysées to be completely – but not quite inexorably – degraded and popularised, by which they mean the same thing.

In recent years, the municipality has invested US$48 million to regain some of the 72-metre-wide Champs-Élysées' former sparkle and prestige. The pavements have been widened to 21 metres (their original width) and paved with granite, new light standards with emerald globes have been raised, and retro news kiosks have replaced the old aluminium and glass ones. Hundreds of 30-year-old plane trees, brought by truck from Germany, have increased the greenery.

The even-numbered side of Ave des Champs-Élysées between Rond Point des Champs-Élysées and Rue de Berri is perforated by a series of **shopping arcades** (M7).

Rue du Faubourg Saint Honoré

Rue du Faubourg Saint Honoré (the western continuation of Rue Saint Honoré), 400 metres north of the Champs-Élysées, links Rue Royale (metro Concorde) with Place des Ternes (metro Ternes). It is home to some of Paris' most renowned couture houses (see Fashion in the Shopping chapter). Other luxury items available here include jewellery and fine antiques.

The most noteworthy of the avenue's 18th-century mansions is the **Palais de l'Élysée** (M7), at the intersection of Rue du Faubourg Saint Honoré and Ave de Marigny. The official residence of the French president and symbol of his extensive powers, it was built in 1718 and has housed 19 French presidents since 1873.

Musée du Petit Palais

The Petit Palais (M7; ☎ 01 42 65 12 73; metro Champs-Élysées Clemenceau) on Ave Winston Churchill, built for the Exposition Universelle of 1900, houses the **Musée des Beaux-Arts de la Ville de Paris**, the Paris municipality's Fine Arts Museum. It specialises in medieval and Renaissance objets d'art (porcelain, clocks), tapestries, drawings and 19th-century French painting and sculpture. The Petit Palais is open Tuesday to Sunday from 10 am to 5.40 pm (last entry at 5 pm). Tickets cost 27FF (14.50FF reduced price), more if there's a temporary exhibition.

Grand Palais

The Grand Palais (M7; ☎ 01 44 13 17 30; metro Champs-Élysées Clemenceau), across Ave Winston Churchill from the Petit Palais (the main entrance faces Ave des Champs-Élysées), houses the **Galeries Nationales du Grand Palais**, which hosts special exhibitions lasting three or four months (closed on Tuesday). Built for the Exposition Universelle of 1900, it has an iron frame and an Art Nouveau-style glass roof.

Palais de la Découverte

This fascinating science museum (M7; ☎ 01 40 74 80 00 or 01 40 74 81 82 for a recording; metro Champs-Élysées Clemenceau) on Ave Franklin D Roosevelt has interactive exhibits on astronomy, biology and medicine, chemistry, mathematics and computer science, physics and earth sciences. Although the signs, explanations and excellent public demonstrations (great for kids) are in French, much of the material is self-explanatory if you still remember a bit of high-school physics and biology. The two **Euréka rooms** have exhibits for young children.

The Palais de la Découverte is open Tuesday to Sunday from 9.30 or 10 am to 6 pm (7 pm on Sunday and holidays). Entrance costs 25FF (15FF for students and people under 18 or over 60; free for half an hour before closing time). The **planetarium**, which has four shows a day (in French), costs an extra 15FF (10FF reduced price).

Triangle d'Or

Many of Paris' richest residents, finest hotels and most fashionable couture houses can be found in the Triangle d'Or (golden triangle), an ultra-exclusive neighbourhood whose corners are at Place de la Concorde, the Arc de Triomphe and Place de l'Alma. Ave Montaigne, home of *haute couture* (see Fashion in the Shopping chapter), is a good place from which to start exploring the area.

Arc de Triomphe

The Arc de Triomphe (M6; ☎ 01 43 80 31 31; metro Charles de Gaulle-Étoile) is 2.2 km north-west of Place de la Concorde in the middle of Place Charles de Gaulle (Place de l'Étoile), the world's largest traffic roundabout and the meeting point of 12 avenues (and three arrondissements – the 8e, 16e and 17e). It was commissioned in 1806 by Napoleon to commemorate his imperial victories but remained unfinished when he started losing – first battles and then whole wars. It was finally completed between 1832 and 1836.

Among the armies to march triumphantly through the Arc de Triomphe were the victorious Germans in

DANIEL ROBINSON

Arc de Triomphe

RACHEL BLACK

Départ des Volontaires (1792), also known as
La Marseillaise

RACHEL BLACK

Details under the Arc de Triomphe

1871, the victorious Allies in 1919, the victorious Germans in 1940 and the victorious Allies in 1944. Since 1920, the body of an Unknown Soldier from WW I taken from Verdun in Lorraine has been interred beneath the arch, his fate and that of countless others like him commemorated by a memorial flame rekindled each evening around 6.30 pm. France's national remembrance service is held here annually at 11 am on 11 November.

The most famous of the four high-relief panels is to your right as you face the arch from the Ave des Champs-Élysées side. Entitled *Départ des Volontaires de 1792* and also known as *La Marseillaise*, it is the work of François Rude. Higher up, a frieze running around the whole monument depicts hundreds of figures, each two metres high.

From the viewing platform on top of the arch you can see the 12 avenues – many of them named after Napoleonic victories and illustrious generals – radiating toward every part of Paris. Ave de la Grande Armée heads north-westward to the new skyscraper district of **La Défense** (see La Défense later in this chapter), where the **Grande Arche**, a hollow cube 112 metres to a side, defines the western end of the Grande Axe (the Louvre-Arc de Triomphe axis). The platform can be visited daily, except on major holidays, Tuesday to Saturday from 9.30 am to 10.30 pm; Sunday and Monday from 9.30 am to 6.30 pm. Closing time may be earlier in the winter. Tickets cost 32FF (21FF if you're 18 to 25; 10FF for children aged 12 to 17) and are sold in the underground passageway.

The only sane way to get to the base of the arch is via the underground passageway (M6) – *not* linked to nearby metro tunnels – that surfaces on the even-numbered side of Ave des Champs-Élysées. The similar northern passage to the Ave de la Grande Armée has been closed for security reasons. Driving around the roundabout is Paris' ultimate driving challenge, especially during rush hour.

Ave Foch

Ultra-exclusive Ave Foch (16e; pronounced 'fosh'), Paris' widest boulevard, links the Arc de Triomphe with the Bois de Boulogne. Grassy areas with shaded paths – perfect for walking neurotic little dogs – separate the main lanes of traffic from the stately (and *very* expensive) apartment buildings along either side. Laid out in 1854, Ave Foch is named after Maréchal Ferdinand Foch (1851-1929), commander of the Allied forces during the last few difficult months of WW I.

Walking in the Champs-Élysées Area

For details on the Voie Triomphale (Triumphal Way), see Louvre Area earlier in this section. The most attractive part of Ave des Champs-Élysées is the shady, grass-covered stretch between Place de la Concorde and Rond Point des Champs-Élysées (M7).

The Petit Palais and Grand Palais are one km north of the Invalides and the nearby Musée Rodin. The Eiffel Tower is separated from the Arc de Triomphe by about two km of the fashionable 16e arrondissement.

PARC DE MONCEAU AREA

(northern 8e)

The elegant residential districts that surround the Parc de Monceau are a bastion of Paris' haute bourgeoisie.

Parc de Monceau

Pass through one of the gates in the elaborate wrought-iron fence around the Parc de Monceau (M7; metro Monceau) and you find yourself amidst Paris' most immaculately tended lawns, flowerbeds, trees and pseudo-classical statues. From the many benches, you can observe the city's best dressed children out with their nannies or on their way home from expensive private schools. Nearby streets are lined with opulent mansions and grand apartment buildings from the mid-19th century. The world's first parachute jump – from a balloon – was made here in 1797. The park is open daily until 8 pm (10 pm from April to October).

Musée Cernuschi

The Cernuschi Museum (M7; ☎ 01 45 63 50 75; metro Monceau) at 7 Ave Velasquez houses a collection of ancient Chinese art (funerary statues, bronzes, ceramics) and works from Japan assembled during the 19th century by the banker Henri Cernuschi. It is open from 10 am to 5.40 pm (closed Monday and holidays). Entry costs 27FF (19FF reduced price).

Musée Nissim de Camondo

The Nissim de Camondo Museum (M7; ☎ 01 45 63 26 32; metro Monceau or Villiers) at 63 Rue de Monceau displays 18th-century furniture, wood panelling, tapestries, porcelain and other objets d'art collected by Count Moïse de Camondo, who established this

museum in memory of his son Nissim, who died in WW
I. It is open from 10 am to 5 pm (closed Monday, Tuesday
and holidays). Tickets cost 27FF (18FF for people under
25 or over 60).

Musée Jacquemart-André

The Jacquemart-André Museum (M7; ☎ 01 42 89 04 91;
metro Saint Philippe du Roule) at 158 Blvd Haussmann
is housed in an opulent residence built during the mid-
19th century. The collection includes furniture,
tapestries and enamels but is most noted for its paintings
by Rembrandt and Van Dyck and the Italian Renaissance
works of Bernini, Botticelli, Carpaccio, Donatello,
Mantegna, Tintoretto, Titian and Uccello. The museum
is open daily, from 10 am to 6 pm, and entry is 45FF.

OPÉRA GARNIER AREA (8e & 9e)

Opéra Garnier, Paris' world-famous opera house, abuts
the Grands Boulevards, broad thoroughfares whose *belle
époque* elegance has been overwhelmed only in part by
the traffic and pedestrian tumult of a modern city.

Opéra Garnier

Paris' renowned opera house (M7 & M8; ☎ 01 40 01 22
63; metro Opéra) at Place de l'Opéra (9e), designed in
1860 by Charles Garnier to showcase the splendour of
Napoleon III's France, is one of the most impressive
monuments erected during the Second Empire. The
extravagant **entrance hall**, with its **Grand Escalier** (great
staircase), is decorated with multicoloured, imported
marble and a gigantic chandelier. The **ceiling** of the
recently renovated auditorium was painted by Marc
Chagall in 1964. Other parts of the building are likely to
undergo repairs until the end of the century.

Known as Opéra Garnier since the opening of the new
Opéra at Place de la Bastille, it is open to visitors daily (unless
there's a daytime rehearsal or performance) from 10 am to
5 pm; ticket sales end at 4.30 pm. The entrance fee is 30FF
(20FF for children, students and seniors; free for under 10s).
Operas and concerts are staged both here and at Opéra
Bastille (see the Entertainment chapter for details).

Blvd Haussmann

Blvd Haussmann (8e & 9e), just north of Opéra Garnier,
is the heart of a commercial and banking district best
known for having some of Paris' most famous depart-

ment stores, including **Galeries Lafayette** (M7) at No 40 and **Printemps** (M7) at No 64 (see the Shopping chapter).

Grands Boulevards

The eight Grands Boulevards (M7 & M8) – Madeleine, Capucines, Italiens, Montmartre, Poissonière, Bonne Nouvelle, Saint Denis and Saint Martin – stretch from elegant Place de la Madeleine (8e; see Place de la Concorde Area) eastward to less-than-elegant Place de la République (3e & 10e), a distance of just under three km. Lined with the kind of grand 19th-century buildings for which Paris is famous, they were established in the 1600s on the site of obsolete fortifications. The Grands Boulevards served as a centre of café and theatre life in the 18th and 19th centuries, reaching the height of fashion during the *belle époque*.

The Grands Boulevards pass by the following sights: Place de l'Opéra, designed by Haussmann; the lively nightlife district along Blvd Montmartre and nearby parts of Rue du Faubourg Montmartre (2e & 10e); a number of 19th-century arcades; and two small triumphal arches, Porte Saint Denis and Porte Saint Martin (see 10e Arrondissement).

19th-Century Arcades

Stepping into the covered shopping arcades off Blvd Montmartre is the best way to visit early 19th-century Paris. The **Passage des Panoramas** (M8; metro Rue Montmartre) at 11 Blvd Montmartre (2e), which was opened in 1800 and received Paris' first gas lighting in 1817, was expanded in 1834 with the addition of four other contiguous passages: Feydeau, Montmartre, Saint Marc and Variétés. The arcades are open daily from 6.30 am to midnight.

On the other side of Blvd Montmartre (9e), between Nos 10 and 12, is **Passage Jouffroy** (M8; metro Rue Montmartre), which leads across Rue de la Grange Batelière to **Passage Verdeau** (M8). Both shelter shops selling antiques, old postcards, antiquarian books, pet toys, imports from Asia and the like. The arcades are open until 10 pm. A bit to the east at 97 Rue de Richelieu (2e) is skylighted **Passage des Princes** (M8; metro Richelieu Drouot).

Walking in the Opéra Garnier Area

The area around Opéra Garnier makes for a stimulating (if congested) stroll. In addition to following the Grands

Boulevards, you could walk south along Rue de la Paix, known for its jewellery shops, to Place Vendôme (see the Louvre Area listing) or head south-east along one-km-long Ave de l'Opéra to the Palais Royal and the Louvre. About 100 metres east of Opéra Garnier, you can explore Rue de la Chaussée d'Antin (9e), an enormously fashionable thoroughfare in the late 1700s.

10e ARRONDISSEMENT

The lively, ethnically mixed working-class area (metro Château d'Eau and Gare de l'Est) around Blvd de Strasbourg and Rue du Faubourg Saint Denis (especially south of Blvd de Magenta) is home to large communities of Indians, Pakistanis, West Indians, Africans, Turks and Kurds. Strolling through **Passage Brady** (M8; metro Château d'Eau) is like stepping into a back alley in Bombay.

Tranquil Canal Saint Martin links the 10e with Parc de la Villette (19e). Rue de Paradis (metro Château d'Eau) is famed for its crystal and tableware shops (see the Shopping chapter).

Porte Saint Denis & Porte Saint Martin

Porte Saint Denis (M8; metro Strasbourg Saint Denis), the 24-metre-high triumphal arch at the intersection of Rue du Faubourg Saint Denis and Blvd Saint Denis, was built in 1672 to commemorate Louis XIV's campaign along the Rhine. On the north side, carvings represent the fall of Maastricht in 1673.

Two blocks to the east, at the intersection of Rue du Faubourg Saint Martin and Blvd Saint Denis, is another triumphal arch, 17-metre-high Porte Saint Martin (M8), erected in 1674 to commemorate the capture of Besançon and the Franche-Comté region by Louis XIV's armies.

Baccarat Crystal Museum

The glittering, incredibly pricey Baccarat showroom (M8; ☎ 01 47 70 64 30; metro Château d'Eau) at 30bis Rue de Paradis is a fine example of Napoleon III-era industrial architecture. The attached museum is filled with stunning pieces of crystal, many of them custom made for princes and dictators of desperately poor ex-colonies. It is open weekdays from 9 am to 6 pm, and on Saturday from 10 am to noon and 2 to 5 pm; entry is free.

Canal Saint Martin

The little-touristed, 4.5-km-long Saint Martin Canal (M9; metro République, Jaurès and others) is one of Paris' hidden delights. Its shaded towpaths – speckled with sunlight filtering through the plane trees – are a wonderful place for a romantic stroll or bike ride past nine **locks**, metal bridges and ordinary Parisian neighbourhoods. Parts of the waterway – built in 1806 to link the Seine with the 108-km Canal de l'Ourcq – are higher than the surrounding land.

Between the Port de Plaisance de Paris-Arsenal (the pleasure-boat marina next to Place de la Bastille) and Square Frédéric Lemaître (10e), Canal Saint Martin disappears under reinforced concrete vaults for over two km. The northern, open-air half of the canal, which links Square Frédéric Lemaître with Parc de la Villette (19e), was saved thanks to the failure of a plan – mooted in the early 1970s – to pave it over and turn it into an autoroute. For information on barge rides, see Organised Tours in the Getting Around chapter.

BERCY (12e)

The area along the Seine between Gare de Lyon and Porte de Bercy spent most of the 1980s as a huge construction site for several of former President Mitterrand's grandiose grands projets. These days, Bercy – long cut off from the rest of the city by railway tracks and the Seine – has some of Paris' most important new buildings, including the striking **American Center** at 51 Rue de Bercy (M1), which closed for lack of funding in 1996; the octagonal **Palais Omnisports de Paris-Bercy** (M1) on Blvd de Bercy, designed to serve as both an indoor sports arena and a concert, ballet and theatre venue; and the giant **Ministry of Finance** (M1) on Blvd de Bercy, whose minions of clerks and economists were dragged here, kicking and screaming, from the beautiful north wing of the Louvre.

13e ARRONDISSEMENT

The generally nondescript 13e arrondissement begins a few blocks south of the Jardin des Plantes (5e).

Bibliothèque Nationale de France

Right across the river from Bercy is the controversial, US$2 billion National Library (M1; metro Quai de la

Gare), sarcastically known – recalling the TGV train – as the Très Grande Bibliothèque (very large library).

Conceived by Mitterrand as a 'wonder of the modern world', no expense was spared to carry out a plan that many people say defies logic: while many of the 12 million books and documents will bake on the shelves in the four sun-drenched, 80-metre-high towers – shaped like half-open books – patrons will sit in artificially lit basement halls built around a forest of 126 50-year-old pines, trucked here from Normandy at a cost of US$22,000 each. Eight km of computer-controlled conveyor belts will deliver books to 150 collection points. When the complex opens in 1997, it will cost about US$260 million a year to run, devouring some 10% of the French government's cultural budget.

Chinatown

In the triangle bounded by Ave de Choisy, Ave d'Ivry and Blvd Masséna, Paris' high-rise Chinatown (M1; metro Tolbiac, Porte d'Ivry or Porte de Choisy) has a distinctly Franco-Chinese ambience, thanks to the scores of East Asian restaurants, shops and travel agencies.

14e ARRONDISSEMENT

The less-than-thrilling 14e is best known for Cimetière du Montparnasse (see Montparnasse Area); **Parc Montsouris** (M1; metro Cité Universitaire), a beautiful park across Blvd Jourdan from the lawns and university dorms of the **Cité Internationale Universitaire** (M1); and the discount clothing outlets along Rue d'Alésia (M1; see Clothes & Fashion Accessories in the Shopping chapter).

Catacombes

In 1785, it was decided to solve the hygienic and aesthetic problems posed by Paris' overflowing cemeteries (especially Cimetière des Innocents, just south of modern-day Forum des Halles) by exhuming the bones and storing them in the tunnels of three disused quarries. One ossuary created during this period is the Catacombes (M1; ☎ 01 43 22 47 63; metro Denfert Rochereau), without a doubt Paris' most macabre tourist site. After descending 20 metres below street level, visitors follow 1.6 km of underground corridors in which the bones and skulls of millions of Parisians from centuries past are neatly stacked along the walls. During WW

II, these tunnels were used by the Résistance as a head-quarters.

The route through the Catacombes begins from the small green building at 1 Place Denfert Rochereau. The site is open Tuesday to Friday from 2 to 4 pm and on weekends from 9 to 11 am and 2 to 4 pm. Tickets cost 28FF (19FF for students and children). Flash photography is no problem but tripods are forbidden. It's a good idea to bring along a torch (flashlight).

The exit (metro Mouton Duvernet), where a guard will check your bag for stolen bones, is on Rue Remy Dumoncel, 700 metres south-west of Place Denfert Rochereau.

MONTMARTRE (18e)

During the 19th century – especially after the Communard uprising of 1871, which began here – Montmartre's bohemian lifestyle attracted artists and writers whose presence turned the area into Paris' most important centre of artistic and literary creativity. Although such activity shifted to Montparnasse around WW I, Montmartre retains a magic, leafy ambience that all the tourists in the world couldn't spoil (though they sometimes seem about to).

In English-speaking countries, Montmartre's mystique of unconventionality has been magnified by the notoriety of the **Moulin Rouge** (M7 & M8; see Cabaret in the Entertainment chapter), a nightclub on the edge of the Pigalle sex district that was founded in 1889 and is known for its nearly naked chorus girls.

Getting Around

The RATP's sleek, ultramodern funiculaire (funicular railway; M8) up Montmartre's south slope – really a glorified slightly horizontal lift – whisks visitors from Square Willette (metro Anvers) to Sacré Cœur. It runs until 12.40 am and costs one metro/bus ticket each way. Weekly and monthly Carte Orange coupons and Paris Visite and Formule 1 passes are also valid.

Montmartrobus, run by the RATP, takes a circuitous route all over Montmartre – maps are posted at bus stops.

Basilique du Sacré Cœur

The Basilique du Sacré Cœur (Sacred Heart Basilica; M8; ☎ 01 42 51 17 02; metro Lamarck Caulaincourt), perched at the very top of Butte de Montmartre (Montmartre

Hill), was built from contributions to fulfil a vow of contrition taken by Parisian Catholics after the humiliating Franco-Prussian War of 1870-71. Construction began in 1873, but the basilica was not consecrated until 1919.

On warm evenings, groups of young people gather on the steps below the church to contemplate the view, play guitars and sing. Although the basilica's domes are a well-loved part of the Parisian skyline, the architecture of the rest of the building, which is typical of the style of the late 19th century, is not very graceful.

A 234-step climb up narrow spiral staircases takes you up to the **dome** (15FF, 8FF for children and students under 25), which affords one of Paris' most spectacular panoramas. The chapel-lined **crypt** (15FF, 9FF reduced price) is huge but uninteresting.

The basilica is open daily from 7 am to 10.30 pm. The dome and the crypt, down the stairs to the right as you exit the basilica, are open daily from 9 am to 6 pm (7 pm from late March to September).

Place du Tertre

Half a block west of the **Église Saint Pierre de Montmartre** (M8), parts of which date from the 12th century as it's the only building left from the great Benedictine abbey of Montmartre, is Place du Tertre (metro Abbesses), once the main square of the village of Montmartre. These days, it's filled with cafés, restaurants, portrait artists and tourists and is always animated. Look for the two **windmills** to the west on Rue Lepic.

Espace Montmartre Salvador Dalí

Over 300 works by Salvador Dalí (1904-89), the flamboyant Catalan surrealist printmaker, painter, sculptor and self-promoter, are on display at this museum (M8; ☎ 01 42 64 40 10; metro Abbesses) at 11 Rue Poulbot, around the corner from Place du Tertre. It is open daily, 10 am to 6 pm, and entry is 35FF (25FF reduced rate). Discount coupons are often available.

Musée du Vieux Montmartre

The Museum of Old Montmartre (M8; ☎ 01 46 06 61 11; metro Lamarck Caulaincourt) at 12 Rue Cortot, also known as the Musée de Montmartre, displays paintings, lithographs and documents relating to the area's politically rebellious and bohemian/artistic past. It's hard to appreciate what the big deal is (and to justify the admission fee) unless you know something about Montmartre's mythology – and can read French. There's a lush and wild little garden out the back. The museum is open Tuesday to Sunday from 11 am to 5.30 pm. Tickets cost 25FF (20FF for students and seniors).

Musée d'Art Naïf Max Fourny

The Museum of Naive Art, founded in 1986, is housed in Halle Saint Pierre (M8; ☎ 01 42 58 72 89; metro Anvers) at 2 Rue Ronsard, across from Square Willette and the base of the funiculaire. The colourful, vivid paintings – gathered from around the world – are immediately appealing, thanks in part to their whimsical and generally optimistic perspective on life. The museum, whose themed exhibitions change frequently, is open daily from 10 am to 6 pm. Tickets cost a pricey 40FF (30FF for students under 26, seniors and teachers).

The **gallery** on the ground floor hosts temporary exhibitions and there's a very pleasant café.

Musée d'Art Juif

The small Museum of Jewish Art (☎ 01 42 57 84 15; metro Lamarck Caulaincourt), on the 3rd floor of the Jewish community centre at 42 Rue des Saules, has a modest collection of synagogue models, paintings and ritual objects from Eastern Europe and North Africa. It is open Sunday to Thursday from 3 to 6 pm (closed on Jewish holidays and in August). Entrance costs 30FF (20FF for students, 10FF for children).

In 1998, the museum's collections will be combined with medieval Jewish artefacts from the Musée National du Moyen Age to create the Musée d'Art et d'Histoire du Judaï (metro Rambuteau), to be housed in the Hôtel de Saint Aignan at 71 Rue du Temple (3e) in the Marais.

Cimetière de Montmartre

Montmartre Cemetery (M7; ☎ 01 43 87 64 24; metro Place de Clichy), established in 1798, is the most famous cemetery in Paris after Père Lachaise. It contains the graves of such people as the writers Émile Zola, Alexandre Dumas the younger, Stendahl and Heinrich Heine; the composers Jacques Offenbach and Hector Berlioz; the painter Edgar Degas; the film-maker François Truffaut; and the dancer Vaslav Nijinsky.

The entrance nearest the Butte de Montmartre is at 20 Ave Rachel, down the stairs from 10 Rue Caulaincourt.

From mid-March to early November, it is open daily from 8 am (8.30 am on Saturday, 9 am on Sunday and holidays) to 6 pm (last entry at 5.45 pm). The rest of the year, it's open from 8 am to 5.30 pm.

Pigalle

Only a few blocks south-west of the tranquil, residential streets of Montmartre is lively, neon-lit Pigalle (9e & 18e; M8), one of Paris' two main sex districts (the other, near Forum des Halles, is along Rue Saint Denis). But Pigalle is more than simply a sleazy red-light district: though the area around Blvd de Clichy between the Pigalle and Blanche metro stops is lined with erotica shops and striptease parlours, there are also plenty of trendy night spots, including La Locomotive disco and the Moulin Rouge (see the Entertainment chapter).

Despite the prostitutes, the peep shows and the blatant but controlled seediness, Pigalle is so filled with people of all sorts (including whole buses of fascinated middle-aged tourists) that even late at night it's not unsafe, especially if you're with other people. However, after nightfall the Abbesses metro stop is considered a more prudent bet than the Blanche, Pigalle and, especially, Château Rouge stations.

Walking in Montmartre

The real attractions of Montmartre, apart from the spectacular view (best when there's not too much haze), are the area's little parks and steep, winding cobblestone streets, many of whose houses seem about to be engulfed by creepers. On the corner of Rue Saint Vincent and Rue des Saules, there's even a small **vineyard** whose annual production – several hundred bottles of undrinkable plonk – is auctioned off for charity.

Lovely streets to explore include Rue de l'Abreuvoir, Rue Saint Vincent, Place Constantin Pecqueur and **Place Émile Goudeau** (M8), where Kees Van Dongen, Max Jacob, Amedeo Modigliani and Pablo Picasso once lived in great poverty in a building at No 13 that Jacob dubbed the **Bateau Lavoir** (floating laundry shed; closed to the public). It was rebuilt in 1978 after burning down in 1970. There's a **kids' playground** and **carousel** (10FF, 7FF for children under 12) at the base of the stairs up to Sacré Cœur.

Place Pigalle and Blvd de Clichy, the lively heart of Pigalle, are 200 metres south of Place des Abbesses with a particularly photogenic metro entrance and sign.

RACHEL BLACK

One of the lovely streets in Montmarte

TONY WHEELER

Kids' merry-go-round at the stairs to Sacré Cœur

19e ARRONDISSEMENT

The 19e is of interest to visitors mainly because of Canal Saint Martin (see 10e Arrondissement) and its eastern continuation, Canal de l'Ourcq, and two large parks: Parc de la Villette, next to Paris' largest science museum, and hilly Parc des Buttes-Chaumont.

Parc de la Villette

This whimsical, 30-hectare park (M1) in the city's far north-eastern corner, opened in 1993, stretches 600 metres from the Cité des Sciences et de l'Industrie (metro Porte de la Villette) southward to the Cité de la Musique (metro Porte de Pantin). Split into two sections by Canal de l'Ourcq, its lawns are enlivened by shaded walkways, imaginative public furniture, a series of themed gardens and whimsical, bright red building-sculptures known as *folies* (follies), one of which contains the splendid Hot Brass jazz club (see Jazz in the Entertainment chapter). Check out the giant sculpture entitled *Bicyclette Ensevelie*, which is just that: a huge 'buried bicycle'.

For kids, there's a **merry-go-round** near the Cinaxe, a **playground** between the Géode and the nearest bridge, and two large play areas: the **Jardin des Vents** (Garden of Winds; M1) and the adjacent **Jardin des Dunes** (Dunes Garden). Divided into three areas for children of different ages, they are across Galerie de la Villette (the covered walkway) from the **Grande Halle** (M1), a former slaughterhouse now used for concerts, theatre performances, expositions and conventions.

For information on barge rides from the Port de Plaisance de Paris-Arsenal to Parc de la Villette, see Organised Tours in the Getting Around chapter.

Cité des Sciences et de l'Industrie

The enormous City of Science & Industry (M1; ☎ 01 40 05 72 23; metro Porte de la Villette), at the northern end of Parc de la Villette, has all sorts of hi-tech exhibits on matters scientific. The dazzle-'em-with-gadgets presentation reflects France's traditionally deferential approach to technology and white lab-coated scientists, whom the public – with the encouragement of the government technocracy – seems to think know best. (This attitude could explain why there has been so little popular opposition in France to nuclear power.)

Explora, the huge main museum, is open daily except Monday from 10 am to 6 pm (7 pm on Sunday). A ticket good for Explora, the planetarium, a 3-D film and the

French Navy submarine *Argonaute* (commissioned in 1957) costs 45FF (35FF for people aged eight to 25, seniors and teachers; 25FF after 4 pm) and lets you leave and enter up to four times during the day. Various combo tickets valid for the Cité des Sciences, the Géode and Cinaxe are available.

A free map-brochure in English and the detailed *Guide to the Permanent Exhibitions* (20FF) are available at the Cité des Sciences' main entrance. Nearby, you can hire **headset tours** in English and other languages (15FF).

Cité des Enfants The highlight of the Cité des Sciences is the brilliant Cité des Enfants, whose colourful and imaginative hands-on demonstrations of basic scientific principles are divided into two sections, one for three to five-year-olds, the other for five to 12-year-olds. Younger kids can explore, among other things, the behaviour of water (waterproof lab ponchos provided), while older children can build toy houses with industrial robots and stage news broadcasts in a TV studio equipped with real video cameras.

The 90-minute visits begin four times a day at two-hour intervals from 9.30 or 10.30 am. Each child is charged 20FF, as is an accompanying adult (required). During school holiday periods, it's a good idea to make reservations two or three days in advance (☎ 01 36 68 29 30 or, by Minitel, 3615 VILLETTE).

Géode

Just south of the Cité des Sciences is the Géode (M1; ☎ 01 36 68 29 30), a 36-metre-high sphere whose mirror-like surface made up of 6433 highly polished, stainless-steel triangles has made it one of the architectural calling cards of modern Paris. Inside, high-resolution, 70-mm nature films lasting 45 minutes are projected onto a spherical, 180° screen that gives viewers a sense of being surrounded by the action. Films begin every hour on the hour from 10 am to 9 pm (closed Monday except perhaps during school holiday periods). Headsets that pick up an English soundtrack are available for no extra charge.

Tickets to the Géode cost 57FF (44FF for under 25s, seniors and teachers; not available on weekends and holidays from 4 to 5 pm). For afternoon shows during school holiday periods and on Tuesday and Thursday from March to June, make advance reservations.

Cinaxe

The Cinaxe (☎ 01 42 09 34 00), a 60-person hydraulic cinema with seating that moves in synchronisation with

RICHARD EVERIST

Cité des Sciences et de l'Industrie and the Géode

BETHUNE CARMICHAEL

Playground in the Parc de la Villette

the action on the screen, is right across the walkway from the south-western side of the Cité des Sciences. This example of proto-virtual reality technology is open from 10 or 11 am to 7 pm (closed Monday) and costs 33FF (24 or 29FF for children, students and seniors). Shows begin every 20 minutes.

Cité de la Musique

On the southern edge of Parc de la Villette, the City of Music (M1; ☎ 01 44 84 45 45; metro Porte de Pantin) on Ave Jean Jaurès, which opened in 1995, is a striking triangular concert hall whose brief is to bring non-elitist music from around the world to Paris' multiethnic masses. Hundreds of rare musical instruments are on display in its **Musée de** la Musique (Music Museum). The free Centre d'Information Musique et Danse, open Wednesday to Sunday from noon to 6.30 pm (8 pm on concert nights), lets you try out interactive CD-ROMs (many of them in English) connected in some way to music – subjects range from Beethoven to Woodstock. For details on concerts (some of them free), see the Entertainment chapter.

Parc des Buttes-Chaumont

Encircled by tall apartment blocks, 25-hectare Buttes-Chaumont Park (M9; metro Buttes-Chaumont or Botzaris) is the closest thing in Paris to Manhattan's Central Park. Great for jogging, cycling or tanning, its lush, forested slopes hide grottoes and artificial water-

TONY WHEELER

Parc des Buttes–Chaumont

falls. The romantic **lake** is dominated by a precipitous temple-topped **island** linked to the mainland by two bridges. Once a quarry and rubbish tip, the park – encircled by Rue Manin and Rue Botzaris – was given its present form by Haussmann in the 1860s. Except in icy conditions, it's open daily from 7 am to 9 pm (11 pm from May to September).

20e ARRONDISSEMENT

The multicultural, working-class 20e, last stronghold of the Commune of 1871 and long a bastion of proletarian radicalism, is a lively, little-touristed corner of the city.

Cimetière du Père Lachaise

The most visited necropolis in the world is Père Lachaise Cemetery (M3; ☎ 01 43 70 70 33; metro Philippe Auguste, Père Lachaise or Gambetta), founded in 1805, whose ornate (and at times ostentatious) tombs of famous people form a verdant, open-air sculpture garden. Among the one million people buried here are the composer Chopin; the writers Molière, Apollinaire, Oscar Wilde, Balzac, Marcel Proust, Gertrude Stein and Colette; the artists David, Delacroix, Pissarro, Seurat and Modigliani; the actors Sarah Bernhardt, Simone Signoret and Yves Montand; the singer Édith Piaf; the dancer Isadora Duncan; and even those immortal 12th-century lovers, Abélard and Héloïse. The only tomb most younger, English-speaking visitors come to see is the grave (in Division 6) of 1960s rock star **Jim Morrison**, lead singer of the Doors, who died in Paris in 1971.

On 27 May 1871, the last of the Communard insurgents, cornered by government forces, fought a hopeless, all-night battle among the tombstones. In the morning, the 147 survivors were lined up against the **Mur des Fédérés** (wall of the Federalists) and shot. They were buried where they fell in a mass grave.

The cemetery, which has five entrances (two of them on Blvd de Ménilmontant), is open daily from 8 am to 5.30 pm. From mid-March to early November, hours are 7.30 am to 6 pm. Maps indicating the location of noteworthy graves are posted around the cemetery and can be purchased for 10FF.

Belleville

This buoyant and utterly unpretentious working-class 'village' around Blvd de Belleville (M9; metro Belleville) is home to large numbers of immigrants, especially Muslims and Jews from North Africa and Vietnamese and Chinese from Indochina. In recent years, its flimsy, late 19th-century workers' flats have become a trendy address for avant-garde artists in search of cheap housing and the cachet that comes with slumming it. This is one of the best places in Paris to dine on couscous, the meat available either kosher or halal (slaughtered according to Muslim law).

The **Parc de Belleville** (M9; metro Couronnes), a few blocks east of Blvd de Belleville, occupies a hill almost 200 metres above sea level. Opened in 1992, the park offers superb views of the city.

BOIS DE BOULOGNE (16e)

The 8.65-sq-km Boulogne Woods (M1), on the western edge of the city, are endowed with lakes, lawns, forested areas, flower gardens, meandering paths, cycling trails and *belle époque* cafés. The park owes its informal layout to its designer, Baron Haussmann, who took his inspiration from London's Hyde Park rather than the more formal French models.

The southern reaches of the woods take in **Stade Rolland Garros** (M1), home of the French Open tennis tournament, and two horse-racing tracks, the Hippodrome de Longchamp (for flat races) and the Hippodrome d'Auteuil (for steeplechases; M1). For details, see Horse Racing under Spectator Sports in the Entertainment chapter.

Gardens

The enclosed **Parc de Bagatelle** (M1), in the north-western corner of the Bois de Boulogne, is renowned for its beautiful gardens; they surround the **Château de Bagatelle**, built in 1775. There are areas dedicated to roses (which bloom from June to October), irises (May) and water lilies (August).

The **Pré Catelan Park** (M1) includes a garden in which you can see the plants, flowers and trees mentioned in Shakespeare's plays.

Rowboats & Bicycles Rowboats can be hired at **Lac Inférieur** (M1; metro Ave Henri Martin), the largest of the park's lakes and ponds. Paris Cycles (☎ 01 47 47 76 50 for a recorded message) rents bicycles at two locations: on Ave du Mahatma Gandhi (metro Les Sablons) across from the Porte Sablons entrance to the Jardin d'Acclimatation amusement park, and near the Pavillon Royal (metro Avenue Foch) at the northern end of Lac Inférieur. Except when it rains, bicycles are available

MAP 3

Jim Morrison's grave

TONY WHEELER

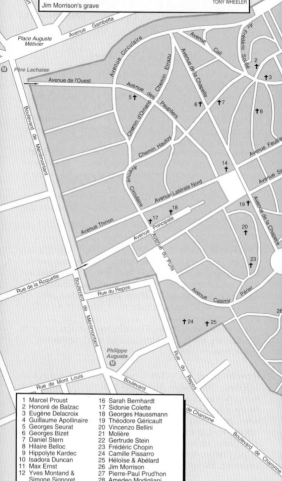

Place Auguste Métivier

Père Lachaise

Avenue Gambetta

Avenue Circulaire

Avenue Cail

Av. Frédéric Sollié

Rue Robineau

Rue Houdart

Avenue de l'Ouest

Chemin Errazu

Avenue Errazu

Avenue de la Chapelle

Avenue des Peupliers

Chemin d'Ornano

Chemin Haytou

Avenue Circulaire

Boulevard de Ménilmontant

Avenue Latérale Nord

Avenue Thinon

Avenue Principale

Avenue Principale

Avenue du Puits

Avenue de la Chapelle

Avenue Saint

Avenue Feuillant

Rue de la Roquette

Boulevard de Ménilmontant

Rue du Repos

Avenue Casimir Périer

Philippe Auguste

Rue du Repos

Rue de Mont Louis

Boulevard

Boulevard de Charonne

de Charonne

Boulevard de Charonne

1	Marcel Proust	16	Sarah Bernhardt
2	Honoré de Balzac	17	Sidonie Colette
3	Eugène Delacroix	18	Georges Haussmann
4	Guillaume Apollinaire	19	Théodore Géricault
5	Georges Seurat	20	Vincenzo Bellini
6	Georges Bizet	21	Molière
7	Daniel Stern	22	Gertrude Stein
8	Hilaire Belloc	23	Frédéric Chopin
9	Hippolyte Kardec	24	Camille Pissarro
10	Isadora Duncan	25	Héloïse & Abélard
11	Max Ernst	26	Jim Morrison
12	Yves Montand &	27	Pierre-Paul Prud'hon
	Simone Signoret	28	Amedeo Modigliani
13	Oscar Wilde	29	Edith Piaf & Théo Sarapo
14	Jacques Louis David	30	Paul Éluard
15	Dominique Ingres	31	Mur des Fédérés

from 10 am to sundown on Wednesday, Saturday and Sunday (daily during school holiday periods and from mid-April to mid-October).

Night-time in the Bois de Boulogne Each night after about 10 pm, especially on weekends, little sections of the Bois de Boulogne are taken over by all manner of prostitutes (the great majority of whom have AIDS, according to a recent study). They are joined by professionals and amateurs with certain sexual preferences and interests: *échangistes* (people interested in partner-swapping), voyeurs, flashers, people who arrange orgies etc. In recent years, the police have cracked down on the park's sex trade, but locals still advise both men and women not to walk through the area alone at night. The areas around the Parc de Bagatelle and the Pré Catelan are also popular gay cruising grounds but, as the *Spartacus Guide* correctly points out, they are definitely AYOR (at your own risk).

Musée National des Arts et Traditions Populaires

The National Museum of Popular Arts & Traditions (M1; ☎ 01 44 17 60 00; metro Les Sablons), near the Jardin d'Acclimatation at 6 Ave du Mahatma Gandhi, has displays illustrating life in rural France before and during the Industrial Revolution. It is open from 9.45 am to 5 pm (closed Tuesday). Tickets cost 20FF (13FF reduced price, available to everyone on Sunday).

Jardin d'Acclimatation

This kids-orientated amusement park (M1; ☎ 01 40 67 90 80; metro Les Sablons) on Ave du Mahatma Gandhi (at the northern edge of the Bois de Boulogne) is open every day, all year long from 10 am to 6 pm. Entrance costs 10FF (5FF reduced price).

Inside the park's Porte Madrid entrance is the **Bowling de Paris** (☎ 01 40 67 94 00), a bowling alley (open daily) where games cost 20 to 33FF per person. The highest tariffs are in force after 8 pm and on weekends. This place also has French and American billiards and snooker.

Musée Marmottan

Two blocks east of the Bois de Boulogne, between Porte de la Muette and Porte de Passy, the Marmottan Museum (M1; ☎ 01 42 24 07 02; metro La Muette) at 2 Rue Louis Boilly (16e) has the world's largest collection of works by the Impressionist painter Claude Monet, as well as paintings by Gauguin and Renoir. It is open Tuesday to Sunday from 10 am to 5.30 pm. Entrance costs 35FF (15FF reduced price).

BOIS DE VINCENNES (12e)

Paris' other large English-style park, the 9.3-sq-km Bois de Vincennes, is in the far south-eastern corner of the city. The **Parc Floral** (Floral Garden; M1; metro Château de Vincennes), just south of the Château de Vincennes (see below), is on Route de la Pyramide. The **Jardin Tropical** (tropical garden; RER stop Nogent-sur-Marne) is at the park's eastern edge on Ave de la Belle Gabrielle.

Every year from the end of March to early May, the Bois de Vincennes hosts a huge amusement park known as the **Foire du Trône**.

Musée National des Arts d'Afrique et d'Océanie

The National Museum of African & Oceanian Art (M1; ☎ 01 44 74 84 80; metro Porte Dorée) at 293 Ave Daumesnil is devoted to the art of the South Pacific, North Africa and western and central Africa. The residents of the **tropical aquarium** include Nile crocodiles. It is open on weekdays except Tuesday from 10 am to noon and 1.30 to 5.30 pm (no midday closure during special exhibitions), and on weekends from 12.30 pm (10 am for the aquarium) to 6 pm. The entry fee is 27FF (18FF if you're 18 to 24 or over 60; free for under 18s).

Zoo

The Parc Zoologique de Paris (M1; ☎ 01 44 75 20 00 or, for a recording, 01 44 75 20 10; metro Porte Dorée), founded in 1934, is on Ave Daumesnil, 250 metres east of the Blvd Périphérique, the ring road around Paris. The park is open daily from 9 am to between 5 and 6.30 pm, depending on the time of year and the day; the last entry is 30 minutes before closing. The rest of the year, the hours are 9 am to 5 pm (5.30 pm on Sunday). The entrance fee is 40FF (30FF reduced tariff, 10FF for students).

Château de Vincennes

The Château de Vincennes (☎ 01 48 08 31 20; metro Château de Vincennes), at the northern edge of the Bois de Vincennes, is a bona fide royal château complete with massive fortifications and a moat. Louis XIV spent his

MAP 4

La Défense

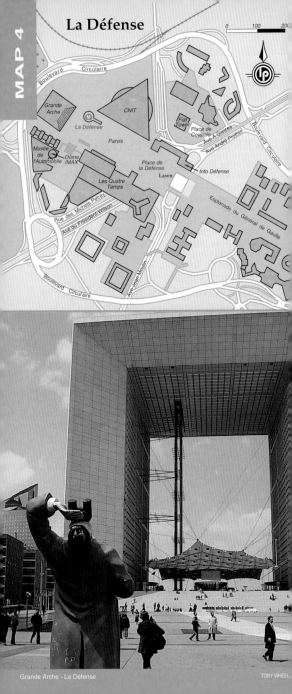

0   100   200

Boulevard   Circulaire

Grande Arche

CNIT

M La Défense

Fiat Tower

Place de Coupole

Ave A Gleizes

Boulevard Circulaire

Parvis

Musée de l'Automobile

Dôme IMAX

Place de la Défense

Info Défense

Les Quatre Temps

Lawn

Esplanade du Général de Gaulle

Rue des Michets Petray

Ave du Président Wilson

Ave Jean Moulin

Ave André Prothim

Boulevard   Circulaire

Grande Arche - La Défense

TONY WHEE

honeymoon in the mid-17th century **Pavillon du Roi**, the westernmost of the two royal pavilions flanking the **Cour Royale** (Royal Courtyard). The 52-metre-high **Donjon**, completed in 1369, was used as a prison during the 17th and 18th centuries. It will be closed for repairs until the end of the century.

You can walk around the grounds for free, but the only way to see the Gothic **Chapelle Royale**, built between the 14th and 16th centuries, is to take a guided tour (in French, with an information booklet in English). Tickets cost 32FF (reduced price 21FF) for a long tour, 22FF (14FF) for a short one. They operate from 10 am to 6 pm in summer.

LA DÉFENSE

La Défense (M4; metro La Défense), Paris' skyscraper district, is three km west of the 17th arrondissement. Set on the sloping west bank of the Seine, its ultramodern architecture and 40-storey office blocks are radically different from centuries-old central Paris – but no less French. This mini-Manhattan is well worth a visit, with vast public spaces surrounded by towering buildings – among them some examples of modern architecture at its best – and adorned with giant works of contemporary art.

La Défense, one of the world's most ambitious urban construction projects, was begun in the late 1950s. Its first major structure was the Centre des Nouvelles Industries et Technologies (Centre for New Industries & Technologies), better known as **CNIT**, inaugurated in 1958 and renovated in 1989. During the mid-1970s economic slump the entire project appeared in jeopardy, but today La Défense has about 50 buildings, the highest of which is the 45-storey, 178-metre-high **Fiat Tower**. There are plans to build a 400-metre-high skyscraper, nick-named the **Tour sans Fin** (endless tower), next to the Grande Arche.

La Défense houses the head offices of 14 of France's 20 largest corporations. A total of 1200 companies of all sizes employ some 110,000 people. Most of the district's 35,000 residents live in high-rise apartment blocks.

Info Défense (☎ 01 47 74 84 24), open daily from 9.30 or 10 am to 6 or 6.30 pm, has a guide to the area's monumental art (15FF) and details on cultural activities.

Grande Arche

The remarkable Grande Arche (☎ 01 49 07 27 57), designed by Danish architect Otto von Spreckelsen, is a hollow cube of white marble and glass measuring 112 metres to a side. Inaugurated on 14 July 1989, it forms the current western terminus of the eight-km-long **Grande Axe** (Great Axis), which stretches from the Louvre pyramid through the Jardin des Tuileries and along the Champs-Élysées to the Arc de Triomphe, Porte Maillot and finally the fountains, elm-shaded squares and plazas of La Défense's Esplanade. The structure, which symbolises a window open to the world, is ever-so-slightly out of alignment with the Grande Axe. Also known as the Tête Défense, it houses government and company offices.

Neither the view from the rooftop nor the temporary exhibitions with human rights themes housed in the under-used top storey justify the ticket price of 40FF (30FF for students, children and seniors). Both are open daily from 10 am to 7 pm, the ticket windows close an hour earlier.

Le Parvis & Esplanade

In a largely successful attempt to humanise the district's somewhat harsh combination of concrete and glass, the Parvis, Place de La Défense and Esplanade du Général de Gaulle, which together form a pedestrian precinct more than one km long, have been turned into a **garden of contemporary art**. The nearly 70 monumental sculptures and murals here – and west of the Grande Arche in the **Quartier du Parc** and **Jardins de l'Arche**, a two-km-long westward extension of the Grande Axe – include colourful and imaginative works by Calder, Miró and Agam.

La Colline de La Défense

This complex, on top of Les Quatre Temps, just south of the Grande Arche, houses the huge **Dôme IMAX** (☎ 01 46 92 45 45), a 460-seat, 180° cinema that gives you the feeling of being inside the films on screen. Tickets cost 55FF (40FF for children under 16, students and seniors). Screenings start every hour from around noon to around 6 pm, later on Saturday.

Of more conventional interest is the superb **Musée de l'Automobile** (☎ 01 46 92 46 00), whose outstanding collection of vintage motorcars includes lots of very early French models. Many of the signs are in English. It's open daily from 12.15 to 7 pm; to 8 pm on Saturday. Entry is 30FF (20FF reduced price).

ACTIVITIES

Paris' weekly entertainment pamphlets, *Pariscope* and *L'Officiel des Spectacles* (see Entertainment Guides under Entertainment), list up-to-date information in French on every imaginable sort of *legal* activity.

Entries entitled Sports-Loisirs, Activités Sportives or Promenades have details on *randonnées pédestres* (hiking in groups), *cyclisme* (cycling, including group rides), *escalade* (rock-climbing excursions), *parachutisme* (parachuting), *piscines* (swimming pools), *patinoires* (ice-skating rinks), *canoë-kayak* (canoeing/kayaking), squash, tennis and golf etc.

Canal Boating

The Paris area's three rivers – the Seine, Marne and Oise – and its canals (Saint Martin, Ourcq) offer a unique vantage point from which to enjoy the delights of the Paris area. A one or two-week rental – less expensive than many hotels if there are four or more of you – can easily be split between quiet canal/river cruises and days spent moored in the city. Within Paris proper, the only places you can stay overnight are Bassin de la Villette (19e; M9) and the Port de Plaisance de Paris-Arsenal (M13; see Houseboats under Places to Stay), but it's possible to stop for an hour or two at a number of quays along the Seine. By the way, heavy traffic and currents make navigating the Seine pretty tricky, but foreigners (unlike French people) are not required to have a special permit.

Europ' Yachting (M13; ☎ 01 43 44 66 77; fax 01 43 44 74 18; metro Bastille) at 11 Blvd de la Bastille (12e), on the ground floor of the Capitainerie of the Port de Plaisance de Paris-Arsenal, rents out boats for four to seven people. From mid-March to mid-October, you can rent by the week (5000 to 10,000FF). On weekends and holidays year round, boats are available for 945 to 1900FF a day, depending on the boat and the period. Reservations should be made three weeks ahead, though boats are sometimes available at the last minute. The office is open Monday to Saturday from 10 am to 1 pm and 2 to 7 pm.

Sports Facilities

For information (in French) on Paris' sporting activities and facilities (including its 36 swimming pools), call Allo Sports on ☎ 01 42 76 54 54 (by Minitel, dial 3615 PARIS). It is staffed on weekdays from 10.30 am to 5 pm (4.30 pm on Friday).

COURSES

Language Courses

All manner of French courses, lasting from two weeks to nine months, are held in Paris and a variety of provincial cities and towns. A number of language schools begin new courses every month or so. Many of the organisations detailed below can also arrange homestays or other accommodation.

The French Cultural Service (see Useful Organisations in the Facts for the Visitor chapter) has reams of information on studying in France, as do French Government tourist offices and French consulates. You might also contact the Ministry of Tourism-sponsored International Cultural Organisation (☎ 01 42 36 47 18; fax 01 40 26 34 45; metro Châtelet) at 55 Rue de Rivoli (1er) in Paris; the mailing address is 55 Rue de Rivoli, BP 2701, 75027 Paris CEDEX.

The many French-language schools in the capital include:

Accord Language School
    52 Rue Montmartre, 75002 Paris (M8; ☎ 01 42 36 24 95; fax 01 42 21 17 91; metro Les Halles). A dynamic language school whose classes get high marks from students. Four-week classes on five levels (beginners to advanced) with a maximum of 14 students (and often less) start at the beginning of each month of the year. They cost 1800FF for the *cours semi-intensif* (10 hours a week for three weeks in summer), held in the afternoon, and 3200FF for the *cours intensif* (25 hours a week for three weeks in summer), held in the morning. The *cours extensif* (three hours a week for three months), which meets at night, costs 2000FF. Another option is the grammar workshop for 950FF. The school's office is open weekdays from 9 am to 8 pm (6 pm on Friday). If there's space, you can sign up until the first day of class.
Alliance Française
    101 Blvd Raspail, 75006 Paris (M11; ☎ 01 45 44 38 28; fax 01 45 44 89 42; metro Saint Placide). The Paris headquarters of a venerable institution whose brief is to promote French language and civilisation around the world. Month-long French courses at all levels – but of variable quality – begin during the first week of each month; registration takes place during the five business days before the start of each session. If there's space, it's possible to enrol for just two weeks. *Intensif* courses, which meet for 3½ hours a day, cost 3200FF a month; *extensif* courses, which involve 1½ or 1¾ hours of class a day, cost 1600FF a month. The enrolment fee is 250FF. The registration office is open Monday to Friday from 9 am to 5 pm.

Bring your passport and a passport-sized photo. Payment, which must be made in advance, can be done with travellers' cheques or credit cards. The mailing address of the Alliance Française is 101 Blvd Raspail, 75270 Paris CEDEX 06.

Cours de Civilisation Française à la Sorbonne
47 Rue des Écoles, 75005 Paris (☎ 01 40 46 22 11; fax 01 40 46 32 29). The Sorbonne's famous French Civilisation Course, from which one of the authors graduated sometime in the late Dark Ages, has courses in French language and civilisation for students of all levels. Very academic and stilted approach to language teaching; don't expect to learn how to haggle in a market or cuss out road hogs even after a year here.

Eurocentre
13 Passage Dauphine, 75006 Paris (☎ 01 43 25 81 40; fax 01 40 46 72 06; metro Odéon). The Paris branch of the Zürich-based, nonprofit Eurocentre chain, which has schools in 10 countries. Two/four-week intensive courses with 12 to 15 participants, well reviewed by Lonely Planet readers, cost 3550/7100FF, including – each week – 25 50-minute lessons, three lectures and five to 10 hours in the multi-media learning centre. New courses begin every two, three or four weeks.

Institut Parisien de Langue et de Civilisation Françaises
87 Blvd de Grenelle, 75015 Paris (M10; ☎ 01 40 56 09 53; fax 01 43 06 46 30; metro Dupleix). Four-week courses with a maximum of 12 students per class cost 3200/5250FF for 15/25 hours a week; six-week courses are 4440/7260FF. The office is open on weekdays from 8.30 am to 5 pm.

Cooking Courses

The major cooking schools include Cordon Bleu (☎ 01 48 56 06 06; fax 01 48 56 03 96; metro Vaugirard) at 8 Rue Léon Delhomme, 75015 Paris, and École de Cuisine La Varenne (☎ 01 47 05 10 16 or 86 63 18 34 in Burgundy; in the USA, ☎ 01 202-337 0073; metro Invalides), based at 34 Rue Saint Dominique, 75007 Paris. Count on paying US$200 to US$500 a day.

The French-American Center (see Language Courses) offers one-week cooking courses.

Places to Stay

ACCOMMODATION SERVICES

Accueil des Jeunes en France (AJF)

No matter what age you are, the AJF can *always* find you accommodation, even in summer. It works like this: you come in on the day (or the day before) you need a place to stay and pay the AJF for the accommodation (plus a 10FF fee). The staff then give you a voucher to take to the hostel or hotel. Prices for doubles start at 230FF and, thanks to special AJF discounts, are often less than the price you'd pay if you contacted the hotel yourself. The earlier in the day you come, the better; the conveniently located and cheap places always go first.

AJF's main office (M12; ☎ 01 42 77 87 80; metro Rambuteau) is at 119 Rue Saint Martin (4e), right across the square from the entrance to the Centre Pompidou. It is open Monday to Saturday from 10 am to 6.45 pm and on Sunday from 12.30 to 2 pm. Be prepared for long queues in summer.

At Gare du Nord, the AJF branch (☎ 01 42 85 86 19; metro Gare du Nord; 10e) operates only in July and August. It's open Monday to Friday from 8 am to 5 pm during those two months. It's on the other side of the SNCF information office from platform 19 – just look for the long queue.

Staying with a French Family

Under an arrangement known as *hôtes payants* (literally, paying guests) or *hébergement chez l'habitant* (lodging with the occupants of private homes), students, young people and tourists can stay with French families. In general you rent a room and enjoy access (sometimes limited) to the family's kitchen and telephone. Many language schools (see Courses in the Facts for the Visitor chapter) arrange homestays for their students.

For details on each agency's prices and conditions, it's a good idea to call, write or fax at least six weeks in advance, though last-minute arrangements are sometimes possible.

Students and tourists alike should count on paying 3000 to 5000FF a month, 1100 to 1500FF a week or, for

short stays, 130 to 300FF a day per person, including
breakfast.

The Paris tourist office (M6) has a number of brochures on homestays, including one on *pensions de
famille*, which are similar to B&Bs.

Accueil France Famille – 5 Rue François Coppée, 75015 Paris
(☎ 01 45 54 22 39; fax 01 45 58 43 25; metro Boucicaut). This
is a nonprofit organisation (membership fee 300FF) that
arranges homestays. In Paris, charges are 1200FF a week
(1400FF for the first week) or 4500FF a month (minimum
two months), including breakfast. The minimum age is
18; there's no maximum age.

Amicale Culturelle Internationale – 27 Rue Godot de Mauroy,
75009 Paris (☎ 01 47 42 94 21; fax 01 49 24 02 67; metro
Havre Caumartin). This agency can arrange stays in
French homes in Paris (1800FF a week including breakfast
and dinner) and elsewhere around France. The minimum
stay is two weeks.

France Lodge – 5 Rue du Faubourg Montmartre, 75009 Paris
(☎ 01 42 46 68 19; fax 01 42 46 65 61; metro Rue Montmartre). This nonprofit organisation arranges accommodation in private homes and apartments. In Paris, prices
start at about 130FF a night per person (cheaper by the
month). Annual membership costs 85FF, and payment
must be made in French francs.

Accueil Familial des Jeunes Étrangers – 23 Rue du Cherche
Midi, 75006 Paris (☎ 01 45 49 15 57; fax 01 45 44 60 48;
metro Sèvres Babylone). This organisation can find you a
room with a family for 3000 to 3500FF a month, including
breakfast. For stays of less than a month, expect to pay
about 140FF a day. There's a 500FF subscription fee
(1000FF for stays of over three months).

Short-Term Flats

Allo Logement Temporaire (M15; ☎ 01 42 72 00 06; fax
01 42 72 03 11; metro Hôtel de Ville) at 64 Rue du Temple
(3e) is a nonprofit organisation that acts as a liaison
between flat owners and foreigners looking for furnished apartments for periods of one week to one year.
Small studios of about 20 sq metres cost 1000 to 2000FF
a week.

October, when university classes resume, is the
hardest month to find a place, but over the summer it's
usually possible to find something within a matter of
days. Before any deals are signed, the company will
arrange for you to talk to the owner by phone, assisted
by an interpreter if necessary. There is a 300FF annual
membership fee and, in addition to the rent (paid
directly to the owner), a charge of 200FF for each month

you rent. The office is open Monday to Friday from noon to 8 pm.

Serviced Flats

Flatotel (M10; ☎ 01 45 75 62 20; fax 01 45 79 73 30; metro Charles Michels) at 14 Rue du Théâtre (15e) has 35-sq-metre studios (750FF a day) and two to five-room apartments at 1200 to 2900FF; all are equipped with kitchen facilities. The minimum stay is one day. The office is open weekdays from 9 am to 6 pm.

Renting a Flat

For general information on renting an apartment in France, see Renting an Apartment under Accommodation in the Facts for the Visitor chapter. The hardest time to find a place in Paris is October, when everyone is back from their summer holidays and students are searching for academic-year digs. Moderately priced places are easiest to come by toward the end of university semesters, ie between Christmas and early February and over the summer, from July to September.

About 2000FF a month will get you a tiny garret room (nine sq metres minimum) with a washbasin but with no telephone, no proper place to cook and no private toilet. There may not even be a communal shower. These rooms, often occupied by students, are frequently converted *chambres de bonne* (maids' quarters) on the 6th or 7th floor of old apartment buildings without lifts but in good neighbourhoods.

Small (15 to 30 sq metre), unfurnished/furnished studios with attached toilet start at about 100/120FF a sq metre per month. The per-metre cost theoretically goes down the larger the place is and the farther away it is from the city centre.

If you've exhausted your word-of-mouth sources (expats, students, natives of your country living temporarily in Paris), it's a good idea to check out the bulletin boards at the American Church (see Cultural Centres under Information). People who advertise there are unlikely to fear renting to foreigners, may speak some English and might be willing to sign a relatively short-term contract. *France USA Contacts (FUSAC)*, a free periodical issued every two weeks and available at English-language bookshops, and the bulletin board at Shakespeare & Co (see Bookshops under Information) might also have a few leads.

If you know a bit of French (or someone who does), you'll be able to consult several periodicals available from newsagents: *De Particulier à Particulier* (14FF) and *La Centrale des Particuliers* (13FF), both issued each Thursday, and the new *A Vendre A Louer* (7FF). You might also try the daily newspaper *Le Figaro*. You'll have to do your calling in French though. If you have access to a telephone, you could place an apartment-wanted ad in *De Particulier à Particulier* and have people call you.

Houseboats

For groups of four or more, it can be cheaper – and a lot more fun – to stay on a rented canal boat than in a mid-range hotel: count on about 1400FF per person a week, including mooring fees. For details on rentals, see Canal Boating under Activities in the Things to See & Do chapter.

If you arrive by pleasure boat (or rent one), you can anchor it quite cheaply at the Port de Plaisance de Paris-Arsenal (M13) (4e & 12e), which stretches for 500 metres from the Seine (metro Quai de la Rapée) to Place de la Bastille (metro Bastille). About 200 moorings for vessels up to 25 metres long are available by the day, month or year. The daily rates for a six to eight-metre boat up to 2.5 metres wide are between 45FF (October to March) and 87FF (June to August); monthly rates are quite a bit cheaper. Larger 10 to 12-metre boats range from 87 to 163FF. Electricity and water link-ups are included in the daily rates. Showers, mail service, fuel and laundry facilities are also available; long-term renters can have telephones installed. About 75% of the people staying here are foreigners.

The *Capitainerie* (harbour master's office; M13; ☎ 01 43 41 39 32; fax 01 44 74 02 66; metro Quai de la Rapée) at 11 Blvd de la Bastille (12e), open daily from 9 am (8 am in July-August) to 6, 7 or 8 pm, has details on fees and regulations. Reservations are not necessary for short-term stays.

PLACES TO STAY – BOTTOM END

Camping

Camping du Bois de Boulogne (☎ 01 45 24 30 00) on Allée du Bord de l'Eau (16e), the only camping ground within the Paris city limits, is along the Seine at the far western edge of the Bois de Boulogne. Two people with a tent are charged about 67FF (94FF with a vehicle), and reception is staffed 24 hours a day. It's very crowded in summer, but there's always space for a small tent (though not necessarily for a car). The Porte Maillot metro stop, 4.5

km to the east, is linked to the camping ground by RATP bus No 244 (runs 6 am to 8.30 pm) and, from around Easter to September, by privately operated shuttle buses (11FF each way, 30FF for a two-day pass).

Paris' main tourist office (M6) has a sheet listing dozens of other camping grounds in the departments surrounding Paris in the Île de France.

Hostels & Foyers

Paris' hostels and *foyers* (student residence halls) don't come cheap. Beds under 100FF are few and far between, so two people who don't mind sleeping in the same bed may find basic rooms in bottom-end hotels a less expensive proposition. Groups of three or four willing to share two or three beds will save even more.

Many hostels allow guests to stay for a maximum of three nights, particularly in summer, though places that have upper age limits (for example 30) tend not to enforce them. Only official auberges de jeunesse (youth hostels) require that guests present HI cards. Curfews at Paris hostels are generally at 1 or 2 am. Few hostels accept telephone reservations from individuals, but those that do are noted in the text.

Louvre Area (1er) You can't get any more central than the area between the Louvre and the Forum des Halles.

Centre International BVJ Paris-Louvre – 20 Rue Jean-Jacques Rousseau (M12; ☎ 01 42 36 88 18; fax 01 42 33 40 53; metro Louvre-Rivoli). This modern, 200-bed BVJ hostel charges 120FF (including breakfast) for a bunk in a single-sex room for two to 10 people. Guests should be aged under 35. Rooms are accessible from 2.30 pm on the day you arrive and all day long after that. Curfew is at 2 am. Kitchen facilities are not available. There is almost always space in the morning, even in summer. If you're on your way over, you can call and request that they hold a spot for a few hours.

Centre International BVJ Paris-Les Halles – 5 Rue du Pélican (M12; ☎ 01 40 26 92 45; metro Louvre-Rivoli). A 55-bed BVJ hostel with the same tariffs and rules as the BVJ Paris-Louvre right around the corner.

Centre International BVJ Paris-Opéra – 11 Rue Thérèse (M8; ☎ 01 42 60 77 23; metro Pyramides). A 68-bed BVJ hostel with the same tariffs and rules as BVJ Paris-Louvre and Paris-Les Halles.

Marais (4e) The Marais is one of the liveliest and most atmospheric sections of the city centre. Its hostels are among the city's finest.

MIJE Fourcy – 6 Rue de Fourcy (M15; ☎ 01 42 74 23 45; fax 01 40 27 81 64; metro Saint Paul). The Maison Internationale de la Jeunesse et des Étudiants runs three *hôtels de jeunes* (young people's hostels) in attractively renovated 17th and 18th-century residences in the Marais; this 207-bed place is the largest of the three. A bed in a shower-equipped, single-sex dorm room for four to eight people costs 120FF (148F in a double, 168FF in a single), including breakfast. Rooms are closed from noon to 4 pm; curfew is from 1 to 7 am.

Individuals can make reservations for all three MIJE hostels by calling the switchboard – they'll hold you a bed until 4 pm, and the maximum stay is seven nights. During summer and other busy periods, there may not be space after about mid-morning.

Costs and phone number details are the same for the other two: *MIJE Fauconnier*, 11 Rue du Fauconnier (M15; metro Saint Paul or Pont Marie), is a 118-bed hostel two blocks south of MIJE Fourcy. *MIJE Maubuisson*, 12 Rue des Barres (M15; metro Hôtel de Ville), is a 114-bed hostel half a block south of the *mairie* (town hall) of the 4e.

Latin Quarter (western 5e) The lively, student-filled Latin Quarter is ideal for young people.

Centre International BVJ Paris-Quartier Latin – 44 Rue des Bernardins (M15; ☎ 01 43 29 34 80; metro Maubert Mutualité). This hostel has the same tariffs and rules as the other BVJ hostels (see Louvre Area, 1er).

Y & H Hostel 80 Rue Mouffetard – (M12; ☎ 01 45 35 09 53; fax 01 47 07 22 24; metro Place Monge). This clean, friendly, English-speaking place – the name is short for 'young & happy' – is in the hopping, happening centre of the Latin Quarter. Popular with a younger crowd, it is closed from 11 am to 5 pm. A bed in a cramped room with washbasin for two to six people costs 97FF, not including breakfast; showers are 10FF. The 2 am curfew is strictly enforced. The TV in the lounge area receives CNN and MTV. Reservations can be made if you make a deposit for the first night. In summer, the best way to get a place is to stop by at about 9 am.

9e Arrondissement Just down the hill from rowdy Pigalle, this is a quiet, residential quarter.

Woodstock Hostel – 48 Rue Rodier (M8; ☎ 01 48 78 87 76; metro Anvers). A dorm bed in a room for three to six people costs 75FF; in a double room a bed is 87FF.

11e & 12e Arrondissements The untouristed 11e and 12e (the area east and south-east of Place de la Bastille) are unpretentious and working class.

Auberge Internationale des Jeunes – 10 Rue Trousseau, 11e (M13; ☎ 01 47 00 62 00; fax 01 47 00 33 16; metro Ledru Rollin). This friendly hostel, 700 metres east of Place de la Bastille, attracts a young, international crowd and is very full in summer. Beds cost just 81FF from November to February, 91FF from March to October, including breakfast. They'll hold a bed for you if you call from the train station.

Résidence Bastille – 151 Ave Ledru Rollin, 11e (M13; ☎ 01 43 79 53 86; metro Voltaire). The AJF's only year-round hostel is about 900 metres north-east of Place de la Bastille. Beds in rooms for two to four people cost 120FF. Reception is open for check-in from 7 am to 12.30 pm and 2 to 10 pm. Curfew is at 1 am – if you'll be coming back later, inform them in advance.

Maison Internationale des Jeunes – 4 Rue Titon, 11e (M13; ☎ 01 43 71 99 21; fax 01 43 71 78 58; metro Faidherbe Chaligny). This MIJPC, 1.3 km east of Place de la Bastille, charges 110FF for a bed in a spartan dorm room for up to eight people, including breakfast. Curfew is at 2 am. The upper age limit of 30 is not strictly enforced. Telephone reservations are accepted – your chance of finding a place is greatest if you call (or stop by) between 8 and 10 am. The maximum stay is theoretically three days, but you can usually stay for a week.

Auberge de Jeunesse Jules Ferry – 8 Blvd Jules Ferry, 11e (M9; ☎ 01 43 57 55 60; metro République or Oberkampf). This official youth hostel, a few blocks east of Place de la République, is a bit institutional, but the atmosphere is fairly relaxed and – an added bonus – they don't accept groups. Beds cost 110FF in a four or six-person room and 118FF in a double, including breakfast. Rooms are locked from 10.30 am to 2 pm. There is a Franprix supermarket down the block at 28 Blvd Jules Ferry.

Centre International de Séjour de Paris Ravel – 4-6 Ave Maurice Ravel, 12e (M1; ☎ 01 44 75 60 00; metro Porte de Vincennes). The 230-bed CISP Ravel, on the south-eastern edge of the city, charges 105FF per bed in a 12-person dormitory, 135FF in a two to five-person room and 181FF in a single, including breakfast. There are no upper age limits. Reception is open from 6.30 am to 1.30 am. Individuals (as opposed to groups, which predominate) can make telephone reservations up to two days ahead. To get there from the Porte de Vincennes metro station, walk south on Blvd Soult, turn left onto Rue Jules Lemaître and then go right onto Rue Maurice Ravel.

13e, 14e & 15e Arrondissements Paris' southern three arrondissements are not particularly exciting places, but neither are they very far from the Left Bank's major sights.

Three Ducks Hostel – 6 Place Étienne Pernet, 15e (M10; ☎ 01 48 42 04 05; metro Félix Faure or Commerce). Named after three ducks who used to live in the courtyard, the friendly, down-to-earth Trois Canards, at the southern end of Rue du Commerce, is a favourite with young backpackers, whose more exuberant exponents may get a bit noisy at night. A bunk bed in a basic room for two to eight people costs 97FF (85FF from November to April). Telephone reservations are accepted on the day of arrival. Kitchen facilities are available.

Aloha Hostel – 1 Rue Borromée, 15e (☎ 01 42 73 03 03; metro Volontaires). Run by the same people (and with the same prices) as the Three Ducks Hostel, this place is about one km west of Gare Montparnasse. Rooms are closed from 11 am to 5 pm. Curfew is at 2 am.

Foyer International d'Accueil de Paris Jean Monnet – 30 Rue Cabanis, 14e (M1; ☎ 01 45 89 89 15; metro Glacière). FIAP Jean Monnet, a few blocks south-east of Place Denfert Rochereau, has modern, carpeted rooms for eight/four/two people – pretty luxurious by hostel standards – for 126/151/171FF per person (including breakfast); singles are 261FF. Rooms specially outfitted for disabled people (*handicapés*) are available. Curfew is at 2.30 am. From March to July, there's usually a maximum stay of a few days. Telephone reservations are accepted up to 15 days ahead, but priority is given to groups.

Centre International de Séjour de Paris Kellermann – 17 Blvd Kellermann, 13e (M1; ☎ 01 44 16 37 38; metro Porte d'Italie). The 350-bed CISP Kellermann has the same prices and rules as CISP Ravel (see 11e & 12e Arrondissements). Facilities for disabled people are available. Except on Friday and Saturday nights, curfew is at 1.30 am. The maximum stay is five or six nights. Kitchen facilities are not available. Telephone reservations can be made up to 48 hours before you arrive.

Maison des Clubs UNESCO – 43 Rue de la Glacière, 13e (M1; ☎ 01 43 36 00 63; metro Glacière). This rather institutional place charges 120FF for a bed in a large, unsurprising room for three or four people; singles/doubles are 160/140FF per person. In the multi-bed rooms, priority is given to 18 to 30-year-olds but older travellers are accepted if there's space. Beds booked by telephone are usually held until 2 pm – if you'll be arriving later, ring them on the day of your arrival.

Foyer des Jeunes Filles – 234 Rue de Tolbiac, 13e (M1; ☎ 01 44 16 22 22; fax 01 45 65 46 20; metro Glacière). Also known as Foyer Tolbiac, this friendly, Protestant-run dormitory accepts women travellers only, with no minimum or maximum stay and no upper age limit from mid-June to mid-September (and, if there's space, during the rest of the year). A single room costs 120FF (including breakfast) plus an annual fee of 30FF. There are kitchens on each floor. Reservations can be made by phone or fax, and reception is open 24 hours a day. There's no curfew. The foyer is about 600 metres south of the nearest metro stop so you might want to take bus No 21 or 62. Orlybus stops nearby.

Student Accommodation

The Union Nationale des Étudiants Locataires (National Union of Student Renters; M1; ☎ 01 45 41 58 18; by Minitel: 3615 UNEL; metro Pernety) at 2 Rue Pernety (14e) will let anyone with a student card who pays the 105FF annual fee (photo required) consult its lists of available apartments and chambres de bonne. The usual rental period is 12 months, though six-month or one-semester leases do exist. The office is open on weekdays from 10 am to noon and 2 to 6 pm (open afternoons only from about January to April); year round, Wednesday hours are 10 am to 8 pm.

The Paris tourist office's sheet entitled *Logements pour Étudiants* lists other organisations that can help find accommodation for students who'll be in Paris for at least a semester.

Hotels

In rooms without a bath or shower in this category you may be charged 10FF to as much as 30FF each time you use the hall shower. Breakfast typically costs 15 to 30FF.

1er Arrondissement
Very few cheapies are left anywhere in the 1er.

Hôtel de Lille – 8 Rue du Pélican (M12; ☎ 01 42 33 33 42; metro Palais Royal). At this 13-room place clean singles/doubles (190/220FF) come with washbasin, bidet and cheap ceiling tiles. Doubles with shower are 270FF. A token for a 15-minute shower costs an appalling 30FF.

Marais (4e)
Despite gentrification, the Marais still has a few cheapies left.

Hôtel Rivoli – 44 Rue de Rivoli (M15; ☎ 01 42 72 08 41; metro Hôtel de Ville). This hotel on the corner of Rue des Mauvais Garçons is one of the best deals in town. Basic and somewhat noisy rooms with washbasin start at 140FF; doubles with bath but no toilet are 160 to 190FF; and a double with bath and toilet is 220FF. The hall shower (20FF) is sometimes lukewarm. The front door is locked from 2 to 6.30 am.

Hôtel de la Pointe Rivoli – 125 Rue Saint Antoine (M15; ☎ 01 42 72 14 23; metro Saint Paul). The 28 rooms of this old place have been spared upgrading thanks to the municipality's strict rules concerning historic buildings. Very basic rooms with washbasin cost 100 to 140FF; large doubles with shower and toilet are 220FF. The hall shower is 15FF. Reception is open daily from 9 am to 6.30 pm, 10 am to 6 pm on Sunday.

Hôtel Le Palais de Fès – 41 Rue du Roi de Sicile (M15; ☎ 01 42 72 03 68; fax 01 42 60 49 33; metro Hôtel de Ville). Fairly large, modern doubles cost 200FF (with washbasin) and 280FF (with shower and toilet). Singles start at 150FF. Hall showers are 15FF. Reception is in the ground-floor Moroccan restaurant.

Hôtel Moderne – 3 Rue Caron (M15; ☎ 01 48 87 97 05; metro Saint Paul). The basic singles/doubles come with washbasin and start at 130/160FF; doubles with shower are 190FF (220FF with toilet). There's a toilet and shower (15FF) on the stairs halfway between each floor. Telephone reservations are accepted up to a week before your scheduled arrival.

Hôtel Pratic – 9 Rue d'Ormesson (M15; ☎ 01 48 87 80 47; fax 01 48 87 40 04; metro Saint Paul). This is a 23-room hotel with nondescript singles/doubles from 150/230FF (250/275FF with shower). Doubles/triples with bath and toilet are 340/420FF.

Hôtel Sully – 48 Rue Saint Antoine (M15; ☎ 01 42 78 49 32; metro Bastille). You'll find one-star doubles for 200FF with washbasin, 250FF with shower and 265FF with shower and toilet at this hotel, only one block south of Place des Vosges. A two-bed triple with shower and toilet costs 300FF. The hall shower is free.

Hôtel de la Herse d'Or – 20 Rue Saint Antoine (M15; ☎ 01 48 87 84 09; metro Bastille). This is a friendly place with unsurprising, serviceable singles/doubles with washbasin from 160/200FF; doubles with toilet and a small shower are 260 to 280FF. Hall showers are 10FF.

Île de la Cité & Île Saint Louis (4e & 1er)

Île de la Cité and Île Saint Louis are an easy walk from all of central Paris. Believe it or not, Île de la Cité's *only* hotel is a cheapie.

Hôtel Henri IV – 25 Place Dauphine, 1er (M14; ☎ 01 43 54 44 53; metro Cité, Saint Michel). This old-fashioned, very popular hotel is a bit tattered and worn but has 22 adequate rooms with one bed from 110 to 250FF, two beds from 195 to 270FF. Showers (15FF) and toilets are in the hall. Reception is open until 8 pm but make reservations a month in advance. Credit cards are not accepted and we've had reports of indifferent service.

Latin Quarter (western 5e) Real cheapies are nearly extinct in the Latin Quarter.

Port Royal Hôtel – 8 Blvd de Port Royal (M1; ☎ 01 43 31 70 06; metro Les Gobelins). The clean, quiet and well-kept singles/doubles at this older, one-star place start at 146/183FF (270FF with shower and toilet). Hall showers are 15FF.

Hôtel de Médicis – 214 Rue Saint Jacques (M14; ☎ 01 43 54 14 66 for reception, 43 29 53 64 for the public phone in the hall; metro Luxembourg). This is exactly what a cockroach-infested, dilapidated Latin Quarter dive for impoverished students should be like. Very basic singles start at 75FF, but they're usually occupied; doubles/triples are 140/225FF. Reservations are not accepted.

Hôtel du Centre – 5 Rue Saint Jacques (M14; ☎ 01 43 26 13 07; metro Saint Michel). This is a run-down establishment with only basic singles/doubles which start at 100/150FF; doubles with shower are 180FF, triples 300FF. Hall showers are 20FF. Reservations are not accepted.

Gare Saint Lazare & Grands Boulevards (9e) The better deals are away from Gare Saint Lazare but there are several places along Rue d'Amsterdam beside the station.

Hôtel du Calvados – 20 Rue d'Amsterdam (M7; ☎ 01 48 74 39 31; fax 01 48 74 33 75; metro Saint Lazare). Singles start at 160FF while doubles are 180 to 220FF or 260 to 300FF with toilet and shower.

Gare du Nord Area (10e) This area of Paris has some pretty good bottom-end deals.

Hôtel de Milan – 17 Rue de Saint Quentin (M8; ☎ 01 40 37 88 50; fax 01 43 57 75 65; metro Gare du Nord). This friendly, old-fashioned one-star establishment is equipped with an ancient (and temperamental) lift. Clean, quiet singles and doubles are available at all sorts of prices from 143 to 216FF (the more expensive rooms have toilets). Doubles with toilet and shower are 256 to 326FF, while triples and quads cost from 309 to 489FF. Breakfast is included, and hall showers cost 18FF.

Hôtel Bonne Nouvelle – 125 Blvd de Magenta (M8; ☎ 01 48 74 99 90; metro Gare du Nord). The 'Good News' is a modest hotel with simple, clean, shower-equipped doubles for 160 to 220FF. A bed for a third person costs 66FF. Hall toilets are on the landing.

Grand Hôtel Magenta – 129 Blvd de Magenta (M8; ☎ 01 48 78 03 65; metro Gare du Nord). Clean, spacious rooms are available with washbasin and bidet, with shower, or with shower and toilet from 200 to 350FF. Larger rooms for three to five people are 300 to 450FF. Hall showers are 20FF.

Hôtel Vieille France – 151 Rue La Fayette (M8; ☎ 01 45 26 42 37; fax 01 45 26 99 07; metro Gare du Nord). A 50-room place with spacious, pleasant and soundproofed doubles for 200FF (with washbasin and bidet) and 250 to 320FF (with bath or shower and toilet). Hall showers are 15FF.

Gare de l'Est Area (10e)

This lively, working-class area of Paris has its own attractions even if your train doesn't pull into the Gare de l'Est. The 10e has some of Paris' grungiest flophouses, but the few diamonds in the rough offer some real bargains.

Sibour Hôtel – 4 Rue Sibour (M8; ☎ 01 46 07 20 74; fax 01 46 07 37 17; metro Gare de l'Est). This friendly, one-star place has 45 recently renovated rooms, including old-fashioned singles/doubles from 165/190FF (280FF with shower, toilet and TV). Hall showers cost 15FF.

Hôtel d'Alsace – 85 Blvd de Strasbourg (M8; ☎ 01 40 37 75 41; metro Gare de l'Est). An old but well-maintained hostelry with bright, clean singles/doubles/quads with washbasin for 134/187/247F. Doubles with shower are 227FF. The fireplaces give the rooms a bit of old-time charm. Hall showers cost 10FF. The entrance is on the left-hand side of the driveway.

Hôtel Liberty – 16 Rue de Nancy, 1st floor (M8; ☎ 01 42 08 60 58; fax 01 42 40 12 59; metro Château d'Eau). Clean, plain singles/doubles start at 130/160FF (160/185FF with shower, 190/220FF with shower and toilet). A bed for a third person costs 40FF. Hall showers are 10FF.

Hôtel Pacific – 70 Rue du Château d'Eau (M8; ☎ 01 47 70 07 91; metro Château d'Eau). An older one-star place, the Pacific has spacious, unpretentious and clean doubles/triples for 130/220FF (250FF with shower). Hall showers are 15FF.

Hôtel Château d'Eau – 61 Rue du Château d'Eau (M8; ☎ 01 48 24 67 09; metro Château d'Eau). If you like your linoleum with cigarette burns, this run-down, partly residential hotel is for you. Large, basic singles/doubles cost 120/150FF (220FF with shower). Hall showers are 15FF.

11e Arrondissement

The area just east of Place de la Bastille (ie around Rue de Lappe) has become one of Paris' trendiest nightlife areas since the construction of the new opera house. Farther east is an ungentrified, typically Parisian working-class neighbourhood whose hotels cater mainly to French businesspeople of modest means. The 11e has Paris' best selection of respectable, old-time cheapies. The best deals are away from Place de la Bastille.

Hôtel Baudin – 113 Ave Ledru Rollin (M13; ☎ 01 47 00 18 91; fax 01 48 07 04 66; metro Ledru Rollin). This once grand, old-fashioned, one-star hostelry has mercifully unmodernised singles/doubles from 120/180FF (250/300FF with bath and toilet); triples are 100FF more. Hall showers are free.

Hôtel de France – 159 Ave Ledru Rollin (M13; ☎ 01 43 79 53 22; metro Voltaire). At this one-star establishment, decent, well-maintained singles/doubles/triples with shower go for 150/200/280FF. All the toilets are off the hall.

Hôtel de Savoie – 27 Rue Richard Lenoir (M13; ☎ 01 43 72 96 47; metro Voltaire). Nondescript but serviceable singles/doubles at this hotel start at 100/150FF; showers are free. Rooms with shower are 150/220FF.

Hôtel Familial – 33 Rue Richard Lenoir (M13; ☎ 01 43 67 48 24; metro Voltaire). This family-run, old-time cheapie with basic, slightly run-down singles/doubles with washbasin start from 100/120FF. Hall showers are 15FF.

Hôtel Camélia – 6 Ave Philippe Auguste (M1; ☎ 01 43 73 67 50; metro Nation). This family-run, one-star establishment has pleasant, well-kept rooms from 150FF, 210FF with shower and 220 to 250FF with shower and toilet. Hall showers cost 20FF. The hotel is closed late July to late August.

Hôtel Central – 16 Ave Philippe Auguste (M1; ☎ 01 43 73 73 53; metro Nation). The proprietor of this hotel is somewhat choosey when it comes to clients, but the place is quiet and clean. Doubles/quads with washbasin and bidet are 155/260FF. Hall showers cost 20FF (less if you stay for a few days).

Hôtel Saint Amand – 6 Rue Trousseau (M13; ☎ 01 47 00 90 55; metro Ledru Rollin). The linoleum-floored, washbasin-equipped singles/doubles spread over six lift-less floors are nothing fancy, but the prices begin at only 101/122FF. Hall showers are 20FF.

Hôtel Bastille Opéra – 6 Rue de la Roquette (M13; ☎ 01 43 55 16 06; metro Bastille). This ageing, 20-room place, just off Place de la Bastille, has basic singles/doubles starting at 130/170FF. Showers are free. Reception, open 24 hours, is on the 1st floor – push the intercom button to get in. Telephone reservations are not accepted, but if you call from the train station they'll hold a room for an hour or two. There are other hotels along Rue de la Roquette.

Vix Hôtel – 19 Rue de Charonne (M13; ☎ 01 48 05 12 58; metro Bastille or Ledru Rollin). This place is a bit dreary and not exactly spotless, but it has plenty of basic singles/doubles from 100/120FF; hall showers are 15FF. Doubles with shower cost 140 to 150FF. Telephone reservations are not usually accepted.

13e Arrondissement

Paris' Chinatown is south of Place d'Italie along Ave d'Ivry and Ave de Choisy. The 13e may not be electrifying, but it has some good deals.

Hôtel Tolbiac – 122 Rue de Tolbiac (M1; ☎ 01 44 24 25 54; fax 01 45 85 43 47; metro Tolbiac). Well-lit, quiet and spotlessly clean singles/doubles go for 125/150FF with washbasin, 145/175FF with shower or 190FF with shower and toilet. Hall showers are free. Reception closes at 9 pm.

Arian Hôtel – 102 Ave de Choisy (M1; ☎ 01 45 70 76 00; fax 01 45 70 85 53; metro Tolbiac). This motel-ish, one-star place has small doubles from 160FF; doubles and triples with shower and toilet are 230 to 280FF.

Hôtel des Beaux-Arts – 2 Rue Toussaint Féron (M1; ☎ 01 44 24 22 60; metro Tolbiac). Singles/doubles start at 160/180FF and go up to 220 to 270FF with shower or bath and toilet.

Gare Montparnasse & 14e Arrondissement
The untouristed and less-than-thrilling 14e nonetheless has a number of good deals. The 14e's bottom-end places don't see many foreign tourists.

Celtic Hôtel – 15 Rue d'Odessa (M11; ☎ 01 43 20 93 53, 01 43 20 83 91; metro Edgar Quinet). The Celtic is an old-fashioned, one-star place that has suffered only partial modernisation. It has bare singles/doubles at 190/220FF, doubles/twins/triples with shower at 260/300/340FF and with shower and toilet at 280/320/360FF.

Hôtel de l'Espérance – 45 Rue de la Gaîté (M11; ☎ 01 43 21 63 84; metro Gaîté). A 14-room place whose doubles (165FF with washbasin, 185FF with shower) are a bit frayed and dreary. A bed for a third person is 50FF. Hall showers cost 15FF.

Hôtel Aviatic – 10 Rue de Brézin (M1; ☎ 01 45 40 59 75; fax 01 45 40 67 48; metro Mouton Duvernet). The clean, basic singles/doubles, which at this family-run hotel-bar come equipped with steel-frame beds and linoleum floors, start at 100/130FF (200FF with shower and toilet). Hall showers are 10FF.

Hôtel L'Espérance – 1 Rue de Grancey (M1; ☎ 01 43 21 41 04; fax 01 43 22 06 02; metro Denfert Rochereau). This 17-room place has doubles from 190FF (260 to 325FF with shower but no toilet).

Montmartre (18e)
Montmartre is one of the most charming, leafy neighbourhoods in Paris. The flat area around the base of the hill has some surprisingly good deals. The lively, ethnically mixed area east of Sacré Cœur can be a bit rough – some people say its prudent to avoid the Château Rouge metro stop at night.

Hôtel Saint Pierre – 3 Rue Seveste (M8; ☎ 01 46 06 20 73; metro Anvers). This friendly, family-run establishment in a renovated older building with 36 simple but serviceable singles/doubles costs from 120/140FF (170/180FF with shower and toilet).

Hôtel Audran – 7 Rue Audran (M8; ☎ 01 42 58 79 59; metro Abbesses). Basic singles/doubles start at 100/140FF; rooms with shower and toilet are also available. Each floor has a toilet; the 1st and 3rd floors have showers (10FF).

Idéal Hôtel – 3 Rue des Trois Frères (M8; ☎ 01 46 06 63 63; fax 01 42 64 97 01; metro Abbesses). This is an older place whose simple but adequate singles/doubles start at 125/170FF. A shower usually costs 20FF. Rooms with shower, but still no toilet, are 250FF. If you ring from the station, they'll hold a room for a few hours.

Hôtel du Cheval Blanc – 20 Rue d'Orsel (M8; ☎ 01 46 06 38 77; metro Anvers). This 38-room place has singles/doubles/triples from 120/150/200FF (170/200/240FF with shower). Hall showers cost 20FF.

Hôtel de Rohan – 90 Rue Myrha (M8; ☎ 01 42 52 32 57; metro Château Rouge). Basic, tidy singles/doubles at this one-star establishment go for 110/140FF (170 to 200FF with shower). Showers cost 20FF.

Hôtel de Carthage – 10 Rue Poulet (M8; ☎ 01 46 06 27 03; fax 01 46 06 28 38; metro Château Rouge). This 40-room cheapie with basic but serviceable singles costs 90 to 110FF; doubles are 140 to 160FF. Hall showers cost 15FF. Curfew is at 1 am.

PLACES TO STAY – MIDDLE

Even in this category not all places will come with a bath or shower.

1er Arrondissement

You won't find many bargains in the 1er.

Hôtel Saint Honoré – 85 Rue Saint Honoré (M12; ☎ 01 42 36 20 38; fax 01 42 21 44 08; metro Châtelet). This recently renovated but cramped one-star place offers doubles/quads from 280/450FF; more spacious doubles are 320 to 350FF.

Marais (4e)

The Marais' middle-range places generally offer good value.

Hôtel de Nice – 42bis Rue de Rivoli (M15; ☎ 01 42 78 55 29; fax 01 42 78 36 07; metro Hôtel de Ville). The English-speaking owner of this especially warm, family-run place has 23 comfortable doubles/triples/quads for 400/500/600FF. Many rooms have balconies on which guests have been known to sunbathe.

Hôtel Le Compostelle – 31 Rue du Roi de Sicile (M15; ☎ 01 42 78 59 99; fax 01 40 29 05 18; metro Hôtel de Ville). This three-star place whose 27 singles/doubles come with TV (from 300/400FF) is tasteful but not fancy.

Hôtel de la Place des Vosges – 12 Rue de Birague (M15; ☎ 01 42 72 60 46; fax 01 42 72 02 64; metro Bastille). Superbly situated right next to Place des Vosges, this 16-room, two-star place has rather average rooms with shower for 315FF, nicer rooms with bathrooms at 450 or 460FF. There's a tiny lift from the 1st floor.

Hôtel Castex – 5 Rue Castex (M15; ☎ 01 42 72 31 52; fax 01 42 72 57 91; metro Bastille). This cheery, 24-room establishment has been run by the same family since 1919. Quiet, old-fashioned (but immaculate) singles/doubles with shower cost 220/300FF (240 to 320FF with toilet, too). If possible, reserve at least four weeks ahead.

Latin Quarter (western 5e)

The Latin Quarter has dozens of two and three-star hotels, including a cluster near the Sorbonne on Rue Victor Cousin and nearby Rue Cujas and another grouping along lively Rue des Écoles. The following list includes several almost-cheapies.

Grand Hôtel du Progrès – 50 Rue Gay Lussac (M14; ☎ 01 43 54 53 18; metro Luxembourg). Washbasin-equipped singles at this older, 36-room hotel start at 150FF; large, old-fashioned doubles with a view and morning sunlight are 240FF (330FF with shower and toilet), including breakfast. Hall showers are free. From May to mid-October, the minimum stay is three days. Credit cards are not accepted. The hotel is closed in August.

Hôtel Gay Lussac – 29 Rue Gay Lussac (M14; ☎ 01 43 54 23 96; metro Luxembourg). This family-run, one-star place with a bit of character and a lift has small rooms starting from around 200FF, rooms with toilet for 240 to 260FF and rooms with shower or bath and toilet for 310 to 340FF. Fairly large doubles/three-bed quads with shower, toilet and high ceilings are 360/500FF.

Familia Hôtel – 11 Rue des Écoles (M12; ☎ 01 43 54 55 27; fax 01 43 29 61 77; metro Cardinal Lemoine). This is a welcoming, well-situated, two-star establishment with 30 upbeat, functional rooms. Doubles go for 370 to 480FF and triples are 585FF.

Hôtel Saint Jacques – 35 Rue des Écoles (M14; ☎ 01 43 26 82 53; fax 01 43 25 65 50; metro Maubert Mutualité). This two-star hotel hasn't lost its old-time charm. Spacious doubles/triples, many with ornamented ceilings and balconies, start at 405/535FF.

Hôtel Marignan – 13 Rue du Sommerard (M14; ☎ 01 43 25 31 03; metro Maubert Mutualité). This friendly, one-star place has pleasant, old-fashioned singles/doubles triples/quads with washbasin for 190/290/390/480FF, including breakfast. About half of the 30 rooms have toilets. A washing machine (10FF) and a drier (free) are available.

Grand Hôtel Saint Michel – 19 Rue Cujas (M14; ☎ 01 46 33 33 02; fax 01 40 46 96 33; metro Luxembourg). This two-star hotel's simple but serviceable singles/doubles (some with balconies) cost from 305/355; triples are from 500FF. Reserve as far in advance as possible, especially from Easter to September.

Hôtel Cluny Sorbonne – 8 Rue Victor Cousin (M14; ☎ 01 43 54 66 66; fax 01 43 29 68 07; metro Luxembourg). The lift in this two-star hotel, which has pleasant, well-kept doubles from 370FF, is the size of a telephone booth. If you'll be checking in before 1 pm, you can usually reserve a room by telephone without sending a deposit.

6e Arrondissement

The places listed below are the least expensive hotels the 6e has to offer.

Hôtel de Nesle – 7 Rue de Nesle (M14; ☎ 01 43 54 62 41; metro Odéon, Mabillon). The Nesle is a spirited, often *too* jolly hostelry that's been a favourite with young travellers since it was established in 1971. It remains a good place to meet other travellers. A bed in a double is 135FF, including breakfast; if you come alone they'll find you a roommate. Singles start at 195FF; doubles with toilet and shower are 350 to 400FF. Reservations are not accepted – the only way to get a place is to stop by in the morning.

Hôtel Saint Michel – 17 Rue Gît le Cœur (M14; ☎ 01 43 26 98 70; metro Saint Michel). Comfortable but pretty standard, soundproofed rooms start from 190FF with nothing, from 285FF for rooms with shower but no toilet, and from 325 to 370FF for rooms with shower and toilet. The hall shower costs 12FF.

Delhy's Hôtel – 22 Rue de l'Hirondelle (M14; ☎ 01 43 26 58 25; fax 01 43 26 51 06; metro Saint Michel), through the arch from 6 Place Saint Michel. This 21-room, one-star hotel has neat, simple washbasin-equipped singles/doubles for as low as 150/250FF; with toilet they're 250/290FF, while a double with toilet and shower is 370FF. Hall showers cost 25FF. Breakfast (35FF) is usually obligatory during summer and holiday periods.

Hôtel Petit Trianon – 2 Rue de l'Ancienne Comédie (M14; ☎ 01 43 54 94 64; metro Odéon). Plain singles/doubles with washbasin and bidet are 170/260FF; doubles with shower begin at 320FF. Doubles/triples with shower and toilet are 370/450FF.

Hôtel Saint André des Arts – 66 Rue Saint André des Arts (M14; ☎ 01 43 26 96 16; fax 01 43 29 73 34; metro Odéon). Rooms at this 34-room hotel, situated on a lively, restaurant-lined thoroughfare, start at 295/420/520/540FF for one/two/three/four people, including breakfast. The three singles with washbasin cost 230FF.

Hôtel des Académies – 15 Rue de la Grande Chaumière (M11;
☎ 01 43 26 66 44; metro Vavin). This truly charming hotel
has been run by the same friendly family since 1920 and
has singles with washbasin for 190FF; shower-equipped
doubles are 255FF or 295 to 310FF with shower and toilet.

Gare Saint Lazare & Grands Boulevards (9e)

There are quite a few two and three-star hotels along Rue
d'Amsterdam, which runs along the eastern side of Gare
Saint Lazare.

Hôtel Britannia – 24 Rue d'Amsterdam (M7; ☎ 01 42 85 36 36;
fax 01 42 85 16 93; metro Saint Lazare). The Hôtel Britannia
is a two-star place with narrow hallways and pleasant,
clean doubles/triples (425/525FF) that are a bit on the
small side.
Hôtel Chopin – 46 Passage Jouffroy (M8; ☎ 01 47 70 58 10; fax
01 42 47 00 70; metro Rue Montmartre). This 36-room,
two-star hotel near 10-12 Blvd Montmartre is down one
of Paris' most delightful 19th-century shopping arcades.
Singles/doubles/triples cost from 405/450/565FF. After
the arcade closes at 10 pm, ring the illuminated *sonnette
de nuit* (night doorbell).

Gare du Nord Area (10e)

There are lots of two-star hotels around Gare du Nord.

Nord Hôtel – 37 Rue de Saint Quentin (M8; ☎ 01 45 26 43 40;
fax 01 42 82 90 23). This hotel, right across from Gare du
Nord, has clean, quiet singles for 275 to 330FF or doubles
for 330 to 360FF. An extra person costs 95FF.

Gare de l'Est Area (10e)

There are quite a few two and three-star places near the
Gare de l'Est.

Hôtel Français – 13 Rue du 8 Mai 1945 (M8; ☎ 01 40 35 94 14;
fax 01 40 35 55 40; metro Gare de l'Est). A 71-room place
with attractive, almost luxurious, singles/doubles/
triples – some with balconies – for 370/410/470FF. Children with parents are free.
Grand Hôtel de Paris – 72 Blvd de Strasbourg (M8; ☎ 01 46 07
40 56; fax 01 42 05 99 18; metro Gare de l'Est). This well-run
(though extravagantly named) establishment has 49
pleasant, soundproofed singles/doubles/triples/quads
(300/350/400/450FF) and a tiny lift. If you stay at least
four days in the off-season, they may throw in breakfast
(30FF) for free.

11e Arrondissement

Two-star comfort is less expensive in the 11e than in the inner arrondissements.

Hôtel et Résidence Trousseau – 13 Rue Trousseau (M13; ☎ 01 48 05 55 55; fax 01 48 05 83 97; metro Ledru Rollin). This hotel is perfect for families or groups of friends. The three-star-quality, kitchenette-equipped rooms or apartments for two/three/four/six people are large and modern and cost 500/770/1000/1350FF (including weekly maid service) if you stay at least three nights. Parking costs 80FF a day.

Hôtel Bastille – 24 Rue de la Roquette (M13; ☎ 01 47 00 06 71; fax 01 43 38 54 27; metro Bastille). The youthful staff at this friendly, two-star establishment offer neat, modern singles/doubles/triples for 320/380/430FF, including breakfast. From June to September and around Christmas, a bed in a single-sex shared triple with shower and toilet costs 115FF, including breakfast.

Hôtel Pax – 12 Rue de Charonne (M13; ☎ 01 47 00 40 98; fax 01 43 38 57 81; metro Bastille or Ledru Rollin). Large, spotless rooms start at 200 to 250FF with toilets and showers. Triples and quads without toilet are 230 to 380FF.

Hôtel Lyon Mulhouse – 8 Blvd Beaumarchais (M13; ☎ 01 47 00 91 50; fax 01 47 00 06 31; metro Bastille). This two-star, 41-room hotel offers quiet, predictable singles at 300 to 350FF, and doubles with shower and toilet at 450FF; there are also triples and quads available.

Gare Montparnasse & 14e Arrondissement

Just east of Gare Montparnasse, there are a number of two and three-star places on Rue Vandamme and Rue de la Gaîté; the latter street is dotted with sex shops.

Petit Palace Hôtel – 131 Ave du Maine (M1; ☎ 01 43 22 05 25; fax 01 43 21 79 01; metro Gaîté). The same family has run this friendly, ambitiously named place since 1952. It has small-ish but spotless doubles/triples for 230/300FF with washbasin and bidet and 290/360FF with shower and toilet. Hall showers are 20FF.

Hôtel de Blois – 5 Rue des Plantes (M1; ☎ 01 45 40 99 48; fax 01 45 40 45 62; metro Mouton Duvernet). This one-star establishment offers smallish singles/doubles with washbasin and bidet for 220/260FF; doubles/triples with shower and toilet are 270/360FF.

Hôtel Floridor – 28 Place Denfert Rochereau (M1; ☎ 01 43 21 35 53; fax 01 43 27 65 81; metro Denfert Rochereau). Shower-equipped singles/doubles go for 259/287FF (277/305FF with toilet as well), including breakfast served in your room.

15e Arrondissement

Although the 15e is not particularly exciting it's conveniently close to the Eiffel Tower and the other attractions of the Left Bank. There are a number of mid-range hotels along Blvd de Grenelle, particularly around metro La Motte Picquet Grenelle.

Hôtel Saphir Grenelle – 10 Rue du Commerce (M10; ☎ 01 45 75 12 23; fax 01 45 75 62 49; metro La Motte Picquet Grenelle). Conveniently close to restaurants and metro lines, this small hotel has modern singles/doubles at 390/460FF.

Montmartre (18e)

The attractive two-star places on Rue Aristide Bruant are generally less full in July and August than in spring and autumn.

Hôtel des Arts – 5 Rue Tholozé (M8; ☎ 01 46 06 30 52; fax 01 46 06 10 83; metro Abbesses). This is a friendly, attractive place with singles/doubles from 345/440FF (490FF with two twin beds).

Tim Hôtel – 11 Rue Ravignan, Place Émile Goudeau (M8; ☎ 01 42 55 74 79; fax 01 42 55 71 01; metro Abbesses). This is a good choice if you place more value on location than room size. The 60 neat, modern singles/doubles cost 450/550FF; a third bed for a child under 12 is 140FF. Some of the rooms on the 4th and 5th floors have stunning views of the city. Buffet breakfast is 49FF.

Hôtel Utrillo – 7 Rue Aristide Bruant (M8; ☎ 01 42 58 13 44; fax 01 42 23 93 88; metro Abbesses). The 30 singles/doubles/triples start at 305/380/525FF and buffet breakfast is 40FF.

Hôtel Capucines Montmartre – 5 Rue Aristide Bruant (M8; ☎ 01 42 52 89 80; fax 01 42 52 29 57; metro Abbesses). Singles/doubles with TV and minibar cost 250/300 to 325/350FF. A bed for a third person is 80FF.

Hôtel du Moulin – 3 Rue Aristide Bruant (M8; ☎ 01 42 64 33 33; fax 01 46 06 42 66; metro Abbesses) is the third of this useful cluster and has rooms with toilet and bath or shower at 290/350FF.

Hôtel Luxia – 8 Rue Seveste (M8; ☎ 01 46 06 84 24; fax 01 46 06 10 14; metro Anvers). This 45-room hotel takes mainly groups, but at least a few rooms are almost always left for independent travellers. Plain, clean singles/doubles/triples with shower, toilet and TV are 280/300/390FF.

Airports

Both airports have a wide selection of places including mid-range Ibis hotels.

Hôtel Ibis – next to the Aéroport Charles de Gaulle 1 train station (☎ 01 49 19 19 19; fax 01 49 19 19 21). This large, modern chain hotel with two stars and 556 rooms has doubles and triples for 395FF. The hotel is linked to all three terminals by the SK mini-metro or shuttle bus.

Hôtel Ibis – Orly Airport (☎ 01 46 87 33 50; fax 01 46 87 29 92). This 300-room chain hotel is linked to both terminals by the Navette ADP (airport shuttle bus). Doubles cost 385FF.

PLACES TO STAY – TOP END

1er Arrondissement

Three-star places this central don't come cheap. The 1er and the eastern end of the 8e are home to some of the most luxurious hotels in the world.

Grand Hôtel de Champagne – 17 Rue Jean Lantier (M12; ☎ 01 42 36 60 00; fax 01 45 08 43 33; metro Châtelet). This very comfortable, three-star hotel has rooms from 596 to 721FF (in July and August) up to 652 to 812FF (in June and from September to November).

Hôtel Brighton – 218 Rue de Rivoli (M7; ☎ 01 42 60 30 03; fax 01 42 60 41 78; metro Tuileries). This is a three-star, 70-room establishment with lovely singles/doubles/triples starting at 530/560/990FF, less in the off season. The rooms that overlook the Jardin des Tuileries are the most popular; those on the 4th and 5th floors afford views over the trees.

Hôtel de Crillon – 10 Place de la Concorde, 8e (M7; ☎ 01 44 71 15 00; fax 01 44 71 15 02; metro Concorde). The colonnaded, two-centuries-old Crillon, whose sparkling public areas are sumptuously decorated with chandeliers, original sculptures, gilt mouldings, tapestries and inlaid furniture, is the epitome of French luxury. Spacious singles/doubles with pink marble bathrooms start at 2550/3200FF or from 2900/3500 in May-June and September-October. The cheapest suites are 4900FF and breakfast is another 155FF (continental) or 230FF (American).

Hôtel Ritz – 15 Place Vendôme (M7; ☎ 01 43 16 30 30; fax 01 43 16 36 68; metro Opéra). As one of the world's most celebrated and expensive hotels, the 140-room, 47-suite Ritz has sparkling singles/doubles starting at 2750/3350FF (10% more in May-June and September-October). Junior suites begin at 4950FF; regular suites are 5500FF and up. Breakfast is 180FF (continental) or 230FF (for the heartier 'American' version). Facilities include a deluxe health club, a swimming pool and squash courts. The hotel restaurant, L'Espadon, has two Michelin stars.

Hôtel Meurice – 228 Rue de Rivoli (M7; ☎ 01 44 58 10 10; fax 01 44 58 10 15; metro Tuileries). The Meurice's stunning public spaces, modelled on Versailles, positively ooze elegance: designed at the turn of the century, they are

decorated with gilded furniture, chandeliers and trompe
l'œil paintings. Singles/doubles start at 2300/2600FF;
suites go for 5500 to 8500FF. Continental/American
breakfasts are 150/195FF.

Marais (4e)

There are a number of top-end hotels in the vicinity of
elegant Place des Vosges.

Grand Hôtel Malher – 5 Rue Malher (M15; ☎ 01 42 72 60 92; fax
01 42 72 25 37; metro Saint Paul). The 31 nicely appointed
singles/doubles at this family-run, three-star establishment start from 470/570FF (570/670FF during high-
season periods).

Gay Hotel Paris has only one all-gay hotel, and not
surprisingly it's in the heart of the Marais.

Hôtel Central Marais – 2 Rue Sainte Croix de la Bretonnerie
(M15; ☎ 01 48 87 56 08; fax 01 42 77 06 27; metro Hôtel de
Ville). This seven-room, mostly gay male hotel also
welcomes lesbians. Singles/doubles with one bathroom
for every two rooms are 400/485FF. After 3 pm, reception
is around the corner in the bar (33 Rue Vieille du Temple).
Reservations should be made four to six weeks ahead –
they'll hold a room if you give them a Visa or MasterCard
number.

Île de la Cité & Île Saint Louis (4e & 1er)

Île Saint Louis is one of the most expensive
neighbourhoods in Paris in which to live – and rent a
hotel room.

Hôtel Saint Louis – 75 Rue Saint Louis en l'Île, 4e (M15; ☎ 01
46 34 04 80; fax 01 46 34 02 13; metro Pont Marie). The 21
doubles (595/795FF with one/two beds) at this three-star
establishment are appealing but unspectacular. The basement breakfast room dates from the early 1600s; breakfast
costs 45FF.

Latin Quarter (western 5e)

The Latin Quarter generally offers better value than the
nearby 6e.

Hôtel de L'Espérance – 15 Rue Pascal (M1; ☎ 01 47 07 10 99; fax
01 43 37 56 19; metro Censier Daubenton). Just a couple of
minutes walk south of colourful Rue Mouffetard, this
quiet and pleasantly elegant 38-room hotel has doubles

with shower and toilet for 350FF, with bath for 380FF or larger rooms with two beds at 420FF. Breakfast is 35FF.

Hôtel Saint-Christophe – 17 Rue Lacépède (M12; ☎ 01 43 31 81 54; fax 01 43 31 12 54; metro Place Monge). A classy small hotel with 31 well-equipped rooms at 650FF, although discounts are often available.

6e Arrondissement

Three-star hotels in Saint Germain des Prés are pricey places to stay.

Hôtel Michelet Odéon – 6 Place de l'Odéon (M14; ☎ 01 46 34 27 80; fax 01 46 34 55 35; metro Odéon). Only a one-minute walk from the Jardin du Luxembourg, the Hôtel Michelet Odéon has tasteful, generously proportioned singles for 400FF, doubles for 480 to 520FF, triples for 645 to 695FF and quads for 700 to 800FF. Rooms with bath rather than shower are slightly more expensive.

Hôtel des Deux Continents – 25 Rue Jacob (M14; ☎ 01 43 26 72 46; fax 01 43 25 67 80; metro Saint Germain des Prés). This 40-room establishment has spacious, flowery doubles from 695 to 815FF and triples for 1020FF; breakfast is 45FF.

Hôtel des Marronniers – 21 Rue Jacob (M14; ☎ 01 43 25 30 60; fax 01 40 46 83 56; metro Saint Germain des Prés). This 37-room place has less-than-huge singles/doubles/ triples from 520/715/1040FF and a charming garden out the back.

Citadines Aparthôtel – 121 Blvd du Montparnasse (M11; ☎ 01 43 35 46 35; fax 01 40 47 43 01; metro Vavin). At the southern boundary of the 6e, quite near Gare Montparnasse, the apartment-style rooms feature kitchen areas. Prices vary during the year from 600 to 670FF for a small 'studette', 710 to 780FF for a two-person studio or 1250 to 1300FF for a two-bedroom apartment.

Gare Saint Lazare (8e)

As well as several mid-range hotels in this vicinity, you'll also find the top-end Atlantic Hôtel.

Atlantic Hôtel – 44 Rue de Londres (M7; ☎ 01 43 87 45 40; fax 01 42 93 06 26; metro Saint Lazare). On the northern side of the station, this stylishly renovated three-star hotel has 93 rooms at 510 to 780FF with shower or 540 to 890FF with bath.

Gare Montparnasse & 14e Arrondissement

If you need to be near Gare Montparnasse, you can't beat the Miramar for convenience.

Hôtel Miramar – 6 Place Bienvenüe (M11; ☎ 01 45 48 62 94; fax 01 45 48 68 73; metro Montparnasse Bienvenüe). Soundproofed, smallish and typically three-star singles/doubles/triples cost 450/500/800FF.

Montmartre (18e)

There are several larger hotels near the entrance to the Cimetière de Montmartre.

Citadines Aparthôtel – 16/18 Ave Rachel (M7, ☎ 01 453 42 43 44; metro Blanche). Right by the entrance to the cemetery, and on a quiet street, this branch of the apartment-style hotel chain has small 'studettes' from 510FF, larger studios from 580FF and two-bedroom apartments from 890FF. Parking is 45FF a night or 250FF a week.

Places to Eat

FOOD

The cuisine of France is remarkably varied, with a great many regional differences based on the produce and gastronomy of each region. Eating well is still of prime importance to most French people, who spend an amazing amount of time thinking about, talking about and consuming food.

Many of the pubs, clubs and bars listed under Entertainment also serve snacks and light meals.

VEGETARIAN FOOD

Vegetarians form only a small minority in France and are not very well catered for, as specialised vegetarian restaurants are few and far between. Some restaurants have at least one vegetarian dish on the menu. Unfortunately, very few set *menus* include vegetarian options.

The Vegan Guide to vegetarian restaurants in Paris is available from the Société Végan, 12 Allée Jacques Becker, 93300 Aubervilliers, France.

ETHNIC CUISINES

France has a considerable population of immigrants from its former colonies and protectorates in North and West Africa, Indochina, the Middle East, India, the Caribbean and the South Pacific, as well as refugees from every corner of the globe, so an exceptional variety of reasonably priced ethnic food is available.

MEALS IN FRANCE

The French start the day with a *petit déjeuner* (breakfast), usually consisting of a croissant and a light bread roll with butter and jam, followed by a *café au lait* (coffee with lots of hot milk), a small black coffee or hot chocolate.

For many French people, lunch is still the main meal of the day. Dinner usually begins around 8.30 pm.

RESTAURANTS & BRASSERIES

Restaurants usually specialise in a particular variety of food (eg regional, traditional, North African), whereas brasseries serve more standard fare.

Restaurants are usually open only for lunch and dinner, whereas brasseries stay open from morning until night and serve meals at all times of the day.

Most restaurants offer you the choice of ordering à la carte or ordering one fixed-price, multicourse meal known in French as a *menu* or a more restricted *formule*. A *menu* almost always costs much less than ordering à la carte. Note, however, that the word '*menu*' is one of the false friends between English and French. If you really want a menu, ie a list of the dishes available, you must ask for *la carte*.

CAFÉS

Cafés are an important focal point for social life in France, and sitting in a café to read, write, talk with friends or just daydream is an integral part of many French people's day-to-day existence. Only basic food is available in most cafés. A baguette filled with Camembert or pâté is a common option.

SALONS DE THÉ

Salons de thé (tearooms) are trendy and somewhat pricey establishments that usually offer quiches, salads, cakes, tarts, pies and pastries in addition to tea and coffee.

FAST FOOD

American fast-food companies, including McDonald's, Burger King, Pizza Hut, Haagen Daz and KFC, have busy branches all over Paris, which must mean that the average French person is a lot more open to Anglo-Saxon culinary ideas than some defenders of French civilisation seem to believe. There's even a local hamburger chain called Quick.

CHAIN RESTAURANTS

A number of restaurants have several outlets around Paris with standard menus. They're a definite step up from the fast-food companies and can be good value in places like the Ave des Champs-Élysées, where restaurants tend to be expensive or bad value or both.

RICHARD NEBESKY

Café in Place de la Bastille

Hippopotamus

There are about 15 branches of this hugely popular national chain that specialises in solid, steak-based meals. *Menus* are available at 60 and 100FF and they are typically open daily from 11.30 am to 1 am.

Batifol

There are a dozen branches in Paris of these attractive and popular 1930s-style bistros with their jazz-theme décor. Specialities include *pot au feu* (stewed beef and vegetables; 64FF) and *moelle* (beef marrow on bread; 40FF). The generous plats du jour cost 60 to 70FF and there's a *menu* with wine for 78FF. Meals are served daily from noon to midnight.

Léon de Bruxelles

The dozen branches of this restaurant are dedicated to only one thing: the preparation of *moules* (mussels). Meal-size bowls of the bivalves, served with chips and fresh bread, start at 60FF. They're open daily from 11.45 am to midnight, and to 1 am on Friday and Saturday nights.

Other Chains

There are five *Indiana Cafés* serving blandly safe Tex-Mex food in popular tourist areas. They're open daily from 7 am to midnight or 1.30 am, and apart from the Ave des Champs-Élysées branch they all have a 5 to 8 pm happy hour. *Pizza Pino* is open from 11.30 am until 5 am at three of their four Paris branches. The pizzas aren't bad and again they provide reasonably priced food in often expensive districts.

SELF-CATERING

One of France's culinary delights is stocking up on fresh breads, pastries, cheese, fruit, vegetables and prepared dishes and sitting down for a gourmet *pique-nique*. Many food shops are closed on Sunday afternoon and Monday, and almost all supermarkets close all day on Sunday.

Fresh bread is baked and sold at *boulangeries*; mouthwatering pastries are available at *pâtisseries*; the owner of a *fromagerie* can supply you with cheese that is *fait* (ripe) to the exact degree that you request; a *charcuterie* offers sliced meats, pâtés etc; and fresh fruits and vegetables are sold at greengrocers, supermarkets and open-air markets.

A general butcher is a *boucherie*, but for specialised poultry you have to go to a *marchand de volaille*. A *boucherie chevaline*, easily identifiable by the gilded horse's head above the entrance, sells horse meat, which some people prefer to beef or mutton. Fresh fish and seafood are available from a *poissonnerie*.

DRINKS

Nonalcoholic Drinks

Soft Drinks Soft drinks can be hideously expensive at Paris cafés. One relatively inexpensive café drink is *sirop* (squash), served either *à l'eau* (mixed with water), with *soda* (carbonated water) or Perrier. Restaurants will supply tap water if you ask for it, although touristy places may try to push mineral water. Ask for a *carafe*

JAMES LYON

Mouth-watering pâtisseries

d'eau or raise a smile by asking for *Château Tiberi* (Monsieur Tiberi is the Mayor of Paris).

Coffee A cup of coffee can take various forms, but the most ubiquitous is espresso. A small, black espresso is called *un café noir*, *un express* or simply *un café*. You can also ask for a *grand* (large) version.

Un café crème is espresso with steamed milk or cream. A small café crème is a *petit crème*. *Un café au lait* is lots of hot milk with a little coffee served in a large cup or even a bowl. A *noisette* (literally, hazelnut) is an espresso with just a dash of milk. A coffee in a café can be as little as 6FF if you drink it standing up at the counter. Sit down and the price will double or even triple on the Champs-Élysées.

Tea & Hot Chocolate *Thé* (tea) is unlikely to be up to the English standard but will be served with milk if you ask for *un peu de lait frais*. Herbal tea is popular and is called a *tisane* or *infusion*. *Chocolat chaud* (hot chocolate) can be excellent or undrinkable.

Wine

Two regions produce the most celebrated wines in France: Bordeaux and Burgundy. Burgundy of the right vintage can be extraordinary but Bordeaux is more reliable. Beaujolais, a light Burgundy, is generally drunk very young (about two months old).

Other Alcoholic Drinks

Apéritifs Meals are often preceded by an appetite-stirring *apéritif* such as *kir* (white wine sweetened with a syrup such as cassis, ie blackcurrant syrup). Port is drunk as an apéritif rather than after the meal.

Digestifs France's most famous brandies are Cognac and Armagnac. The various other sorts of brandies are known collectively as *eaux de vie* (literally, waters of life). Calvados is an apple brandy which ages beautifully. Well-known liqueurs include Cointreau, Bénédictine and Chartreuse.

Beer Beer *(bière)*, which is served by the *demi* (about 33 ml), is usually either Alsatian (like Kronenbourg from Strasbourg, 33 or Pelforth) or imported from Germany or Belgium. A draught beer is a *bière à la pression*.

LOUVRE & LES HALLES AREAS

The area between the Forum des Halles and the Centre Pompidou is filled with scores of *branché* (plugged-in or trendy) restaurants, but few of them (except the many fast-food joints) are particularly inexpensive. Streets lined with places to eat include Rue des Lombards, bar and bistro-lined Rue Montorgueil, and the narrow streets north and east of Forum des Halles.

French

The 1er and 4e have a diverse selection of French eating establishments.

Chain Restaurants – There are branches of the following chain restaurants at Les Halles: *Batifol*, 14 Rue Mondétour, 1er (M12; ☎ 01 42 36 85 50; metro Les Halles); *Léon de Bruxelles*, 120 Rue Rambuteau, 1er (M12; ☎ 01 42 36 18 50; metro Les Halles); and *Hippopotamus*, 29 Rue Berger (M12; ☎ 01 45 08 00 29; metro Les Halles).

Au P'tit Rémouleur – 2 Rue de la Coutellerie, just west of the Hôtel de Ville, 4e (M15; ☎ 01 48 04 79 24; metro Hôtel de Ville). This small, typically French fish restaurant includes bouillabaisse (55FF), mussels and a 63FF *menu* amongst its specialities. Main dishes cost 49 to 74FF. It is open Monday to Saturday from noon to 3 pm and 7 to 11 pm.

Brasserie Paoli – 104 Rue de Rivoli, 1er (M12; ☎ 01 42 33 98 53; metro Châtelet). This brasserie, decorated with brass, mirrors and grape-bunch lamps, is open 365 days a year, 22 hours a day (it's closed from 6 to 8 am). Meals – including the two-course 72FF *menu* – are served from 11 am to 5 am. Beer is 15 to 29FF and coffee from 11FF, depending on the hour.

Au Pied de Cochon – 6 Rue Coquillère, 1er (M12; ☎ 01 42 36 11 75; metro Les Halles). Onion soup, pieds de cochon (pigs' trotters; from 82FF) and other pork dishes (eg tripe; 75FF) from this venerable establishment long satisfied the appetites of both market porters and theatre-goers. The clientele has become more uniformly up-market (and touristy) since Les Halles was moved to the suburbs, but Au Pied de Cochon is still open 24 hours a day, seven days a week. The same block has a number of other restaurants in the same price bracket.

Le Grand Véfour – 17 Rue de Beaujolais, at the northern edge of the Jardin du Palais Royal, 1er (M8; ☎ 01 42 96 56 27; fax 01 42 86 80 71; metro Pyramides). A dining favourite of the Paris élite since 1784, the traditional French and Savoyard cuisine and 18th-century elegance have earned this restaurant two Michelin stars. Count on spending 800 to 1000FF per person for dinner. A lunch *menu* is available for 325FF, not including wine. Closed on Saturday and Sunday and during August.

Reservations for dinner should be made about 10 days ahead; for lunch, one or two days should suffice.

Café Beaubourg – 49 Rue Saint Merri, just opposite the Centre Pompidou, 1er (M15; ☎ 01 48 87 63 96; metro Châtelet-Les Halles). This high-tech café draws in an arty crowd and there's always free entertainment on the large square in front. Sunday brunch is excellent. It's open daily from 8 am to 1 am (2 pm on weekends).

Japanese

Businesspeople from Japan in search of real Japanese food flock to Rue Sainte Anne and other streets of Paris' 'Japantown', which is just west of the Jardin du Palais Royal. Many of the restaurants offer surprisingly good value.

Lamen Higuma – 32bis Rue Sainte Anne, 1er (M8; ☎ 01 47 03 38 59; metro Pyramides). Stepping into this place is like ducking into a corner noodle shop in Tokyo. To the delight of the almost exclusively Japanese clientele (the only French people we saw there were chatting in Japanese), the high-temperature woks are forever filled with furiously bubbling soups and simmering vegetables. A meal-sized bowl of soup noodles costs 40 to 48FF. It is open daily from 11.30 am straight through to 10 pm. The *menus* (60 to 70FF) are not served from 3 to 5 pm.

Matsuri Sushi – 36 Rue de Richelieu (M8; ☎ 01 42 61 05 73; metro Pyramides). Plates of sushi (21FF at lunch, 23 to 30FF in the evening) make their way around this sushi bar on a little conveyor belt. It is open weekdays from noon to 2.30 pm and 7 to 10.30 pm (11.30 pm on Friday), and on Saturday from 7 to 11.30 pm.

Other Cuisines

This part of Paris is a fast-food lovers' paradise, with a variety of chain outlets close to the Centre Pompidou and Les Halles.

Restaurant China – 70 Rue de la Verrerie, 4e (M15; ☎ 01 42 71 78 82; metro Hôtel de Ville). The all-you-can-eat buffet for 59FF (66FF at night) at this friendly Chinese restaurant is one of the Right Bank's great bargains. It is open daily from noon to 3.30 pm and 6 to 11 pm.

Chicago Meatpackers – 8 Rue Coquillère, 1er (M12; ☎ 01 40 28 01 83; metro Châtelet-Les Halles). The décor and ambience of this huge place is about as American as any place with English bartenders could be. Culinary specialities include American-style hamburgers (70 to 79FF), ribs and Haagen Daz ice cream. The restaurant section is open every day of the year from 11.45 am to 1 am. The bar at the back charges 33FF for a pint of beer.

Mélodine Cafeteria – 42 Rue Rambuteau, across from the north side of the Centre Pompidou, 4e (M15; ☎ 01 40 29 09 78; metro Rambuteau). The food at this huge, self-service cafeteria is better than you might expect, and may satisfy finicky kids. Main dishes cost only 25 to 40FF. Salads are available. Food is served daily from 11 am to 10 pm.

Pizza Pino – 43 Rue Saint Denis, 1er (M12; ☎ 01 40 26 39 07; metro Châtelet-Les Halles). A nicely located outlet of the French pizza chain.

Self-Catering

There are a number of options along Ave de l'Opéra and Rue de Richelieu, as well as around Forum des Halles, including a *Monoprix* at 21 Ave de l'Opéra (M8), a *Franprix* at 35 Rue Berger and a bargain-priced *Ed l'Épicier* at 80 Rue de Rivoli. *Fine food shops* can be found on the Rue de Richelieu.

MARAIS

The Marais, filled with small eateries of every imaginable kind, is one of Paris' premier neighbourhoods for eating out. The pretty little Place du Marché Sainte Catherine (M15; metro Saint Paul) is a square surrounded by small restaurants. They're all a bit pricey but you're paying for the pleasant outdoor location.

French

The French places in the area tend to be small and intimate although you'll also find the big Bofinger and

RICHARD NEBESKY

Bistrot du Dome, off Place de la Bastille

chain establishments like Hippopotamus and Léon de Bruxelles clustered by the Place de la Bastille.

Brasserie Bofinger – 5-7 Rue de la Bastille, 4e (M13; ☎ 01 42 72 87 82; metro Bastille). This is reputedly the oldest brasserie in Paris (founded in 1864), with Art Deco-style brass, glass and mirrors. Specialities include choucroute (80 to 120FF) and seafood (120 to 140FF). The 169FF *menu* includes half a bottle of wine. It is open daily from noon to 3 pm and 6.30 pm to 1 am (no afternoon closure on weekends and holidays). Reservations are necessary for dinner, especially on the weekend, and for Sunday lunch. Ask for a seat downstairs, under the *coupole* (stained-glass dome) if possible.

Le Dôme Bastille – 2 Rue de la Bastille, 4e (M13; ☎ 01 48 04 88 44; metro Bastille). Opposite Bofinger, this superb restaurant, a distant cousin of the better known Le Dôme Brasserie in Montparnasse, specialises in superbly prepared (and pricey) fish dishes. The blackboard menu has main courses at 75 to 130FF.

Chain Restaurants – *Hippopotamus*, 1 Blvd Beaumarchais, 4e (M13; ☎ 01 42 72 98 37; metro Bastille), and *Léon de Bruxelles*, 3 Blvd Beaumarchais, 4e (M13; ☎ 01 42 71 75 55; metro Bastille).

Le P'tit Gavroche – 15 Rue Sainte Croix de la Brettonerie, 4e (M15; ☎ 01 48 87 74 26; metro Hôtel de Ville). This bar/restaurant, which is also known as Bistro du Marais, attracts tables of raucous working-class regulars; it isn't the place for a quiet date. Solid, basic meals are served from noon to 2.30 pm and 7 pm to midnight (closed Saturday at noon and on Sunday). The bar is open from 8 am to 2 am. The *menus*, available until about 10 pm (or whenever they run out), cost about 48FF. Main dishes are around 50FF; a small carafe of wine is 12FF.

Le Petit Picard – 42 Rue Sainte Croix de la Bretonnerie, 4e (M15; ☎ 01 42 78 54 03; metro Hôtel de Ville). Mainly gay and very popular, the cuisine is very traditional French. The *menus* cost 64FF (lunch only) and 84FF. Closed for lunch on the weekends and all day Monday.

Le Gai Moulin – 4 Rue Saint Merri, 4e (M15; ☎ 01 42 77 60 60; metro Rambuteau). Traditional French cuisine, including a 99FF *menu*, is served from noon to 2 pm and 7.30 to 11.30 pm (closed Tuesday) at this small, modern place with a mainly (but not exclusively) gay clientele. In July and August, it's open only for dinner, seven days a week.

Marais Plus – corner of Rue des Francs Bourgeois and Rue Payenne, 3e (M15; ☎ 01 48 87 01 40; metro Saint Paul). This mellow salon de thé specialises in tartes salées (quiches; 50FF) and tarts (pies; 35FF). It is open daily from 10 am to 7.30 pm.

Restaurant L'Amadeo – 19 Rue François Miron, 4e (M15; ☎ 01 48 87 01 02; metro Saint Paul). This restaurant is decidedly gay, although hetero diners are very welcome, and it produces delicious and stylish food at a standard price of 165FF for almost any starter, main course and dessert on their menu.

Coffee Shop – 3 Rue Sainte Croix de la Bretonnerie, 4e (M15; ☎ 01 42 74 46 29; metro Hôtel de Ville). A small, almost exclusively gay café that's open daily from noon to midnight. Bottled beer, officially served only with the two-course meals (60FF; available all day long), costs 17FF. Coffee is 16FF.

Le Petit Dragon – 32 Rue Saint Paul, 4e (☎ 01 42 78 52 73, metro Saint Paul). This is a small Chinese restaurant with some Thai and Vietnamese flavours to its low-priced and very well prepared dishes.

Jewish

The kosher and kosher-style restaurants along Rue des Rosiers serve specialities from North Africa, Central Europe and Israel. Many are closed on Friday evening, Saturday and Jewish holidays.

Takeaway falafel and shwarma are available all along Rue des Rosiers.

Chez Rami et Hanna – 54 Rue des Rosiers, 4e (M15; ☎ 01 42 78 23 09; metro Saint Paul). Israeli dishes, including the assiette royale (a plate of seven salads; 60FF), are served daily from 11 am to 2 am.

Café des Psaumes – 14-16 Rue des Rosiers, 4e (M15; ☎ 01 48 04 74 77; metro Saint Paul). This is a strictly kosher brasserie with dishes from Tunisia, Central Europe and Israel. It is open from noon to midnight (closed Saturday, Jewish holidays and from mid-afternoon on Friday).

Jo Goldenberg – 7 Rue des Rosiers, 4e (M15; ☎ 01 48 87 20 16; metro Saint Paul). Founded in 1920, this kosher-style restaurant-delicatessen has become Paris' most famous Jewish eatery. The starters (30FF) and apple strudel (29FF) are excellent, but the plats du jour (70FF) don't measure up to New York standards. It is open 364 days a year (closed Yom Kippur) from 8.30 am until midnight or 1 am.

Finkelsztajn Bakeries – *Florence Finkelsztajn* is on the corner of Rue des Écouffes and Rue des Rosiers, 4e (M15; ☎ 01 48 87 92 85; metro Saint Paul), and *Sacha Finkelsztajn* is at 27 Rue des Rosiers (M15; ☎ 01 42 72 78 91; metro Saint Paul). These places have scrumptious Jewish-style Central European breads and pastries, including apple strudel and poppy-seed cakes. Florence's is also a deli. At least one of the two is open daily except Tuesday until 7 pm.

Vegetarian

The 4e has an excellent selection of meatless restaurants.

La Truffe – 31 Rue Vieille du Temple, 4e (M15; ☎ 01 42 71 08 39; metro Hôtel de Ville). This organic, vegetarian restaurant specialises in dishes made with mushrooms. The poêlée champignons (129FF) and vegetable lasagne (79FF) are

superb. A savoury tarte served with vegetables is 59 to
79FF. It is open daily from noon to 4 pm and 7 to 11 pm.

Piccolo Teatro – 6 Rue des Écouffes, 4e (M15; ☎ 01 42 72 17 79;
metro Saint Paul). The *menus* at this intimate place with
stone walls, beamed ceiling and cosy little tables cost 53
and 75FF for lunch and 90 and 115FF for dinner; the tasty
assiette végétarienne (vegetarian plate) is 60FF. It is open
from noon to 3 pm and 7 to 11 pm (closed Monday and
Tuesday); often busy in the evening, especially on Friday
and Saturday.

Aquarius – 54 Rue Sainte Croix de la Bretonnerie, 4e (M15; ☎ 01
48 87 48 71; metro Rambuteau). The calming, airy atmosphere of this healthy restaurant makes you think of fresh
bean sprouts – great if you're in the mood for something
light. The two-course *menu* costs 56FF. It is open Monday

TONY WHEELER

Boulangerie in the Marais

to Saturday from noon to 10 pm; the plat du jour is available from noon to 2 pm and 7 to 10 pm.

Other Cuisines

The area has a good selection of ethnic places as well.

Woolloomooloo – 36 Blvd Henri IV, 4e (M15; ☎ 01 42 72 32 11; metro Bastille). Paris' one and only Australian restaurant, opened in 1994. The dishes, served in a bright, open dining area, bring together the culinary traditions of South-East Asia and the Mediterranean. Two and three-course *menus* are 120 and 140FF. The extensive Australian wine list generally costs 100 to 300FF a bottle. It is open from noon to 2.30 pm and 7.30 or 8 to 11 pm (closed all

TONY WHEELER

Jewish delicatessen store in Rue des Rosiers

day Monday and Tuesday at noon); brunch is served on
Sunday from noon to 3 pm.

Resto' Pouce – 8 Rue de Rivoli, 4e (M15; ☎ 01 40 27 93 07; metro
Saint Paul). A cheap Tunisian eatery with couscous (49 to
69FF), steak and chips (39FF), three-course *menus* (49 and
59FF) and take-out falafel (23FF). It is open daily from 10
am to 7 pm.

404 – 69 Rue des Gravilliers, 3e (M15; ☎ 01 42 74 57 81; metro
Arts et Métiers). 404 has some of the best couscous and
tagine (a meat-and-vegetable 'stew' cooked in a domed
earthenware pot) in Paris (both 90 to 105FF). It also has
excellent grills from 90FF, aniseed bread and *menus* at 59
and 78FF, which are great value. The restaurant, done up
like the inside of an old Moroccan home, is owned by the
French-Arab comedian Smain, so the atmosphere is
always upbeat. It's open seven days a week for lunch and
dinner. The Sunday brunch berbère (Berber brunch) is
available from noon to 5 pm.

Minh Chau – 10 Rue de la Verrerie, 4e (M15; ☎ 01 42 71 13 30;
metro Hôtel de Ville). For only 26 to 32FF you can enjoy
tasty main dishes at this tiny but welcoming Vietnamese
place. It is open Monday to Saturday from 11.30 am to 3
pm and 5.30 to 11 pm.

Restaurant The Studio – 41 Rue du Temple, 4e (M15; ☎ 01 42 74
10 38; metro Rambuteau). This popular and trendy place
is Texas as only the French could imagine it! Tacos, enchi-
ladas and chimichangas go for 68 to 82FF and there are
two-course *menus* at 100FF and 150FF, including a show
at 10 pm. While dining you can watch flamenco, tap, jazz
and rock & roll lessons at the dance school around the
courtyard. It is open on weekdays from 7.30 pm to midnight and on weekends from 12.30 to 3.30 pm (for brunch)
and 7.30 pm to 12.30 am.

La Perla – 26 Rue François Miron, 4e (M15; ☎ 01 42 77 59 40;
metro Saint Paul). A favourite with younger Parisians,
this trendy California-style Mexican place is more bar
than restaurant. Specialities include guacamole (29FF),
nachos (30FF) and burritos (from 42FF). Meals are served
Monday to Friday from noon to 3 pm and 7 to 11 pm, and
on weekends nonstop from noon to 11 pm. Monday to
Friday happy hour is 6 to 8 pm.

Self-Catering

There's a whole bunch of *food shops* on the odd-numbered side of Rue Saint Antoine between the *Monoprix*
supermarket at No 71 and the *Supermarché G20* at No 117
(open Monday to Saturday from 9 am to 8.30 pm).

G Millet Fromager – 77 Rue Saint Antoine, 4e (metro Saint Paul).
This store sells Poilâne sourdough bread as well as
cheeses (closed from 1 to 4 pm, on Sunday afternoon and
on Monday).

Gourmaud – 91 Rue Saint Antoine, 4e (metro Saint Paul). This is one of the few gourmet shops in Paris where you can assemble an entire picnic – everything from escargots (5.80FF each) to eclairs – in one stop (open 365 days a year from 9 am to 10 pm).

ÎLE SAINT LOUIS

Famed for its ice cream, the Île Saint Louis is generally an expensive place to eat. It's best suited to those looking for a light snack or the finest ingredients for lunch beside the Seine. Rue Saint Louis en l'Île has several salons de thé, and there are lots of restaurants along this street but they tend to be either touristy and disappointing or expensive (or both).

Brasserie de l'Île Saint Louis – 55 Quai de Bourbon, 4e (M15; ☎ 01 43 54 02 59; metro Pont Marie). Founded in 1870, this spectacularly situated brasserie features Alsatian-style choucroute garnie (sauerkraut with charcuterie) for 85FF, but you can enjoy the location by ordering coffee/beer (6/15FF at the bar, 12/20FF at a table or on the terrace). It is open from 11.30 am (6 pm on Thursday) to 1 am (closed Wednesday and in August).

Berthillon – 31 Rue Saint Louis en l'Île, 4e (M15; ☎ 01 43 54 31 61; metro Pont Marie). This ice-cream parlour is reputed to have Paris' most delicious frozen delicacies. While the fruit flavours are justifiably renowned, the chocolate, coffee and Agenaise (Armagnac & prunes) flavours are incomparably richer. The takeaway counter is open from 10 am to 8 pm (closed Monday, Tuesday and during school holiday periods); one/two/three tiny scoops cost 9/16/20FF. The *salon dégustation* (sit-down area) is open the same days from 1 pm (2 pm on weekends) to 8 pm. Other places on the Île Saint Louis also feature Berthillon ice cream but without the big queues.

Les Fous de L'Île – 33 Rue des Deux Ponts (M15; ☎ 01 43 25 76 67; metro Pont Marie). An exception to the touristy nature of the Île Saint Louis, a meal at this friendly and down-to-earth establishment will run from 120 to 150FF per person. It's open Tuesday to Friday from noon to 11 pm, Saturday from 3 to 11 pm and Sunday from noon to 7 pm.

Self-Catering

The Île Saint Louis, home to some of Paris' finest and priciest food shops, is a great place to assemble a gourmet picnic. Along Rue Saint Louis en l'Île, 4e (M15; metro Pont Marie) there are a number of *Fromageries* & *Groceries* which tend to be closed on Sunday afternoon and Monday. There are more *food shops* on Rue des Deux Ponts.

TONY WHEELER

Café, Pont Saint Louis

Le Moule à Gâteau – 47 Rue Saint Louis en l'Île, 4e (M15; metro Pont Marie). This store has some of the most delicious fancy breads in all of France as well as fantastic brownies and chocolate cakes (10FF). It is open from 8.30 am to 8 pm (closed Monday).

LATIN QUARTER

Rue Mouffetard is filled with scores of places to eat. It's especially popular with students, in part because of the unparalleled selection of stands selling baguette sandwiches, panini (Italian toasted bread with fillings) and crêpes. Rue Soufflot (metro Luxembourg) is lined with cafés.

TONY WHEELER

Mexican restaurant in Rue Mouffetard

Avoid Rue de la Huchette (metro Saint Michel) unless you're after chawarma (ie shwarma), available at several places around No 14.

French

The western 5e has some of Paris' best reasonably priced French places.

Crêpes Stand – 61 Rue Mouffetard (M12; metro Place Monge). This sidewalk stand serves some of the best discount crêpes in Paris. Savoury crêpes are only 11 to 23FF; sweet crêpes are 7 to 22FF. It is open daily from 11 am to 12.30 am (2 am on Friday and Saturday nights).

Perraudin – 157 Rue Saint Jacques (M14; ☎ 01 46 33 15 75; metro Luxembourg). If you fancy bœuf Bourguignon (59FF), gigot d'agneau (leg of lamb; 59FF) or confit de canard (59FF), try this reasonably priced traditional French restaurant that hasn't changed much since the turn of the century. At lunch time, there's a *menu* for 63FF. It is open from noon to 2.15 pm and 7.30 to 10.15 pm (closed Saturday and Monday at noon and all day Sunday).

Chez Léna et Mimille – 32 Rue Tournefort, a block west of Rue Mouffetard (M14; ☎ 01 47 07 72 47; metro Censier Daubenton). The terrace of this elegant French restaurant overlooks a lovely little park. The lunch/dinner *menus* cost 98/185FF. It closes on Saturday at noon and in winter on Sunday.

L'Étoile de Berger – 42 Rue de la Montagne Sainte Geneviève (M14; ☎ 01 43 26 38 87; metro Maubert Mutualité). This Savoyard restaurant, decorated like a mountain chalet, specialises in raclette and fondue (75 to 110FF). It is open daily. There are numerous other restaurants nearby.

Le Navigator – 63 Rue Galande, two blocks from Notre Dame (M14; ☎ 01 43 54 35 86; metro Maubert Mutualité). This restaurant serves traditional French cuisine from 11.45 am to 2.30 pm and 6.45 to 11 pm (closed Monday). *Menus*, including wine, are available for 90, 130, 150 and 200FF.

Moissonnier – 28 Rue des Fossés Saint Bernard (M12; ☎ 01 43 29 87 65; metro Cardinal Lemoine). Excellent Lyon-inspired cuisine has been served at this elegant restaurant since 1960. Count on a full meal costing about 250FF. It is open from noon to 1.30 pm and 7 pm to 9.30 pm (closed on Sunday night and Monday and in August). There are a number of other classy restaurants along the same street.

Dodin Bouffant – 25 Rue Frédéric Sauton (M14; ☎ 01 43 25 25 14; metro Maubert Mutualité). This classic French restaurant has lunch-time and dinner *menus* at 180FF and 245FF. Reservations are recommended.

La Tour d'Argent – 15 Quai de la Tournelle, 6th floor (M15; ☎ 01 43 54 23 31; metro Cardinal Lemoine). Famous for its canard (duck), La Tour d'Argent was the shock story in the 1996 Michelin *Guide Rouge* when it was downgraded from three to two stars. You can still expect to pay over 1000FF per person for dinner. Lunch reservations should be made eight to 10 days in advance; for dinner, reserve three weeks ahead.

D'Ici ou d'Ailleurs – 4 Rue des Fossés Saint Jacques (M14; ☎ 01 40 51 83 11; metro Luxembourg). An attractive, laid-back salon de thé with very reasonable prices and a good selection of vegetarian dishes. Mariage frères teas (15 kinds) and homemade hot chocolate (nine kinds) are 12 to 20FF. Meal-size salads are 30 to 42FF, hot and cold sandwiches start at 13FF. It is open weekdays from 10.30 am to 8.30 pm. From October to March, Sunday brunch is served from noon to 4 pm.

L'Arbre à Cannelle – 14 Rue Linné (M12; ☎ 01 43 31 68 31; metro Jussieu). A bright, upbeat salon de thé known for its brunches (90 to 120FF). It is open daily from noon to 6.30 pm.

Tea Caddy – 14 Rue Saint Julien le Pauvre (M14; ☎ 01 43 54 15 56; metro Saint Michel), a half-block from the Seine. A fine place to enjoy English tea for 27FF. It is open from noon to 7 pm (closed Tuesday and Wednesday).

Pan-Asian

The Latin Quarter has restaurants serving cuisines from every corner of Asia, from west Asia eastward.

Al-Dar – 8-10 Rue Frédéric Sauton (M14; ☎ 01 43 25 17 15; metro Maubert Mutualité). This Lebanese restaurant has a great snack-traiteur (deli) section on the corner. The latter, open daily from 7 am to midnight, serves delicious dishes of the highest quality, including meat pizzas (15FF) and stuffed grape leaves (4FF each). The restaurant, open daily from noon to 3 pm and 7 pm to midnight, has lunch *menus* for 89 and 150FF, main courses at 60 to 75FF.

Saveurs d'Asie – 29 Place Maubert (M14; ☎ 01 44 07 05 55; metro Maubert Mutualité). Small and crowded, with excellent Vietnamese food, open Monday to Saturday from noon to 8 pm. There's a pricier version of the same restaurant next door.

La Voie Lactée – 34 Rue du Cardinal Lemoine (M12; ☎ 01 46 34 02 35; metro Cardinal Lemoine). The 'Milky Way' is a Turkish place with modern and traditional Anatolean cuisine, including a buffet of Turkish salads. The evening *menus* cost 85 to 120FF. It is open from noon to 3 pm and 7 to 11 pm (closed on Sunday).

Koutchi – 40 Rue du Cardinal Lemoine (M12; ☎ 01 44 07 20 56; metro Cardinal Lemoine). The décor of this Afghan restaurant is reminiscent of a Central Asian caravanserai. Specialities include Afghan salads (25FF), soups (28FF), meat dishes (65 to 80FF) and desserts (25 to 30FF). The evening *menu* costs 98FF; lunch *menus* are cheaper. It is open from noon to 2.30 pm and 7 to 11 pm (closed Saturday at noon and on Sunday).

Tashi Delek – 4 Rue des Fossés Saint Jacques (M14; ☎ 01 43 26 55 55; metro Luxembourg). Lunch *menus* at this intimate Tibetan restaurant (whose name means 'bon jour' in Tibetan) cost 58 to 65FF; the 105FF dinner *menu* includes wine. It is open Monday to Saturday from noon to 2.30 pm and 7 to 10.30 pm.

Au Coin des Gourmets – 5 Rue Dante (M14; ☎ 01 43 26 12 92; metro Maubert Mutualité). This place serves decent (if not ground-breaking) hybrid Indochinese food. It is open from noon to 2.30 pm and 7 to 10.30 pm (closed Tuesday). Reservations are recommended on weekends.

Chez Maï – 65 Rue Galande (M14; ☎ 01 43 54 05 33; metro Maubert Mutualité). This hole-in-the-wall Vietnamese place is open daily from noon to 3 pm and 7 to 11 pm. Main dishes (including excellent shrimp) cost only 25 to 30FF; soup is 20FF.

Le Petit Légume – 36 Rue des Boulangers (M12; ☎ 01 40 46 06 85; metro Cardinal Lemoine). A good place for a quick vegetarian lunch.

Other Cuisines

Not all the Peruvians in Paris play Andean music in the metro – some run restaurants – and not all Greek restaurants deal in moussaka.

Machu Pichu – 9 Rue Royer Collard (M14; ☎ 01 43 26 13 13; metro Luxembourg). This small Peruvian restaurant, with main dishes for 60 to 80FF and a 48FF lunch *menu*, is open from noon to 2 pm and 7.30 to 11 pm (closed Saturday at noon and on Sunday).

Aleka – 187 Rue Saint Jacques (M14; ; ☎ 01 44 07 02 75; metro Luxembourg). This small, postmodernist eatery, owned by an affable Greek couple, has some of the freshest Greek-style hors d'œuvres (from 23FF) and grilled salmon and tuna (79FF) in Paris. Aleka is open weekdays for lunch and every night to 2 am for dinner.

Self-Catering

Barbecued publishers are no longer available in this area (Place Maubert is where Rabelais' publisher, Étienne Dolet, was burned at the stake in 1546), but on Tuesday, Thursday and Saturday from 7 am to 1 pm, the square (M14; metro Maubert Mutualité) is transformed into a lively *food market*. *Food shops* are found at Place Maubert and parts of nearby Rue Lagrange.

There's another *food market* on Rue Mouffetard, at the bottom end, around Rue de l'Arbalète (M12; metro Censier Daubenton). The stalls tend to close on Sunday afternoons and Mondays. This is one of Paris' oldest and liveliest market areas, with many interesting shops along the street. Rue Saint Jacques, just south of Rue Soufflot (M14; metro Luxembourg), also has a variety of food shops and another *food market* can be found at Place Monge (M12; metro Place Monge). It's open Wednesday, Friday and Sunday mornings until 1 pm. Nearby is a cheap *Ed l'Épicier supermarket* at 37 Rue Lacépède.

For sandwiches to take to the Jardin du Luxembourg, try the popular hole-in-the-wall *Paris Douce* at 7 Rue Royer Collard (M14; metro Luxembourg), where the lunch-time line of Sorbonne students confirms the quality of their 13FF sandwiches. The nearby *D'Ici ou d'Ailleurs* (see the Entertainment chapter) also has good takeaway sandwiches.

6E ARRONDISSEMENT

Rue Saint André des Arts (metro Saint Michel or Odéon) is lined with restaurants, including a few down the covered passage between Nos 59 and 61. There are lots of places between Église Saint Sulpice and Église Saint Germain des Prés, especially along Rue des Canettes, Rue Princesse and Rue Guisarde. Place Carrefour de l'Odéon (metro Odéon) has a cluster of lively bars, cafés and restaurants.

French

Place Saint Germain des Prés is home to three famous cafés: Brasserie Lipp is listed below; Les Deux Magots and Café de Flore are covered under 6e Arrondissement in the Entertainment chapter.

Crêmerie Restaurant Polidor – 41 Rue Monsieur le Prince (M14; ☎ 01 43 26 95 34; metro Odéon). A meal here is like a quick trip back to Victor Hugo's Paris – the restaurant and its décor date from 1845 – but everyone knows it and the place has become somewhat touristy. Guests are seated together at tables of six, 10 or 16. *Menus* of tasty, family-style French cuisine are available for 55FF (lunch only) and 100FF. Specialities include bœuf Bourguignon (50FF), blanquette de veau (veal in white sauce; 68FF) and the most famous tarte tatin (caramelised apple pie) in Paris. It is open daily from noon to 2.30 pm and 7 to 1 am (11 pm on Sunday). Neither reservations nor credit cards are accepted.

Les Mouettes – 27 Rue de Vaugirard (M11 & M14; ☎ 01 45 48 22 31; metro Saint Sulpice). Traditional, family-style French cuisine is served at this neighbourhood restaurant from noon to 3 pm and 7 to 11 pm (closed on Sunday). The *menus* cost from 75FF (for lunch) and 88FF (for dinner).

L'Arbuci – 25 Rue de Buci (M14; ☎ 01 44 41 14 14; metro Mabillon). Opened in 1992, this large, animated retro-style restaurant's specialities include seafood and spit-roasted beef, chicken, pork, salmon and bananas. Lunch *menus* cost 72 or 99FF, dinner is 129FF. All-you-can-eat access to oysters of modest size costs 135FF. It is open daily from noon to 1 am. From 10 pm to closing time there's live jazz in the basement from Tuesday to Saturday (not during July and August).

Brasserie Lipp – 151 Blvd Saint Germain (M11 & M14; ☎ 01 45 48 53 91; metro Saint Germain des Prés). Politicians rub shoulders with intellectuals and editors, while tuxedoed waiters serve pricey à la carte dishes at this old-time, wood-panelled café-brasserie. The *menu* costs 195FF and wine costs from 26FF a glass. Many people make a big fuss about sitting downstairs rather than upstairs, which is considered Nowheresville; the nonsmoking section is upstairs. It is open daily from 8.30 am to 1 am.

Le Petit Zinc – 11 Rue Saint Benoît, 6e (M14; ☎ 01 42 61 20 60; metro Saint Germain des Prés). This wonderful (and expensive – main courses at 100 to 150FF) place serves regional specialities from the south-west of France in true Art Nouveau splendour. There's a *menu* at 168FF. Try to get a table on the raised level in order to enjoy all the goings-on. It's open daily from noon to 2 am.

Lina's – 27 Rue Saint Sulpice, 6e (M14; ☎ 01 43 29 14 14; metro Odéon). A conveniently situated and comfortable member of a chain with classy sandwiches in the 20 to 40FF range.

Vegetarian

Surprisingly, vegetarian restaurants are relatively rare on the Left Bank.

Guenmaï – 2bis Rue de l'Abbaye (M14; ☎ 01 43 26 03 24; metro Saint Germain des Prés or Mabillon). Macrobiotic, organically grown meals are served from Monday to Saturday from 11.45 am to 3.30 pm. The plat du jour is 61FF.

Pan-European

The cuisines of southern, central and eastern Europe are well represented in the 6e.

La Datcha des Arts – 56 Rue Saint André des Arts (M14; ☎ 01 46 33 29 25; metro Mabillon). Light meals of smoked fish, herring, blini (blintzes; from 25FF), piroshki (35FF), bortch (borscht; 53FF) and Russian-style salads are served at simple wooden tables in an informal dining/delicatessen area plastered with posters of arts shows past. It is open daily from 11 am to 4 pm and 6 pm to midnight (or later), with live Russian music from 8 pm to midnight.

Le Golfe de Naples – 5 Rue de Montfaucon (M14; ☎ 01 43 26 98 11; metro Mabillon). Italians resident in Paris say this restaurant/pizzeria has the best pizza and home-made pasta in a city not generally celebrated for its Italian food, which many French people don't consider 'serious' enough. Pizzas start at 48FF and don't forget to try the grilled fresh vegetables.

Osteria del Passe-Partout – 20 Rue de l'Hirondelle, through the arch from 6 Place Saint Michel (M14; ☎ 01 46 34 14 54; metro Saint Michel). Pasta, meat dishes and tiramisu with an excellent reputation are served at this modern Italian place with medieval touches. Open from noon to 2.30 pm and 7.30 to 11 pm (closed Saturday at noon and on Sunday). The *menus* start at 86FF (64FF at lunch time).

Self-Catering

With the Jardin du Luxembourg nearby, this is the perfect area for a picnic lunch. See the Latin Quarter section for more picnic suggestions.

Poilâne – 8 Rue du Cherche Midi (M11; metro Saint Sulpice). This is the most famous boulangerie in France. Its delicious sourdough bread, baked in wood-fired ovens every two hours, has a crunchy, slightly burnt crust (19FF for a small round loaf). Open from 7.15 am to 8.15 pm (closed on Sunday).

Pâtisserie Viençoise – 8 Rue de l'École de Médicine (M14; ☎ 01 43 26 60 48; metro Odéon). This shop has a delightful selection of apple-cinnamon strudel (15FF), Sacher torte (17FF) and tourtes (quiche-like pies; 25FF). It is open Monday to Friday from 9 am to 7.15 pm (closed from mid-July to the end of August).

Food shops – Rue de Seine and Rue de Buci (metro Mabillon). This is the largest cluster of shops in the 6e.

Champion – 79 Rue de Seine (M14). This supermarket is open
  Monday to Saturday from 8.40 am to 9 pm.
Chez Jean-Mi – 10 Rue de l'Ancienne Comédie (M14; metro
  Odéon). This boulangerie and restaurant is open 24 hours
  a day, 365 days a year.
Monoprix – 50-52 Rue de Rennes (M14; metro Saint Germain
  des Prés). This store's supermarket, at the back of the
  basement level, is open Monday to Saturday from 9 am to
  about 8 pm.
Marché Saint Germain – Rue Lobineau, just north of the eastern
  end of Église Saint Germain (M14; metro Mabillon). This
  covered market reopened in 1995 after extensive renovation.

MONTPARNASSE

Since the 1920s, Blvd du Montparnasse has been one of
the city's premier avenues for enjoying that most Parisian of pastimes: sitting in a café and watching the world
go by. However, many younger Parisians now consider
the area dull and lacking in personality.

There are several *crêperies* across the street from 21 Rue
d'Odessa and several more around the corner on Rue du
Montparnasse. An alternative to the all-night Au Pied de
Cochon, if the idea of a gelatinous trotter at 5 am turns
your stomach inside out and your face green, is the
Mustang Café at 84 Blvd du Montparnasse, 14e (M11;
☎ 01 43 35 36 12; metro Montparnasse-Bienvenüe), with
passable Tex-Mex until the very wee hours. There are
plenty of other chain restaurants in the vicinity (see map
M11) including branches of *Pizza Pino*, *Batifol*, *Léon de
Bruxelles* and three *Hippos*.

French

Blvd du Montparnasse, around the Vavin metro stop, is
home to a number of legendary establishments, made
famous between the wars by writers (F Scott Fitzgerald,
Hemingway) and avant-garde artists (Dalí, Cocteau).
Before the Russian Revolution, the area's cafés attracted
exiled revolutionaries such as Lenin and Trotsky. The
intellectual café scene shifted to Saint Germain des Prés
after WW II.

La Coupole – 102 Blvd de Montparnasse, 14e (M11; ☎ 01 43 20
  14 20; metro Vavin). La Coupole's famous mural-covered
  columns (decorated by artists including Brancusi and
  Chagall), dark wood panelling and indirect lighting have
  hardly changed since the days of Sartre, Soutine, Man Ray
  and Josephine Baker. Mains at this 450-seat brasserie,
  which opened in 1927, cost about 100FF, so count on

spending about 175FF per person for a meal. A lunch-time express *menu* is 89FF including wine. It is open daily from 7.30 am to 2 am. There's dancing on Tuesday (Mambomania night), when a 15-member Latin American band plays.

Le Select – 99 Blvd du Montparnasse, 6e (M11; ☎ 01 45 48 38 24 or 42 22 65 27); metro Vavin). Another Montparnasse legend, the Select's décor has changed very little since 1923. The *menu* costs 90FF, and tartines (buttered bread) made with pain Poilâne start at 28FF. Drinks are served at the tiny, round sidewalk tables, each equipped with Parisian café-style rattan chairs. It is open daily from 7 am to 2.30 am.

Chez Dummonet – 117 Rue du Cherche Midi, 6e (M11; ☎ 01 42 22 81 19, 45 48 52 40; metro Falguière). The rôtisserie *menu* costs 150FF, including wine and coffee; à la carte meals cost more. It is closed Monday and Tuesday and in August.

Le Caméléon – 6 Rue de Chevreuse, 6e (M11; ☎ 01 43 20 63 43; metro Vavin). If you want to eat at a 'nouveau' bistro or a brasserie – the distinction isn't clear even to the French any more – that serves fresh, innovative food in a traditional setting, you couldn't do better than at Le Caméléon. Their 79FF lobster ravioli, amongst other dishes, is worth dying for. It also has an excellent wine selection.

La Cagouille – 10-12 Place Brancusi, facing 23 Rue de l'Ouest, 14e (M1; ☎ 01 43 22 09 01; metro Gaîté). Chef Gerard Allemandou, one of the flavours of the 1990s, gets rave reviews for his fish and shellfish dishes (baked black scallops from Brest, fresh fried anchovies) at this café-restaurant. The *formule* costs 150FF, a *menu* is 250FF and bookings are essential.

Self-Catering

Right by the Tour Montparnasse there's an *Inno* supermarket and a *food market* on Blvd Edgar Quinet, open Wednesday and Saturday mornings until 1 pm.

CHAMPS-ÉLYSÉES AREA

Few places along touristy Ave des Champs-Élysées offer good value.

French

Don't come to the 8e looking for cheap eats.

Fauchon – 26-30 Place de la Madeleine, 8e (M7; ☎ 01 47 42 60 11; metro Madeleine). Paris' most famous luxury food store (see Self-Catering) also has five eat-in areas, including a *café*, in the basement at No 30 – where you can purchase hot drinks, cold dishes, sandwiches and exqui-

site pastries. It is open Monday to Saturday from 8.15 am
to 6.30 pm. From 7 pm to 1 am, the café turns into a
brasserie with live music; the *menus* cost 115, 120 and
145FF. *La Trattoria* (☎ 01 47 42 90 30), an Italian restaurant
on the 1st floor at No 26, is open from noon to 3 pm and
7 to 11 pm (closed on Sunday and holidays).

La Maison d'Alsace – 39 Ave des Champs-Élysées, 8e (M7; ☎ 01
43 59 44 24; metro Franklin D Roosevelt). A pricey, Alsa-
cian-style brasserie where you can dine 24 hours a day,
365 days a year. Specialities include seafood (oysters are
117 to 168FF a dozen), choucroute Strasbourgeoise (Stras-
bourg-style sauerkraut with garnishes; 83FF) and fish and
meat dishes (79 to 148FF). Beer is 24FF for a demi.

Maison Prunier – 16 Ave Victor Hugo, 16e (M6; ☎ 01 44 17 35
85; metro Charles de Gaulle-Étoile). This venerable fish
and seafood restaurant, founded in 1925, is famed for its
Art Deco interior. First courses generally cost 70 to 250FF,
mains are 140 to 270FF. It is open from noon to 2.30 pm
and 7 to 11 pm (closed on Sunday night and Monday).
Make reservations at least two days ahead.

Chain Restaurants – The Champs-Élysées also has branches of
a number of the French chains, including: *Hippo Citroën*,
42 Ave des Champs-Élysées (M7; ☎ 01 45 63 40 84; metro
George V), and *Batifol*, 76 Ave des Champs-Élysées (M7;
☎ 01 45 62 64 93; metro George V).

Other Cuisines

Nowadays, young Parisians flock to restaurants that bill
themselves as 'American'.

Chicago Pizza Pie Factory – 5 Rue de Berri, 8e (M6 & M7; ☎ 01
45 62 50 23; metro George V), just off Ave des Champs-
Élysées. A vastly popular eatery that specialises in
Chicago-style deep-dish pizzas (86 to 149FF for the two-
person size, 50% cheaper between 4 and 7 pm except on
Sunday). Weekday lunch *menus* are available for 51, 62
and 71FF. It is open daily from 11.45 am to 1 am. Happy
hour at the bar is from 6 to 8 pm.

Planet Hollywood – 78 Ave des Champs-Élysées (M7; ☎ 01 53
83 78 27; metro George V). The Paris version of this
show-biz hamburger chain offers pizzas at 65 to 78FF,
burgers at 69 to 75FF, desserts at 38 to 45FF, beers at 30 to
38FF and wine by the glass for 20FF. It's open daily from
11 am to 1 am.

Pizza Pino – 33 Ave des Champs-Élysées (M7; ☎ 01 43 59 23 89;
metro Franklin D Roosevelt). One of the French pizza
chain.

Self-Catering

Place de la Madeleine (metro Madeleine) is the luxury
food centre of one of the world's food capitals. The

delicacies on offer don't come cheap, but even travellers on a modest budget can turn a walk around La Madeleine into a gastronomic odyssey. Most places are open from Monday to Saturday.

Prisunic – 62 Blvd des Champs-Élysées, 8e (M7; metro Franklin D Roosevelt). This store's supermarket section is in the basement. It is open Monday to Saturday from 9 am to midnight.

Fauchon – 26-30 Place de la Madeleine, 8e (M7; ☎ 01 47 42 60 11; metro Madeleine). Six departments sell the most incredibly mouth-watering (and expensive) delicacies, such as foie gras for 1000 to 2000FF per kg. The fruits – the most perfect you've ever seen – include exotic items from South-East Asia (eg mangosteens and rambutans). Fauchon is open daily except on Sunday and holidays, and also has five eat-in options. To place an order from abroad, contact Fauchon's *service export* (☎ 01 47 42 60 11; fax 01 47 42 83 75).

La Maison du Miel – 24 Rue Vignon, a block north of Fauchon, 9e (M7; metro Madeleine). This store stocks over 40 kinds of honey made from the pollen of different types of flowers. It is open Monday to Saturday from 9 am to 7 pm.

Hédiard – 21 Place de la Madeleine, 8e (M7; metro Madeleine). This famous luxury foods shop consists of two adjacent sections selling prepared dishes, tea, coffee, jams, wine, pastries, fruit and vegetables etc. It is open from 9.30 am to 9 pm (closed on Sunday and certain holidays).

Maison de la Truffe – 19 Place de la Madeleine, 8e (M7; metro Madeleine). If you've always wanted to taste fine truffles – black French ones from late October to March, white Italian ones from mid-October to December (over 2000FF per 100 grams) – this may be your chance. This place also has a small sit-down area (open from noon to closing time) where you can sample dishes made with the prized fungus (260FF for the *menu*) or fresh foie gras (125 to 240FF). It is open Monday to Saturday from 9 am to 9 pm (8 pm on Monday).

Caviar Kaspa – 17 Place de la Madeleine, 8e (M7; metro Madeleine). This place sells caviar from the Iranian and Russian sections of the Caspian Sea for 450 to 1200FF per 100 grams, depending on the quality. It is open from 9 am to 1 am (closed on Sunday and some holidays). The *restaurant* (☎ 01 42 65 33 32) is open from noon to 1 am.

GRANDS BOULEVARDS

Neon-lit Blvd Montmartre (metro Rue Montmartre or Richelieu Drouot) and nearby bits of Rue du Faubourg Montmartre (neither of which are anywhere near the neighbourhood of Montmartre) form one of Paris' most animated café and dining districts.

French

This area is home to two of Paris' most reasonably priced
historic restaurants.

Le Drouot – 103 Rue de Richelieu (1st floor), 2e (M8; ☎ 01 42 96
68 23; metro Richelieu Drouot). The décor and ambience
of this inexpensive restaurant haven't changed since the
late 1930s; dining is like a trip back to prewar Paris. A
three-course traditional French meal with wine should
cost less than 100FF: fish and meat main courses are 40 to
50FF, a demi of cider or beer is 12FF. It is open 365 days a
year from 11.45 am to 3 pm and 6.30 to 10 pm. Reservations are not accepted.

Chartier – 7 Rue du Faubourg Montmartre, 9e (M8; ☎ 01 47 70
86 29; metro Rue Montmartre). A real gem that is justifiably famous for its 330-seat, *belle époque* dining room,
virtually unaltered since 1896. The prices and fare are
similar to those at Le Drouot (the management is the
same). It is open every day of the year from 11 am to 3 pm
and 6 to 9.30 pm. Reservations are not accepted, so don't
be surprised if there's a queue.

Vegetarian

Vegetarian dining is possible right near Opéra Garnier.

Country Life – 6 Rue Daunou, 2e (M7 & M8; ☎ 01 42 97 48 51;
metro Opéra). A food shop/restaurant that serves an
all-you-can-eat buffet from 11.30 am to 2.30 pm and 6.30
to 10 pm (closed on Friday night, Saturday and Sunday).

Other Cuisines

The 'exotic' cuisine of North America draws large
crowds to Blvd Montmartre.

North African-Jewish restaurants – Rue Richer, Rue Cadet and
Rue Geoffroy Marie (all 9e; M8). These kosher places are
just south of the Cadet metro stop.

Hard Rock Café – 14 Blvd Montmartre, 9e (M8; ☎ 01 42 46 10 00;
metro Rue Montmartre). Housed in the former theatre
where Maurice Chevalier made his debut, Paris' hopping
Hard Rock Café attracts businesspeople for lunch and a
mix of tourists and young, trendy Parisians at night.
Salads are 52 to 80FF, burgers 62 to 100FF, main courses
78 to 99FF, desserts 28 to 55FF. It is open every day of the
year except Christmas Day from 11.30 am straight
through to 1 or 1.30 am. The boutique (open daily from 10
am to 1 am) does a roaring business selling T-shirts,
bomber jackets and other fashion items.

10E ARRONDISSEMENT

The tiny restaurants off Blvd de Strasbourg, many open throughout the afternoon, serve Paris' best Indian and Pakistani food.

French

There's a cluster of brasseries and bistros opposite the façade of Gare du Nord, all M8 and metro Gare du Nord.

Brasserie Terminus Nord – 23 Rue de Dunkerque (M7; ☎ 01 42 85 05 15; metro Gare du Nord). The copper bar, white tablecloths and brass fixtures – reflected brightly in the mirrored walls – look much as they did between the wars. Also known as Brasserie 1925, this Art Deco palace is a fine spot for a last, nostalgically Parisian meal before boarding the Eurostar back to Old Blighty. Breakfast (45FF) is available daily from 7 to 11 am; full meals are served from 11 am straight through to 12.30 am. The 119FF *menu du garçon* is not available from 6 to 10 pm; the late-night (after 10 pm) *faim de nuit menu* costs 121FF.

Chain Restaurants – They include a *Hippopotamus*, 27 Rue de Dunkerque (☎ 01 48 78 29 26) and *Batifol*, 9 Blvd de Denain (☎ 01 42 80 34 74). *Menus* are in the 65 to 75FF range.

Indian & Pakistani

The 10e has Paris' best cheap South Asian food, although it's not generally of the same consistent standard as in Britain.

Ambala – 11 Rue Jarry (M8; ☎ 01 48 01 06 98; metro Château d'Eau). This takeaway joint with eat-in counter space does a roaring business serving snacks and copious main dishes from 25FF. It is open Monday to Saturday from 9 am to 8.30 pm.

Passage Brady – Running between Blvd de Strasbourg and Rue du Faubourg Saint Denis, the tiny Passage Brady is a covered arcade that could easily be in Bombay or Calcutta. The incredibly cheap (and usually crowded) Indian and Pakistani places are generally open for one of the best lunch deals in Paris (meat curry, rice and a tiny salad from 25FF) and for dinner. They include *Salma, La Rose du Kashmir, Kamathenu, Shalimar, Bhai Bhai, Kashmir Express* and *Pooja*.

Other Cuisines

The 10e is home to a large community of Francophone Africans.

Restaurant Paris-Dakar – 95 Rue du Faubourg Saint Martin (M8; ☎ 01 42 08 16 64; metro Gare de l'Est). *Menus* at this Senegalese restaurant cost 59FF (lunch only), 99 and 149FF. Specialities include tiepboudienne (rice, fish and vegetables; 98FF), yassa (chicken or fish marinated in lime juice and onion sauce; 70FF) and mafé (beef sautéed in peanut sauce; 69FF). It is open from noon to 3 pm and 7 pm to midnight (closed on Monday).

Self-Catering

Rue du Faubourg Saint Denis (metro Strasbourg Saint Denis), north of Blvd Saint Denis, is one of the cheapest places in Paris to buy food. It has a distinctively Middle Eastern air, and quite a few of the groceries offer Turkish and North African specialities. Many of the food shops, including the fromagerie at No 54 (M8), are closed on Sunday afternoon and Monday.

Marché Saint Quentin – Opposite 86 Blvd de Magenta (M8; metro Gare de l'Est or Gare du Nord). This huge covered market is open from 8 am to 1 pm and 3.30 to 7.30 pm (closed on Sunday afternoon and Monday).
Franprix – 57 Blvd de Magenta. Open Monday to Saturday until 7.30 pm.

BASTILLE AREA

Narrow, scruffy Rue de Lappe may not look the part during the day, but it's one of the trendiest café and nightlife streets in Paris, attracting a young, alternative crowd. Many of the places speak with a Spanish accent – Tex-Mex, tapas and Cuban food can all be found. Things really start to pick up late at night.

French

Yes, even traditional French food can be found in the Bastille Area.

Le Tabarin – 3 Rue du Pasteur-Wagner, corner of Rue Amelot (M13; ☎ 01 48 07 15 22; metro Bréguet Sabin). On the Marais-Bastille border, this friendly café/restaurant manages to combine tradition with a modern approach. Excellent and reasonably priced food like grilled salmon costs from 66 up to 80FF. Open daily until midnight.
Café de l'Industrie – 16 Rue Saint Sabin (M13; ☎ 01 47 00 13 53; metro Bréguet Sabin). At this very popular restaurant main courses are in the 50 to 70FF bracket and the desserts are delicious. It's open until 1 am every night except Saturday and it's wise to book.

Chez Paul – 13 Rue de Charonne, at the end of Rue de Lappe (M13; ☎ 01 47 00 34 57; metro Ledru Rollin). This is a convivial and extremely popular bistro with traditional French cuisine. Mains cost 60 to 85FF, so count on paying about 150FF for a meal with wine. It is open daily from noon to 3 pm and 7.30 pm to 12.30 am.

Restaurant Relais du Massif Central – 16 Rue Daval (M13; ☎ 01 47 00 46 55; metro Bastille). The culinary inspiration of this small, family-run French restaurant comes from the Massif Central. The *menus* cost 64FF and 84FF, and the food is very conservative and traditional. It is open Monday to Saturday from noon to 3 pm and 7.30 to midnight.

Crêpes Show – 51 Rue de Lappe (M13; ☎ 01 47 00 36 46; metro Ledru Rollin). This small restaurant specialises in sweet and savoury Breton crêpes and buckwheat galettes (18 to 39FF) and has *menus* at 43FF (lunch) and 59FF. Quite a few vegetarian dishes are also available, including salads (from 35FF). It is open from 11 am to 3 pm and 7 pm to 2 am (closed for lunch on weekends and, in winter, all day Sunday).

Melac – 42 Rue Léon-Frot (M13; ☎ 01 43 70 59 27; metro Charonne). Farther east from the Bastille, Melac's regional specialities include a plat du jour at 58FF. It's open from Monday to Friday.

Other Cuisines

National cuisines from all over the world are found along Rue de la Roquette and Rue de Lappe, just east of Place de la Bastille, but Tex-Mex (usually rather bland in Paris) is the major attraction. The *Mustang Café* at 20 Rue de la Roquette (☎ 01 49 23 73 73; metro Bastille) and the *Indiana* at 14 Place de la Bastille (☎ 01 43 43 42 76, metro Bastille) are both represented here and at other locations around Paris.

Havanita Café – 11 Rue de Lappe (M13; ☎ 01 43 55 96 42; metro Bastille). A bar/restaurant decorated with posters and murals inspired – like the food and drinks – by Cuba. Draught beers are 20 to 24FF, cocktails 32 to 45FF, starters 34 to 46FF and the excellent main courses 54 to 86FF. It's open daily from noon to 3 pm and 5 pm to 2 am.

Hamilton's Fish & Chips – 51 Rue de Lappe (M13; ☎ 01 48 06 77 92; metro Ledru Rollin). Paris' one and only fish-and-chips shop gets good reviews from homesick Brits. A small/large battered cod is 22/30FF; chips cost 12/23FF. It is open weekdays from noon to 2.30 pm and 6 pm to midnight (1 am on Friday) and on Saturday from noon to 1 am.

La Pirada Bar Tapas – 7 Rue de Lappe (☎ 01 47 00 73 61; metro Bastille). This popular place also has live music at night. Other nearby Tex-Mex options are *Café 66* (named after Route 66) at No 8 and *Del Rio Café* at No 26.

Barbecue Coréen Chez Heang – 5 Rue de la Roquette (M13; ☎ 01 48 07 80 98; metro Bastille). You cook your food on a gas grill in the middle of your table at this turquoise (outside) and pink and grey (inside) Korean barbecue restaurant. *Menus* are 68 to 148FF. It is open daily from noon to 2.30 pm and 6.30 to midnight.

Restaurant Babylon – 21 Rue Daval (M13; ☎ 01 47 00 55 02; metro Bastille). This small Middle Eastern grill has excellent shwarma (20FF takeaway, 25FF eat in) and falafel. The tables are round and very tiny. It is open Monday to Saturday from 11 am to 1 am.

La Magnani – 21 Rue Chanzy (M13; ☎ 01 43 71 27 48; metro Charonne). At this pleasant Italian restaurant main courses are in the 50 to 80FF range and there's a *menu* at 98FF. It's open daily except Sunday.

Self-Catering

There are lots of *food shops* and supermarkets along Rue de la Roquette up toward Place Léon Blum (metro Voltaire). There's a *Monoprix* at 97 Rue du Faubourg Saint Antoine (metro Ledru Rollin), diagonally across the intersection from *Ed l'Épicier*, the discount supermarket store.

RUE OBERKAMPF & RUE DE BELLEVILLE

In the northern part of the 11e, east of Place de la République, Rue Oberkampf and Rue de Belleville are becoming increasingly popular at night, particularly for their low-priced ethnic restaurants. Rue de Belleville is dotted with Chinese, Vietnamese and Turkish places.

Au Trou Normand – 9 Rue Jean-Pierre Timbaud (M9; ☎ 01 48 05 80 23; metro Oberkampf). Hosted by a trio of grannies, this very French and very cosy little restaurant has some of the lowest prices in Paris. Starters are 10 to 15FF, main courses from 30FF.

Aux Délices du Cameroun – 69 Rue Jean-Pierre Timbaud (M9; ☎ 01 43 55 50 51; metro Parmentier). In complete contrast, here's African food with main courses at 65 to 90FF. It's closed Saturday lunch time and on Sunday.

Le Café Charbon – 109 Rue Oberkampf (M9; ☎ 01 43 57 55 13; metro Parmentier). More café than restaurant, Saturday or Sunday brunch for 70FF is just right at a place that's not too chic, not too trendy, not too young and not too conservative.

Favela Chic – 131 Rue Oberkampf (M9; ☎ 01 43 57 15 47; metro
  Ménilmontant). Very branché Brazilian is the story at this
  small place with main courses at 40 to 70FF.

La Piragua – 6 Rue Rochebrune (M13; ☎ 01 40 21 35 98; metro
  Saint Ambroise). Colombian food and good Latino music
  feature at this small and friendly restaurant. Count on
  around 200FF per person including wine; it's closed on
  Sunday.

PLACE DE LA NATION

There are lots of restaurants on the roads fanning out
from Place de la Nation.

Khun Akorn – 8 Ave de Taillebourg, 11e (M1; ☎ 01 43 56 20 03;
  metro Nation). In this airy Thai restaurant most main
  courses are 70 to 80FF. It's open for lunch and dinner daily
  except Monday.

CHINATOWN

Dozens of East Asian restaurants line the main streets of
Paris' Chinatown, including Ave de Choisy, Ave d'Ivry
and Rue Baudricourt. The cheapest *menus*, which go for
49FF, are usually available only at lunch on weekdays.

Château de Choisy – 44-46 Ave de Choisy, 13e (M1; ☎ 01 45 82
  40 60; metro Porte de Choisy). This Chinese-Vietnamese
  place has an all-you-can-eat buffet (10 starters and four
  mains) for 84 or 94FF (69FF for lunch on weekdays).

15e ARRONDISSEMENT

There are quite a few places to eat to the south of Blvd
de Grenelle.

Feyrous – 8 Rue de Lourmel, 15e (M10; ☎ 01 45 78 07 02; metro
  Dupleix). A bright, busy and outgoing Lebanese restaurant with *menus* at 58 and 80FF at lunch and 98FF at
  dinner. It's open daily from 7 am to 2 am.

Le Tipaza – 150 Ave Émile Zola, 15e (M10; ☎ 01 45 79 22 25;
  metro Émile Zola). This classy Moroccan restaurant has
  good couscous and other Moroccan specialities with
  menus at 75FF at lunch and 130FF at dinner.

Le Café du Commerce – 51 Rue du Commerce, 15e (M10; ☎ 01
  45 75 03 27; metro Émile Zola). Its slogan proclaims that
  there's 'finally a restaurant which is not à la mode', and
  inside this resolutely old-fashioned place you can enjoy
  traditional French dishes with *menus* at 85 or 110FF
  including a drink.

MONTMARTRE & PIGALLE

The restaurants along Rue des Trois Frères are a much better bet than their touristy counterparts at Place du Tertre. Many are open seven days a week but only for dinner.

French & European

Montmartre's French restaurants, like almost everything else on the Butte, are slightly offbeat, although there is a branch of *Batifol* at 3 Place Blanche.

Restaurant Le Petit Chose – 41 Rue des Trois Frères, 18e (M8; ☎ 01 42 64 49 15; metro Abbesses). This elegant, semiformal place serves traditional French cuisine (including some regional dishes) to the accompaniment of jazz and French chansons played on an old gramophone. The *menus* cost 95 and 160FF. It is open daily from 7 to 11 pm.

Refuge des Fondus – 17 Rue des Trois Frères, 18e (M8; ☎ 01 42 55 22 65; metro Abbesses). This establishment has been a Montmartre favourite since 1966. For 87FF you get an aperitif, hors d'œuvre, red wine in a baby bottle (or beer or soft drink) and a good quantity of either fondue Savoyarde (cheese) or fondue Bourguignonne (meat; minimum order for two). It is open daily from 7 pm to 2 am (last seating at midnight or 12.30 am). It's a good idea to phone ahead (at 5 or 6 pm) for reservations, especially at the weekend.

Il Duca – 26 Rue Yvone Le Tac, 18e (M8; ☎ 01 46 06 71 98; metro Abbesses). A neat, tidy, cosy and intimate little Italian restaurant with good, straightforward Italian food, including a lunch-time *menu* for 69FF and main courses at 70 to 82FF.

Other Cuisines

Montmartre has an incredible variety of non-European cuisines.

Le Mono – 40 Rue Véron, 18e (M8; ☎ 01 46 06 99 20; metro Abbesses or Blanche). The friendly Togolese woman who runs this unpretentious restaurant has been serving great West African cuisine for 20 years. Specialities – made with special imported ingredients – include lélé (flat, steamed cakes made from white beans and shrimp and served with tomato sauce; 25FF), mafé (beef or chicken served with peanut sauce; 50FF) and gbekui (a sort of goulash made with spinach, onions, beef, fish and shrimp; 55FF). Vegetarian dishes are prepared upon request. It is open from 7 pm to midnight (later on Friday and Saturday) except on Wednesday.

Restaurant Le Taroudant – 8 Rue Aristide Bruant, 18e (M8; ☎ 01 42 64 95 81; metro Abbesses). Couscous and tagines are served at this Moroccan restaurant for 65 to 100FF. It is closed on Wednesday.

Restaurant Copacabana – 32bis Rue des Trois Frères, 18e (M8; ☎ 01 42 62 24 96; metro Abbesses). Specialities at this Brazilian restaurant include feijoada (black beans and various meats prepared with green cabbage and manioc flour; 85FF). It is open daily from 7 pm until the people who order at midnight finish eating. There's live music after 9 pm at weekends.

Wou Ying – 24 Rue Durantin, 18e (M8; ☎ 01 42 51 24 44; metro Abbesses). This place, open daily from noon to 2.30 pm and 7 to 11.30 pm, is great for cheap Cantonese food, including a *menu* for only 44FF.

Self-Catering

Towards Pigalle there are lots of *groceries* – many of them open until late at night – on the side streets leading off Blvd de Clichy (eg Rue Lepic).

Fromagerie Tissot – 32 Rue des Abbesses, 18e (M8; metro Abbesses). This good fromagerie is closed from 1 to 4 pm and on Sunday and Monday. There is also a grocery at 37bis, open from 7.30 am to 9 or 9.30 pm (closed on Monday).

Charcutier Traiteur – 6 Rue des Trois Frères, 18e (M8; metro Abbesses). This store sells ready-to-eat gourmet dishes daily from 9.30 am to 8.30 pm.

Les Caves de Nîmes – 7bis Rue Tardieu, 18e (M8; metro Abbesses). This wine and cheese shop, next door to Charcutier Traiteur, is closed from 1.30 to 3.30 pm and on Wednesday.

Franprix – 44 Rue Caulaincourt, 18e (M8; metro Lamarck Caulaincourt). This supermarket is open Monday to Saturday from 8.30 am to 7.25 pm (7.45 pm on Friday and Saturday). There's an *Ed l'Épicier* supermarket (M8; metro Anvers) a block south of the bottom of the funiculaire at 31 Rue d'Orsel.

UNIVERSITY RESTAURANTS

Bad cafeteria food is available in copious quantities at Paris' 16 *restaurants universitaires* (student cafeterias), run by the Centre Régional des Œuvres Universitaires et Scolaires (CROUS; ☎ 01 40 51 37 10; by Minitel: 3615 CROUS). Tickets for institutional but filling three-course meals cost 13.20FF for students with ID, 21.10FF if you have an ISIC card (Carte Jeune Internationale) and 26.40FF for nonstudent guests.

CROUS restaurants (usually referred to as *restos U*) have variable opening times that change according to school holiday schedules and weekend rotational agreements. Even during the academic year, only about half are open for dinner; the weekend selection is even more limited. Only one university restaurant stays open during July; a different one is on duty during August. Monthly schedules are generally posted at ticket windows, some of which are open only on weekdays at lunch time. In general, lunch is served from 11.30 am to sometime between 1.45 and 3.30 pm, while dinner time is 6 or 6.30 to 7.45 pm.

About half of the CROUS cafeterias are in the 5e and 6e arrondissements. They include:

Assas – 92 Rue d'Assas (7th floor), 6e (M11; ☎ 01 46 33 61 25; metro Port Royal, Notre Dame des Champs), in the Université de Paris' Faculté de Droit et des Sciences Économiques (Law & Economics Faculty). The ticket window is on the 6th floor.

Châtelet – 8 Rue Jean Calvin, just off Rue Mouffetard, 5e (M14; ☎ 01 43 31 51 66; metro Censier Daubenton).

Bullier – 39 Ave G Bernanos (2nd floor) in Centre Jean Sarrailh, 5e (M14; ☎ 01 43 54 93 38; metro Port Royal).

Mabillon – 3 Rue Mabillon (3rd floor), 6e (M14; ☎ 01 43 25 66 23; metro Mabillon).

Entertainment

ENTERTAINMENT GUIDES

It's virtually impossible to make plans to sample the richness of Paris' entertainment scene without at least perusing *Pariscope* (3FF at any newspaper kiosk) or *L'Officiel des Spectacles* (2FF), both of which come out on Wednesday.

You can hear recorded, English-language information on concerts and other events, prepared by the Paris tourist office, by calling ☎ 01 49 52 53 56 (24 hours).

BOOKING AGENCIES

You can buy tickets for many (but not all) cultural events at several ticket outlets, among them FNAC (1er; M12; ☎ 01 40 41 40 00; metro Châtelet-Les Halles) at 1-7 Rue Pierre Lescot and Virgin Megastore (8e; M7; ☎ 01 49 53 50 50) at 60 Ave des Champs-Élysées. Both accept reservations and ticketing by phone only if you can pay, by post, in French francs with a personal cheque, Eurocheque or *mandat postal* (postal money order). Credit card bookings are not accepted by phone. Tickets cannot be returned or exchanged unless a performance is cancelled.

Reservations for a wide variety of theatre and opera productions can be made using the Minitel (3615 THEA).

DISCOUNT TICKETS

On the day of a performance, the two Kiosque Théâtre outlets (no phone) sell theatre tickets for 50% off the usual price (plus a commission of 16FF). The seats on offer are always the most desirable (in the orchestra or 1st balcony). Tickets to concerts, operas and ballets may also be available.

Both Kiosque Théâtre outlets – across from 15 Place de la Madeleine (8e; M7; metro Madeleine) and halfway between Gare Montparnasse and the nearby Tour Montparnasse (15e; M11; metro Montparnasse Bienvenüe) – are open Tuesday to Saturday from 12.30 to 8 pm and on Sunday from 12.30 to 4 pm.

CINEMAS

Pariscope and *L'Officiel des Spectacles* list the cinematic offerings alphabetically by their French title. Parisian movie-going does not come cheap: expect to pay around 45 to 50FF for a ticket. Students and people under 18 and over 60 usually get discounts of about 25% except on Friday, Saturday and Sunday nights. On Wednesday (and sometimes Monday), most cinemas give discounts to everyone.

If a movie is labelled 'VO' (version originale) it means it will be subtitled rather than dubbed, so Hollywood movies will still be in English. The French cinematic enthusiasm goes far beyond the borders of France; the French passion for Jerry Lewis is well known and Woody Allen movies have a huge following in Paris.

Cinémathèque Française

This government-supported cultural institution (☎ 01 45 53 21 86 or, for a recording, 01 47 04 24 24) almost always leaves its foreign offerings – often seldom-screened classics – in VO. Screenings take place in the far-eastern tip of the Palais de Chaillot on Ave Albert de Mun (16e; M10; metro Trocadéro or Iéna) and at 18 Rue du Faubourg du Temple (11e; M9; metro République). Tickets cost 30FF.

DISCOTHÈQUES

A *discothèque* is just about any sort of place where music leads to dancing. The truly branché crowd considers showing up before 1 am a breach of good taste.

The discothèques favoured by the Parisian 'in' crowd change frequently, and many are officially private. Single men may not be admitted, even if their clothes are subculturally appropriate, simply because they're single men. Women, on the other hand, get in for free on some nights. Generally, though, none of this comes cheap.

Le Balajo – 9 Rue de Lappe, 11e (M13; ☎ 01 47 00 07 87; metro Bastille). A mainstay of the Parisian dance-hall scene since the days of Edith Piaf. The DJs spin the LPs and CDs (rock, disco, funk etc) Wednesday to Saturday nights from 11.30 pm to 5.30 am; dancing begins in earnest at 2 or 3 am. Admission costs 100FF (80FF on Wednesday) and includes one drink. Women can wear pretty much whatever they want, but men should be a bit dressed up. On Friday, Saturday and Sunday afternoons from 3 to 7 pm, DJs play old-fashioned *musette* (accordion music) – waltz, tango, cha-cha – for aficionados of *rétro* tea dancing. Entry is 40FF on Saturday and 50FF on Sunday, including a drink.

La Chapelle des Lombards – 19 Rue de Lappe, 11e (M13; ☎ 01 43 57 24 24; metro Bastille). Antillean, African and South American beats make for a very lively dance scene. Something of a pick-up place, and attracting a more mature crowd, it is open Tuesday to Saturday from 10.30 pm to 5 am (6 am on the weekend). Entry (including one drink) costs 100FF (120FF on Friday and Saturday night). Jeans and running shoes are not permitted.

La Locomotive – 90 Blvd de Clichy, 18e (M7; ☎ 01 42 57 37 37; metro Blanche), in Pigalle. An enormous ever-popular disco that's long been one of the best places in town for dancing until dawn. Music ranges from techno and 'groove sex music' (in the pulsating basement) to Top 40 (on the 1st floor); grunge, psychedelic, rock and the like dominate on the ground floor. It is open nightly from 11 pm (midnight on Monday) to 6 am (7 am on weekends). Entrance costs 70FF (105FF on Friday and Saturday), including one drink. On Sunday night, it's 70FF for men and women pay just 15FF – and even that is deducted from the price of an optional first drink. Dress rules are mellow: jogging suits and sandals are out but almost everything else is decidedly in.

Le Palace – 8 Rue du Faubourg Montmartre, 9e (M8; ☎ 01 42 46 10 87; metro Rue Montmartre). The main dance floor and the bar on the 1st floor are mixed (gay and straight). On Friday and Saturday nights, the basement is reserved for women. It is open from 11.30 pm to 6 am (closed Monday nights). The cover charge (including one drink) is 50, 80 or 100FF. The only real dress rule: sneakers don't cut it. Le Palace's enduringly popular gay tea dance (men only) is held on Sunday from 5 pm (4 pm from October to early May) to 11 pm. Entry costs 60FF including a drink.

L'Entr'acte & Le Scorpion – 25 Blvd Poissonière, 2e (M8; ☎ 01 40 26 01 93; metro Rue Montmartre). On the ground floor: L'Entr'acte, for lesbians only, is open nightly from 11 pm (midnight on Saturday) to 6 am (7 am on Saturday and Sunday mornings). There's no cover charge except on Saturday night. In the cellar: Le Scorpion, gay and straight, is open nightly from midnight to 7 am. There's no cover charge except on Friday and Saturday nights. The music in both sections is mainly techno. Unaccompanied men are not admitted; neither are people wearing jogging suits or military-style clothes.

Queen – 102 Ave des Champs-Élysées, 8e (M6 & M7; ☎ 01 42 89 31 32; metro George V). The most popular gay disco in town (and open to everybody most nights if they can get in) hosts some of the most outrageous theme parties in Paris. Queen is open seven days a week from midnight to dawn. There's no cover charge except on Friday and Saturday nights (80FF, including a drink).

Slow Club – 130 Rue de Rivoli, 1er (M12; ☎ 01 42 33 84 30; metro Châtelet). An unpretentious disco housed in a deep cellar once used to ripen Caribbean bananas. The live bands attract students as well as older couples. The music varies from night to night but includes jazz, boogie and blues. It is open Tuesday to Saturday from 10 pm to 3 am (4 am on Friday and Saturday nights); often crowded after 1.30 am, especially on weekends. The cover charge is 60FF (75FF on Friday and Saturday); students get a small discount. Don't come in shorts, ripped jeans or running shoes.

La Scala de Paris – 188 Rue de Rivoli, 1er (M7; ☎ 01 42 61 64 00; metro Palais Royal). A large disco whose three dance floors and five bars are lit by thousands of little flashing lights. The patrons are mostly in the 18-30 age group and come from all over Europe. It is open nightly from 10.30 pm to dawn. Entry costs 80FF (100FF on Saturday night), including one drink. Women get in for free from Sunday to Thursday except on the eve of public holidays. Jeans and running shoes are OK so long as they're clean and expensive.

Club Zed – 2 Rue des Anglais, 5e (M14; ☎ 01 43 54 93 78; metro Maubert Mutualité), one block north of 70 Blvd Saint Germain. An arched stone basement where the DJs favour rock'n'roll, jazz and the tango. Wednesday is rock night. It is open Wednesday to Saturday from 10.30 pm to 3 am (5 am on Friday and Saturday nights). Entrance costs 50FF (100FF on Friday and Saturday), including a drink. Don't come sloppily dressed (ie no T-shirts) and note that *garçons non accompagnés* may not get in.

La Java – 105 Rue du Faubourg du Temple, 10e (M9; ☎ 01 42 02 20 52; metro Belleville). The original dance hall where Piaf got her first break now reverberates to the sounds of Brazilian and Cuban music, Friday and Saturday nights until 5 am.

Les Bains – 7 Rue du Bourg l'Abbé, 3e (M15; ☎ 01 48 87 01 80; metro Étienne Marcel). A renovated old Turkish bath that still seems to produce steam heat on particularly hot nights. Les Bains is renowned for its surly, selective bouncers on the outside and trendy, star-struck revellers inside.

La Casbah – 18-20 Rue de la Forge Royale, 11e (M13; ☎ 01 43 71 71 89; metro Ledru Rollin). You might want to brave the gorillas and the egos of this club just to check out the décor: over-the-top Moorish from floor to ceiling.

Le Tango – 13 Rue au Maire, 3e (M15; ☎ 01 42 72 17 78; metro Arts et Métiers). An African club on the boil most nights and popular with the frotti/frotta ('rubbing') set. Le Tango is *not* for the shy.

THEATRE

Almost all of Paris' theatre productions, including those written in other languages, are performed in French. There are a few English-speaking troupes around, though – look for ads on metro poster boards and in

English-language periodicals (eg *FUSAC*). For details on the Théâtre du Tourtour, see Other Music Venues.

Comédie Française – 2 Rue de Richelieu, next to the Palais Royal, 1er (M12; ☎ 01 40 15 00 15; metro Palais Royal). The world's oldest national theatre, founded in 1680 under Louis XIV. Its repertoire is based on the works of such French theatrical luminaries as Corneille, Molière, Racine, Beaumarchais, Marivaux and Musset, though in recent years contemporary and even non-French works have been staged. As the beneficiary of some US$26 million in annual state subsidies, it is partly run by the 34 members of the permanent troupe, known as *sociétaires*, who enjoy job security and jealously guarded perks.

The box office is open daily from 11 am to 6 pm. Telephone reservations with credit card payments are possible on weekdays from 2 to 5.30 pm. Tickets for regular seats cost from 50 to 175FF and can be purchased up to 14 days ahead. Tickets for places near the ceiling (25FF) go on sale 45 minutes before curtain time, which is when – subject to availability – people under 25 and students under 27 can purchase any of the better seats remaining for only 50FF.

Odéon Théâtre de l'Europe – Place de l'Odéon, 6e (M14; ☎ 01 44 41 36 36; by Minitel: 3615 ODEON; metro Odéon). This huge, ornate theatre, built in the early 1780s, often puts on foreign plays in their original languages (subtitled in French) and hosts theatre troupes from abroad (30 to 170FF).

The box office is open daily from 11 am to 7 pm. Tickets can be purchased over the phone with a credit card. People over 60 get a discount on the pricier tickets, while students and people under 26 who purchase a Carte Complice Jeune can get good reserved seats at low prices. Half-price tickets are available to anyone 50 minutes before curtain time.

CABARET

Paris' risqué cancan revues – those dazzling, pseudo-bohemian productions featuring hundreds of performers, including female dancers both with and without elaborate costumes – are about as representative of 1990s Paris as crocodile wrestling is of 1990s Australia.

Moulin Rouge – 82 Blvd de Clichy, 18e (M7 & M8; ☎ 01 46 06 00 19; metro Blanche). This legendary cabaret, whose dancers appeared in Toulouse-Lautrec's famous posters, sits under its trademark red windmill (a 1925 copy of the original). Tickets cost 230FF (including a drink) if you stand at the bar; if you prefer to sit down the price jumps to 495FF including half a bottle of champagne. Dinner (at 8 pm) costs 720FF, including champagne. There are shows nightly at 10 pm and, except sometimes in winter, at midnight.

Paradis Latin – 28 Rue du Cardinal Lemoine, 5e (M12; ☎ 01 43 25 28 28; metro Cardinal Lemoine). This establishment is known for its extravagant, nonstop performances of songs, dances and nightclub numbers. The whole staff, including the waiters, often participate. The show begins at 9.45 pm every night except Tuesday and costs 465FF, including half a bottle of champagne or two drinks. Dinner (680FF) begins at 8 pm.

Folies Bergères – 32 Rue Richer, 9e (M8; ☎ 01 44 79 98 98; metro Cadet). Famous for its high-kicking, feather-clad dancers. Tuesday to Saturday, 9 pm; Saturday and Sunday, 3 pm. The show alone is 150 to 320FF; dinner and the show is 535 to 690FF.

Crazy Horse Saloon – 12 Ave George V, 8e (M6 & M7; ☎ 01 47 23 32 32; metro Alma Marceau). The Crazy Horse boasts it has *l'art du nu*; it also had Woody Allen in its dressing (or undressing) rooms in his very first film, *What's New Pussycat?* There are two shows nightly Sunday to Friday, and three shows on Saturday. Prices range from 220FF at the bar with one drink, step by step up to 750FF for the show and dinner.

Le Lido – 116bis Ave des Champs-Élysées, 8e (M6; ☎ 01 40 76 56 10; metro George V). The floorshow gets top marks for the grandiose sets and lavish costumes. Operating since 1946, the nightly shows at 10 pm and midnight cost 510FF for the show with a half bottle of champagne, 345FF to watch from the bar with two drinks and 760 to 940FF for the show and dinner.

CLASSICAL MUSIC & OPERA

The Opéra National de Paris now splits its performances between Opéra Garnier, its old home, and Opéra Bastille, opened in 1989. Both opera houses also stage ballets and concerts put on by the Opéra National's affiliated orchestra, choirs and ballet company. The opera season lasts from mid-September to mid-July.

Paris plays host to dozens of orchestral, organ and chamber music concerts each week.

Opéra Bastille – 2-6 Place de la Bastille, 12e (M13; ☎ 01 44 73 13 99 for enquiries, 01 44 73 13 00 for reservations, 01 43 43 96 96 for a recording in French; by Minitel: 3615 OPERA-PARIS; metro Bastille). Telephone lines are staffed from 11 am to 6 pm daily except Sunday and holidays. It's possible to make reservations by phone from abroad – just make sure you pay for the tickets at least one hour before curtain time. Credit cards are accepted only at the box office, which is open Monday to Saturday from 11 am to 6.30 pm. Ticket sales begin 14 days before the date of the performance.

Opera tickets cost 145 to 590FF. To have a shot at the worst seats in the house (60FF), you have to stop by the ticket office (open Monday to Saturday from 11 am to 6.30 pm) the day tickets go on sale, ie exactly 14 days before the performance you'd like to see (on a Monday if the performance is on a Sunday). Ballets cost 110 to 370FF (50FF for the cheapest seats). Concerts are 85 to 230FF (45FF for the least expensive seats).

If there are unsold tickets, people under 25 or over 65 and students can get excellent seats for about 100FF only 15 minutes before the curtain goes up. Ask for the *tarif spécial*.

Opéra Garnier – Place de l'Opéra, 9e (M7 & M8; same phone and Minitel numbers as Opéra Bastille; metro Opéra). Ticket prices and conditions (including last-minute discounts) are about the same as at Opéra Bastille. For certain non-opera performances, the cheapest regular tickets, which get you a seat with an obstructed view, cost as little as 20 or 30FF.

Opéra Comique – 5 Rue Favart, 2e (M8; ☎ 01 42 44 45 46 for reservations; metro Richelieu Drouot). A century-old hall that plays host to classic and less well known works of opera. The season lasts from late October to early July. Tickets, available from FNAC or Virgin, cost 90 to 490FF; 50FF tickets are available starting 14 days before the performance at the box office (opposite 14 Rue Favart), open Monday to Saturday from 11 am to 7 pm. Subject to availability, students and the young and the old can get big discounts 15 minutes before curtain time.

Théâtre de la Ville – Place du Châtelet, on the eastern side, 4e (M14; ☎ 01 42 74 22 77; metro Châtelet). A municipal hall that plays host to theatre, dance and all kinds of music, with tickets from 80 to 180FF. Depending on availability, people under 25 and students can buy up to two tickets at a 30 to 50% discount on the day of the performance. Credit cards are accepted at the ticket office, which is open Monday to Saturday from 9 am to 8 pm (6 pm on Monday) and on Sunday one hour before the curtain rises. There are no performances in July and August.

Théâtre Musical de Paris – Place du Châtelet, on the western side, 1er (M14; ☎ 01 40 28 28 98 for information, 01 40 28 28 40 for reservations; by Minitel: 3615 CHATELET; metro Châtelet). Named on its exterior as the Théâtre Municipal du Châtelet, this hall plays host to operas (200 to 750FF for the better seats, 60 to 80FF for seats with limited visibility), ballets (90 to 200FF), concerts (including some by the excellent Orchestre de Paris) and theatre performances. Classical music is performed on Sunday at 11.30 am (80FF, free for under 12s) and on Monday, Wednesday and Friday at 12.45 pm (50FF).

The ticket office is open daily from 11 am to 7 pm (8 pm on performance nights); tickets go on sale 14 days before the performance date. Subject to availability, students and people under 25 or over 65 can get seats for all performances, except the operas, for 50FF starting 15 minutes before curtain time. There are no performances in July or August.

Théâtre des Champs-Élysées – 15 Ave Montaigne, 8e (M6 & M7; ☎ 01 49 52 50 50; metro Alma Marceau). A prestigious Right Bank orchestral and recital hall with popular Sunday-morning concerts (11 am).

Salle Pleyel – 252 Rue du Faubourg Saint Honoré, 8e (M6; ☎ 01 45 61 53 00; metro Ternes). A highly regarded, 1920s-era hall that hosts many of Paris' finest classical music concerts and recitals.

Cité de la Musique – in the south-eastern tip of Parc de la Villette on Ave Jean Jaurès, 19e (M1; ☎ 01 44 84 45 45 or, for reservations, 01 44 84 44 84; by Minitel: 3615 CITEMUSIQUE; metro Porte de Pantin). The oval, 1200-seat main auditorium, whose blocks of seats can be reconfigured to suit different types of performances, hosts every imaginable type of music and dance, from Western classical to North African and Japanese. Tickets, usually available from FNAC and Virgin, cost 100 and 160FF for evening concerts. Concerts in the little auditorium on Friday, Saturday and Sunday cost 75FF. The Sunday afternoon performances, which start at 4.30 pm, cost 60 and 100FF; discounts are available for groups of three or more for afternoon concerts.

The 1250 students of the Conservatoire National Supérieur de Musique et de Danse (National Higher Conservatory of Music & Danse; ☎ 01 40 40 45 45) – which is on the other side of the Fontaine aux Lions (Lions Fountain) from the Cité de la Musique – put on free orchestra concerts and recitals several times a week, in the afternoon and/or evening.

Church Venues

Some of the performances held in Paris' historic churches are free, such as those at Notre Dame Cathedral each Sunday at 5.30 pm. From April to October, classical concerts are also held in the Sainte Chapelle (M14; ☎ 01 44 07 12 38) on the Île de la Cité (4e); the cheapest seats are about 100FF (80FF for students under 25). Other noted concert venues are Église Saint Eustache (1er), Église Saint Sulpice (6e), Église Saint Germain des Prés (6e), Église de la Madeleine (8e) and Église Saint Pierre de Montmartre (18e).

Museum Venues

Museums featuring concert series include the Musée du Louvre (☎ 01 40 20 53 17), which holds a series of midday and evening chamber music concerts from September to June; the Musée d'Orsay (☎ 01 40 49 48 84); and the Centre Pompidou (☎ 01 44 78 13 15), where music from

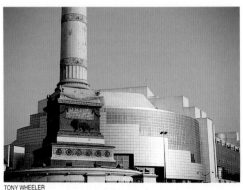

TONY WHEELER

Opéra Bastille in Place de la Bastille

contemporary and avant-garde musicians is performed at the Institut de Recherche et de Coordination Acoustique/Musique (IRCAM).

Other Concert Venues

The city's numerous smaller-scale venues for concerts include:

New Morning – across the street from 10 Rue des Petites Écuries, 10e (M8; ☎ 01 45 23 51 41 for recorded information, 01 42 31 31 31 for reservations; metro Château d'Eau). An informal auditorium that hosts concerts of jazz, funk, salsa, Brazilian music, world music etc three to seven nights a week at 9 or 9.30 pm. The second set ends at about 1 am. Tickets (110 to 130FF), available from FNAC and Virgin, can usually be purchased at the door.

Café de la Danse – 5 Passage Louis-Philippe, 11e (M13; ☎ 01 47 00 57 59 or, for reservations, 01 43 43 28 60; metro Bastille). An auditorium with 300 to 500 seats located only a few metres from 23 Rue de Lappe. Almost every evening at 8 or 8.30 pm, it plays host to rock concerts, dance performances, musical theatre and poetry readings. Tickets (50 to 150FF) are available from FNAC.

Théâtre du Tourtour – 20 Rue Quincampoix, 4e (M15; ☎ 01 48 87 82 48; metro Châtelet). An intimate, 123-seat theatre in a 15th-century cellar. There's something on every night from Tuesday to Saturday: plays by young theatre companies at 7 pm (90FF); classical or modern plays by more experienced actors at 8.30 pm (100FF); and music – anything from rock to French chansons – at 10.15 pm (90FF). Students and people under 25 or over 65 get a 20FF discount. Reservations can be made by phone, usually on the day of the performance, and you can pick up your tickets 20 minutes before show time. Tickets are also available at FNAC and the discount Kiosque Théâtre.

ROCK

Rock concerts are listed in *Pariscope* and *L'Officiel des Spectacles* but you'll get a better idea of what's on by checking booking counters at Virgin or FNAC or by picking up a copy of *LYLO* (an acronym for Les Yeux, Les Oreilles; ie The Eyes, The Ears), a free magazine with excellent listings of rock concerts and other live music. Minitel 3615 LYLO will supply more information.

There's rock at numerous bars, cafés and clubs around Paris, plus a host of venues regularly put on acts by big international performers. It's often easier to see anglophone acts in Paris than back in their home countries. Typically, tickets cost 120 to 220FF. Some of the popular venues for international acts include Zenith at the Cité de la Musique, Bercy, Elysée Montmartre and Olympia.

JAZZ

After WW II, Paris was Europe's most important jazz centre and is again very much à la mode these days; the city's better *boîtes* (clubs) continue to attract top international stars. The Banlieues Bleues (☎ 01 43 85 66 00), a

RICHARD NEBESKY

Rock posters in the Bastille area

jazz festival held in Saint Denis and other Paris suburbs in late March and early April, attracts big-name talent.

For information on New Morning, see Other Concert Venues earlier.

Caveau de la Huchette – 5 Rue de la Huchette, 5e (M14; ☎ 01 43 26 65 05; metro Saint Michel). A medieval *caveau* (cellar) – used as a courtroom and torture chamber during the Revolution – where virtually all the jazz greats have played since 1946. It is open nightly from 9.30 pm to 2.30 am (3.30 am on Friday, 4 am on Saturday and the night before public holidays); sessions begin at 10.15 pm.

The cover charge is 60FF (55FF for students) during the week, 70FF (no discounts) on Friday, Saturday and the night before holidays. Fruit juice/beer start at 22/26FF. Details on coming attractions are posted on the door; the bands change every week or so.

Le Baiser Salé – 58 Rue des Lombards, 1er (M12; ☎ 01 42 33 37 71; metro Châtelet). One of three very hip jazz clubs on the same street (see the following two venues) at which a single membership card (150FF a year) gets you significant discounts. The *salle de jazz* on the 1st floor has concerts of Afro jazz, jazz fusion etc nightly from 10 or 10.30 pm to 3 am. The cover charge is 50 to 70FF (more but including a drink) for the Wednesday jam sessions. On some nights, there's also music (variety shows, rock, blues, jazz) from 8 to 9 pm. The ground-floor bar is open daily from 7 pm to 6 am.

Le Sunset – 60 Rue des Lombards, 1er (M12; ☎ 01 40 26 46 60; metro Châtelet). Musicians and actors (cinema and theatre) are among the jazz fans who hang out at this branché club, whose cellar hosts live concerts of funk, Latino, be-bop and the like nightly from 10 pm to 5 or 6 am. Entry costs 78FF, including a drink; subsequent liquid refreshment is 28FF a go. At the ground-floor bar and restaurant, you can eat until 3 am (closed Sunday); *menus* are 75 and 120FF.

Au Duc des Lombards – 42 Rue des Lombards, 1er (M12; ☎ 01 42 33 22 88; metro Châtelet). An ultra-cool venue decorated with posters of past jazz greats that attracts a far more relaxed (and less reverent) crowd than other jazz venues. The ground-floor bar area vibrates nightly from 10 pm to 4 or 5 am. The cover charge is 50 to 70FF; drinks are 28 to 68FF. Jam sessions take place on the first Tuesday of every month.

La Villa – 29 Rue Jacob, 6e (M14; ☎ 01 43 26 60 00; metro Saint Germain des Prés). This very cool, high-tech place attracts big-name performers from the USA, the rest of Europe and Japan, with local talent thrown in for good measure between sets.

Latitudes – 7-11 Rue Saint Benoît, 6e (M14; ☎ 01 42 61 53 53; metro Saint Germain des Prés). Close to La Villa, Latitudes features a more varied assortment of musicians in a stylish club.

Hot Brass – 211 Ave Jean Jaurès, 19e (M1; ☎ 01 42 00 54 44; metro Porte de Pantin). Serious jazz aficionados won't mind making the trip to this eclectic club, where they can listen to anything from Latin and swing to acid and hip-hop in a bright-red pavilion in the Parc de la Villette.

FRENCH CHANSONS

For details on accordion music at Le Balajo, see Discothèques.

Restaurant du Croquenote – 22 Passage des Panoramas, 2e (M8; ☎ 01 42 33 60 70; metro Rue Montmartre). An intimate French restaurant with dinner (170FF) at 8 pm and chansons – in the styles of Brel, Léo Ferré and Félix Leclerc – at around 10 pm. It is closed on Sunday and in August. Call ahead to reserve a table.

Au Vieux Paris – 72 Rue de la Verrerie, 4e (M15; no phone; metro Hôtel de Ville). An old-time Paris bar (closed Sunday and Monday) that hosts sing-alongs of French chansons, accompanied by an accordionist and Madame Françoise, the feisty proprietress (sheet music provided). The music begins at about 11.45 pm on Thursday, Friday and Saturday nights. The patrons are mostly young Parisians. Come by at around 11 pm to get a seat.

Le Lapin Agile – 22 Rue des Saules, 18e (☎ 01 46 06 85 87; metro Lamarck Caulaincourt). A rustic cabaret venue favoured by turn-of-the-century artists and intellectuals. In 1911 the writer Roland Dorgelès, known for his hatred of modern art, tied a paintbrush to the tail of a donkey and – with the unwitting help of Guillaume Apollinaire, a Lapin Agile regular and a noted exponent of Cubism – managed to get the resulting mess into the Salon des Indépendants art show under the title *Sunset over the Adriatic*.
_20 These days, chansons are performed and poetry read nightly, except Monday, from 9 pm to 2 am. Entry costs 110FF (80FF for students except on Saturday and holidays), including a drink.

Le Piano Zinc – 49 Rue des Blancs Manteaux, 4e (M15; ☎ 01 42 74 32 42; metro Rambuteau). An informal, mainly gay establishment with three levels, including a basement room where, after 10 pm, a pianist accompanies members of the audience overcome by the desire to sing Piaf and Brel favourites. It is open from 6 pm to 2 am; the basements are closed on Monday. There's no cover charge except on Friday, Saturday and the eve of public holidays, when you have to buy a drink. Happy hour is held from 6 to 8 pm.

Chez Louisette – in the Marché aux Puces de Saint Ouen (see Flea Markets under Things to Buy; M1; ☎ 01 40 12 10 14; metro Porte de Clignancourt). One of the highlights of a visit to Paris' largest flea market. Market-goers crowd around little tables to eat lunch and hear an old-time *chanteuse* belt out Edith Piaf numbers to the accompaniment of an accordion. It is open from noon to 6 or 7 pm on Saturday, Sunday and Monday. Main dishes are 65 to 135FF. Chez Louisette is inside the maze of Marché Vernaison not far from 130 Ave Michelet, the boulevard on the other side of the highway from the Porte de Clignancourt metro stop.

PUBS/BARS

1er & 2e Arrondissements

The area around Forum des Halles is filled with 'in' places for a drink.

Café Oz – 18 Rue Saint Denis, 1er (M12; metro Châtelet). An Aussie pub bubbling with the same Down Under, down-home friendliness as the original across the river – see 5e Arrondissement (Latin Quarter) for details.

Willi's Wine Bar – 13 Rue des Petits Champs, 1er (M8; ☎ 01 42 61 05 09; metro Bourse). A civilised yet innovative wine bar run by two British expats with very discerning palates who introduced the wine-bar concept to Paris a decade ago. The lunch *menu* is 140FF, dinner is 180FF. It is open Monday to Saturday from noon to 11 pm.

Joe Allen – 30 Rue Pierre Lescot, 1er (M15; ☎ 01 42 36 70 13; metro Étienne Marcel). A very American bar with great atmosphere and a good selection of Californian wines.

Gay & Lesbian While the Marais is the main centre of gay life in Paris, there are some decent bars west of Blvd de Sébastopol, too.

La Champmesl – 4 Rue Chabanais, 2e (M8; ☎ 01 42 96 85 20; metro Pyramides). A relaxed, dimly lit place that plays mellow music for its patrons, about 75% of whom are lesbians (the rest are mostly gay men). The back room is reserved for women only. Works by a different woman artist are displayed each month. Beer or fruit juice is 25FF. It is open daily from 6 pm to 2 am, and traditional French chansons are performed live every Thursday at 10 pm.

Le Vagabond – 14 Rue Thérèse, 1er (M8; ☎ 01 42 96 27 23; metro Pyramides). A bar/restaurant long popular with older gay men, some of whom have been patrons since the place was founded in 1957. It is open from 6 pm to 3 or 4 am (closed Monday). French cuisine is served from 8.30 pm to 12.15 am; the *menu* is 140FF. To get in, push the white button to the left of the door. For gay men only.

Marais (3e & 4e)

The 4e has quite a few lively places for daytime and after-hours drinks.

Louis-Philippe Café – 66 Quai de l'Hôtel de Ville, 4e (M15; ☎ 01 42 72 29 42; metro Pont Marie), facing the Seine. A mirror-lined café, founded in 1840, with a large terrace. It is open daily from 9 am to 2 am; coffee is 5/10FF at the bar/seated. The restaurant on the 1st floor, reached via a spiral stair-case, is open from noon to 3 pm and 7.30 to 11.30 pm. The 82FF weekday *menu* is not available in the evening during the warm months.

La Tartine – 24 Rue de Rivoli, 4e (M15; ☎ 01 42 72 76 85; metro Saint Paul). A wine bar where little has changed since the

Cafés in the Bastille area

days of gas lighting (the fixtures are still in place). Offers 15 selected reds, whites and rosés for 9.50 to 15.50FF a glass. There's not much to eat except sandwiches and, of course, tartines (5FF). It is open from 8.30 am (noon on Wednesday) to 10 pm (closed Tuesday).

Piment Café – 15 Rue de Sévigné, 4e (M15; ☎ 01 42 74 33 75; metro Saint Paul). This small and cosmopolitan bar changes faces frequently, with tranquil moments punctuated by live music, art on show and good food.

Les Etages – 35 Rue Vieille du Temple, 4e (M15; ☎ 01 42 78 72 00; metro Hôtel de Ville). Head upstairs to the two upper floors for grunge, with graffiti on the walls and big leather armchairs. The drinks aren't cheap but you do get to phone your order on an ancient 1950s phone.

Au Petit Fer à Cheval – 30 Rue Vieille du Temple, 4e (M15; ☎ 01 42 72 47 47; metro Hôtel de Ville). A slightly offbeat bar/restaurant named after its horseshoe-shaped counter; often filled to overflowing with friendly, mostly straight young regulars. The plat du jour changes each day. The all stainless-steel bathroom is straight out of a Flash Gordon film. It is open daily from 9 am (11 am on weekends) to 2 am. Food is available nonstop from noon.

La Chaise au Plafond – 10 Rue du Trésor, 4e (M15; ☎ 01 42 76 03 22, metro Hôtel de Ville). Owned by the same people as Au Petit Fer à Cheval and has a similar cybertoilet. It's warm and wooden with tables outside on a pedestrian-only backstreet. Open daily until 2 am.

Le Pick Clops – Corner of Rue de Roi du Sicile and Rue Vieille du Temple, 4e (M15; metro Hôtel de Ville). Cheap drinks and a great place to watch the world go by on this busy corner.

Stolly's – 16 Rue de la Cloche Percée, 4e (M15; ☎ 01 42 76 06 76; metro Hôtel de Ville). Just off Rue du Rivoli, this Anglo-Saxon bar is always overcrowded, particularly during the 5 to 8 pm happy hour. It's open daily, there are chairs on the pavement and a demi of Guinness is 25FF.

Café des Phares – Place Bastille, 4e (M13; ☎ 01 42 72 04 70, metro Bastille). A pioneering 'philosopher café' where you can argue the meaning of life at 11 am on Sundays. Attempts to resurrect the Paris of Jean-Paul Sartre, but on a commercial basis, are very popular in the 1990s.

Gay & Lesbian

The Marais – especially the area around the intersection of Rue Vieille du Temple and Rue Sainte Croix de la Bretonnerie – has been Paris' main centre of gay social life since the early 1980s.

Bar de l'Hôtel Central – 33 Rue Vieille du Temple, 4e (M15; ☎ 01 48 87 99 33; metro Hôtel de Ville). Founded in 1980, this is one of the oldest gay bars in the city; the clientele is mostly male. A demi costs 15FF (18FF after 10 pm). It is open daily from 2 pm to 1 am (2 am on Friday and Saturday nights).

Amnesia Café – 42 Rue Vieille du Temple, 4e (M15; ☎ 01 42 72 16 94; metro Hôtel de Ville). A cosy, warmly lit and very popular place, most of whose clients are gay. Beers start at 14FF (19FF after 10 pm), cocktails at 45FF. Brunch *menus* are 85 and 125FF. It is open daily from 10 am to 2 am.

Quetzal Bar – on the corner of Rue des Mauvais Garçons (literally, Street of the Bad Boys) and Rue de la Verrerie, 4e (M15; ☎ 01 48 87 99 07; metro Hôtel de Ville). A neon-lit, ultramodern bar so popular with 30-something gay men that the clientele often spills out onto the sidewalk. A demi on tap is 15FF. It is open daily from 2 pm (4 pm on weekends) to 2 am. Happy hour is from 6 to 8 pm and 11 pm to midnight.

Duplex Bar d'Art – 25 Rue Michel Lecomte, 3e (M15; ☎ 01 42 72 80 86; metro Rambuteau). One of the oldest gay bars in Paris, this dark, avant-garde place doubles as something of an art gallery. A gay and lesbian students' group meets here every Wednesday from 8 to 11 pm. It is open daily from 8 pm to 2 am.

Latin Quarter (5e)

The Latin Quarter has Paris' highest concentration of bars catering to Anglophones.

Café Oz – 184 Rue Saint Jacques (M14; ☎ 01 43 54 30 48; metro Luxembourg). A casual, friendly Australian pub with Fosters on tap for 22FF and VB, Coopers, Cascade and Redback as other amber options, plus Australian wines from 20FF. An Aussie pie lunch with salad is 45FF. The nightly happy hour applies to cocktails only but beer is cheaper on Sunday afternoons. It is open daily from 11 am to 1.30 am and the Aussie staff are cluey about jobs, apartments etc.

Le Cloître – 19 Rue Saint Jacques (M14; ☎ 01 43 25 19 92; metro Saint Michel). An unpretentious, relaxed place where the mellow background music goes down well with the students who congregate here. There's beer and Guinness on tap and you can play chess in the back except after 10 pm on weekends and holidays, when it gets too crowded. It is open daily from 3 pm to 2 am.

Polly Maggoo – 11 Rue Saint Jacques (M14; ☎ 01 46 33 33 64; metro Saint Michel). An informal, friendly bar founded in 1967 and still spinning disks from the 1960s. The regulars include English speakers resident in Paris. Chess and backgammon can be played from noon to 8 pm and beer starts at 12FF (18FF after 10 pm). It is open daily from 1 pm to 4 or 5 am.

Le Violon Dingue – 46 Rue de la Montagne Sainte Geneviève (M14; no phone; Maubert Mutualité). A loud, lively and none-too-spotless American-style bar that attracts lots of English speakers in their early 20s. A pint of beer costs 20FF during the 7.30 to 10.30 pm happy hour – when most drinks are half-price – and 34FF the rest of the time. The

TONY WHEELER

Australian bar in the Latin Quarter (5e)

Superbowl (American football) and the NBA (basketball) play-offs are shown on the large-screen TV. It is open daily from 6 pm to 1.30 am (3.30 am on Friday and Saturday).

Le Rallye – 11 Quai de la Tournelle (M15; ☎ 01 43 54 29 65; metro Maubert Mutualité). A 1950s-style Provençal café whose speciality is, as you'd expect, pastis. Most of the daytime clients come from the quartier, some in search of the 50FF lunch *menu*, others to pick up their boules for a game of riverbank pétanque. The evening crowd is young, lively and from all over the city. It is open daily from 8 am to 2 am.

Chez Le Pompier – 13 Quai de la Tournelle (M15; ☎ 01 40 51 77 74; metro Maubert Mutualité). Popular mythology insists that all French women adore *les pompiers* (firemen), and here's a bar dedicated to them. Everything is red, the cocktails include *le baptême de feu* and you can descend from the 1st floor by a fireman's pole.

6e Arrondissement

The 6e has some of Paris most famous cafés.

Les Deux Magots – 170 Blvd Saint Germain (M11 & M14; ☎ 01 45 48 55 25; metro Saint Germain des Prés). A classic café, once the haunt of Jean-Paul Sartre and André Breton, whose name derives from the two wooden *magots* (grotesque figurines) of Chinese dignitaries. On the huge terrace (glassed-in in winter), you can sip coffee (22FF), beer on tap (28FF) and their famous home-made hot chocolate (30FF), served in steaming porcelain pitchers by waiters clad in long white aprons. A continental breakfast costs 80FF. Light meals are available. It is open daily from 7.30 am to 1.30 am.

Café de Flore – 172 Blvd Saint Germain (M11 & M14; ☎ 01 45 48 55 26; metro Saint Germain des Prés). An Art Deco-style café whose red banquettes, mosaic floors, mirrors and marble walls haven't changed since the days Jean Paul Sartre, Simone de Beauvoir, Albert Camus and Picasso sipped the house Pouilly-Fumé. The outdoor terrace (glassed-in in winter) is a sought-after place to sip beer (41FF for 40 cl). It is open daily from 7 am to 1.30 am.

Café de la Mairie – 8 Place Saint Sulpice (M14; ☎ 01 43 26 67 82; metro Saint Sulpice). A bustling and slightly tacky café frequented by students, writers and, since the late 1980s, film producers attracted by its tattered Left Bank ambience. A beer costs 10FF at the counter, double that if you sit down. It is open Monday to Saturday from 7 am to 11 pm or midnight (2 am in the warm months).

Chez Georges – 11 Rue des Canettes (M11 & M14; ☎ 01 43 26 79 15; metro Mabillon). A friendly bar popular with people of all ages, whose smoke-darkened walls are decorated with photos of musicians who played here in the 1960s and 1970s. Beer in bottles starts at 15FF (18FF after 10 pm, 25FF in the cellar), and coffee is 6 to 10FF. It is open Tuesday to Saturday from noon to 2 am (closed in August). The dank cellar, suffused with mellow music, opens at 10 pm.

Le 10 – 10 Rue de l'Odéon (M14; ☎ 01 43 26 66 83; metro Odéon). A pub whose orange lighting adds a warm glow to the smoke-darkened posters on the walls. Popular with local and foreign university students and au pairs, many in their late teens or early 20s. The taped music ranges from jazz and the Doors to Yves Montand. The house speciality is sangria and the second glass is free for men from 5.30 until 8.30 pm and for women from 5.30 pm to 2 am. Beer in bottles is 22 to 32FF. It is open daily from 6 pm to 2 am.

Grands Boulevards (9e & 2e)

The Grands Boulevards are one of the Right Bank's major areas for a night on the town.

Harry's New York Bar – 5 Rue Daunou, 2e (M7 & M8; ☎ 01 42 61 71 14; metro Opéra). Back in the prewar years, when there were several dozen American-style bars in Paris, Harry's was one of the most popular – habitués included Ernest Hemingway and Scott Fitzgerald. The Cuban mahogany interior dates from the mid-19th century and was brought over lock, stock and barrel from Manhattan's 3rd Ave in 1911. Beer costs 28FF (35FF after 10 pm). Drinks at the basement piano bar – there's live music (usually soft jazz) nightly from 10 pm to 2 or 3 am – cost 40 to 70FF. It is open every day of the year except 24 and 25 December from 10.30 am to 4 am. The advertisement for Harry's in the *International Herald Tribune* still reads: 'Tell the Taxi Driver Sank Roo Doe Noo'.

11e Arrondissement (Bastille area)

The area just north of Place de la Bastille has become enormously popular for dining, drinking and dancing until all hours. Rue de Lappe, a dreary narrow laneway in the daytime, comes alive at night. See the Places to Eat chapter for details of some of the many popular bar/restaurants along Rue de Lappe, like the popular Cuban *Havanita* or other Spanish speakers like *La Pirada Bar Tapas*, *Café 66* and *Del Rio Café*.

Le Café du Passage – 12 Rue de Charonne (M13; ☎ 01 49 29 97 64; metro Ledru Rollin). A modern but laid-back wine bar where you can relax in upholstered armchairs while sampling 70 varieties of wine, 10 of them available by the glass (from 18FF). Light food is also available. It is open Monday to Saturday from 6 pm to 2 am.

Iguana Café – 15 Rue de la Roquette (M13; ☎ 01 40 21 39 99; metro Bastille). A chic, two-level café/pub that attracts exceptionally trendy people in their 20s and early 30s. Cocktails are 38 to 59FF; beer on tap is 20 to 28FF (24 to 32FF after 10 pm). It is open daily from 9 am to 5 am.

Rue Oberkampf (northern 11e)

East of Place de la République, Rue Oberkampf and Rue de Belleville are the new up and coming *branché* areas of Paris with a number of interesting cafés and bars, like the popular *Le Café Charbon* (see the Places to Eat chapter).

Cithéa – 112 Rue Oberkampf, 11e (M9; ☎ 01 40 21 70 95; metro Parmentier). This place has acid jazz and funk bands.

Café Cannibal – 93 Rue Jean Pierre Timbaud, 11e (M9; ☎ 01 49 29 95 59; metro Couronnes). So laid-back it's almost asleep, this cosy café and bar is a place where you can either linger over a coffee or grab a quick beer at the bar.

Montmartre & Pigalle (18e & 9e)

In between the sleaze there are some interesting bars at the bottom of the Montmartre hill.

Le Moloko – 26 Rue Fontaine, 9e (M8; ☎ 01 48 74 50 26; metro Blanche). An incredibly 'in' *bar de nuit* whose décor is an eclectic mix of the classic (red velvet) and the provocative. There's jukebox dancing (no charge to choose a tune) on the ground floor. Entry is free most nights, but not on Saturdays, when a female striptease show takes place on

a platform suspended between the two floors. It is open
daily from 10.30 pm to 5.30 or 6 am, but things don't start
to pick up until after midnight.

Bistrot Le Sancerre – 35 Rue des Abbesses, 18e (M8; ☎ 01 42 58
08 20; metro Abbesses). A popular, lively bistro/bar that's
often crowded in the evening. The cheapest beers cost
between 10FF (at the bar during the day) and 20FF (after
10 pm). It is open daily from 7 am to 2 am. Food, including
two plats du jour (55FF), is served from noon to 11 pm.

Le Dépanneur – 27 Rue Fontaine, 9e (M8; ☎ 01 40 16 40 20;
metro Blanche). An old standby whose unstoppable proprietor, Miss Tequila, dispenses same (25FF a shot) faster
than a speeding bullet. Beer is 20FF (35FF from 10 pm to
7 pm). Happy hour is from 6 to 8 pm. A limited selection
of food is always available. The copious brunch, served
from 9 am to 5 pm, costs 95FF. Come to this place and you
may never have to leave. It's open round the clock, seven
days a week.

SPECTATOR SPORT

Football & Rugby

France's national football team and the Paris-Saint
Germain (PSG) football club, one of the best teams in the
French first division, often play at the 50,000-seat Parc
des Princes (16e; M1; ☎ 01 44 26 45 45 for the box office;
metro Porte de Saint Cloud). Tickets are available
through Virgin's Champs-Élysées ticket outlet (see
Booking Agencies). The Parc des Princes also hosts
rugby matches (☎ 01 40 71 91 91 for ticket information),
a sport particularly popular in south-west France.

For details on upcoming sporting events, check the
newspapers, *Figaroscope* (published by *Le Figaro* each
Wednesday) or the colourful sports daily *L'Équipe*. Some
sporting events take place at the Palais Omnisports de
Paris-Bercy (M1; ☎ 01 44 68 44 68; metro Bercy) at 12 Blvd
de Bercy (12e).

Horse Racing

One of the cheapest ways to spend a relaxing afternoon
in the company of Parisians of all ages, backgrounds and
walks of life is to go to the races. The most accessible of
Paris' six racecourses is *Hippodrome d'Auteuil* (M1; ☎ 01
45 27 12 25, 01 49 10 20 26; metro Porte d'Auteuil) in the
south-east corner of the Bois de Boulogne (16e), which
hosts steeplechases from February to early July and from
early September to early December.

Races are held on Sunday as well as other days of the
week, with half a dozen or so heats scheduled between
2 and 5.30 pm. There's no charge to stand on the *pelouse*

(lawn) in the middle of the track; a seat in the *tribune* (stands) costs 25FF (40FF on Sunday and holidays, 50FF during special events). Race schedules are published in almost all national newspapers. If you can read a bit of French, pick up a copy of *Paris Turf*, the horse-racing weekly that comes out each Sunday.

To buy yourself a stake in the proceedings, you can place a bet – the minimum is only 10FF. Information on the horses and their owners, trainers and jockeys is available from the free programmes; additional statistics are printed in *Paris Turf*. The odds are displayed on TV screens near the betting windows. You can bet that your horse will come in *gagnant* (1st place), *placé* (1st or 2nd place) or *placé jumelé* (1st, 2nd or 3rd place). If your horse wins, take your ticket back to any betting window to collect your windfall, which, if you're lucky, will be enough for a beer or two.

Shopping

Paris has shopping options to suit all tastes and all budgets. Garments, for instance, can be selected at the ultra-chic couture houses along Ave Montaigne or plucked from flea-market tables.

BOOKSHOPS

Paris is justly famous for the writers who have graced its cafés, backstreets and boulevards. But a city's literary culture is only as good as its bookshops, and Paris has some of the best.

Shakespeare & Company – 37 Rue de la Bûcherie (5e; M14; no phone; metro Saint Michel). Paris' most famous English-language bookshop has a varied and unpredictable collection of new and used books in English, including novels from 10FF. It is open daily from about 10 am to midnight.

 _Poetry readings are held on most Mondays at 8 pm, and there are two libraries on the 1st floor. The shop is named after Sylvia Beach's bookshop at 12 Rue de l'Odéon (6e), which became famous for publishing James Joyce's *Ulysses* in 1922. It was closed by the Nazis in 1941.

Abbey Bookshop – 29 Rue de la Parcheminerie (5e; M14; ☎ 01 46 33 16 24; metro Cluny-La Sorbonne). A mellow place, not

TONY WHEELER

Shakespeare & Company

far from Place Saint Michel, known for having free tea and coffee, a supply of Canadian newspapers and a good selection of new and used works of fiction. Abbey has readings of prose and poetry about once a month, usually on a Wednesday night. It is open Monday to Saturday from 10 am to 7 pm; Sunday hours vary according to the owner's whim.

Odd Places to Shop

Parisians seem to have a number of special shopping interests, from tiny cars to weird comic books. Here's a selection:

EOL' Modelisme – 55 Rue Blvd St Germain, 5e (☎ 01 43 54 01 43; metro Maubert Mutualité), and two other nearby locations. This shop sells expensive toys for big boys, including every sort of model imaginable – from radio-controlled aircraft to huge wooden yachts. The shop right by the metro entrance has an amazing collection of tiny cars. You can pay over 1000FF for a 10-cm-long miniature version of a rare Ferrari, or a mundane Citroën 2CV for that matter.

Album – 6 & 8 Rue Dante, 5e (☎ 01 43 25 85 19; metro Maubert Mutualité). This shop specialises in *bandes dessinées* – comic books. Comic books have a huge following in France, and this shop has everything from *Tintin* to erotic comics and French editions of the latest Japanese *manga*.

Odimex – 17 Rue de l'Odéon, 6e (☎ 01 46 33 98 96; metro Odéon). This shop sells teapots: little teapots, big teapots, sophisticated teapots, comic teapots and very expensive teapots.

Génération Condom – 6 Rue Thouin, 5e (☎ 01 43 54 43 42; metro Cardinal Lemoine). Every sort of condom, condom accessory, condom joke and condom-related item you could ask for.

Destruction des Animaux Nuisibles – 8 Rue des Halles, 1e (☎ 01 42 36 73 88; metro Châtelet). Got a pest you want to get rid of? This is the place to pick up the perfect pest destroyer, whether it's a roach motel for your cockroach infestation, a mousetrap for some pesky rodent or a box of mosquito coils for your next trip to the tropics. A world-class collection of dead rats, trapped in Les Halles in the old market days, proves they know what they are about.

La Maison de Magnet – 36 Rue Saint André des Arts, 6e (☎ 01 43 29 14 92; metro St Michel). This shop sells nothing but fridge magnets, featuring lots of truly French possibilities, including a collection of escargots in garlic butter. ■

Village Voice – 6 Rue Princesse (6e; M14; ☎ 01 46 33 36 47; metro Mabillon), two blocks south of Saint Germain des Prés. A friendly, helpful shop with an excellent selection of contemporary North American fiction and European literature in translation. It often sponsors readings, usually on Thursday (and perhaps Tuesday) at around 7 pm. It is open on Monday from 2 to 8 pm and Tuesday to Saturday from 11 am to 8 pm.

Brentano's – 37 Ave de l'Opéra (2e; M7 & M8; ☎ 01 42 61 52 50; metro Opéra). Midway between the Louvre and Opéra Garnier, this shop specialises in books from the USA and is open Monday to Saturday from 10 am to 7 pm.

W H Smith – 248 Rue de Rivoli (1er; M7; ☎ 44 77 88 99; metro Concorde). Situated one block east of Place de la Concorde, W H Smith is open from 9.30 am to 7 pm (closed on Sunday). Brace yourself for the prices.

Les Mots à la Bouche – 6 Rue Sainte Croix de la Bretonnerie (4e; M15; ☎ 01 42 78 88 30; metro Hôtel de Ville). Paris' premier gay bookshop specialises in books written by homosexuals or with gay or lesbian themes, and periodicals, including some in English. Most of the back wall is dedicated to English-language books, including lots of novels. It is open Monday to Saturday from 11 am to 11 pm and on Sunday from 2 to 8 pm.

DEPARTMENT STORES

Paris' 'big three' department stores are Printemps, Galleries Lafayette and La Samaritaine.

Printemps – 64 Blvd Haussmann, 9e (M7; ☎ 01 42 82 57 87, 42 82 50 00; metro Havre Caumartin). Printemps has one of the world's largest perfume and cosmetics departments, and is open Monday to Saturday from 9.30 am to 7 pm (10 pm on Thursday). Fashion shows are held on the 7th floor at 10 am every Tuesday and, from March to October, Friday.

Galeries Lafayette – 40 Blvd Haussmann, 9e (M7 & M8; ☎ 01 42 82 36 40; metro Auber or Chaussée d'Antin). This huge store, housed in two adjacent buildings linked by a pedestrian bridge, features over 75,000 brand-name items, and has a wide selection of fashion accessories. It is open Monday to Saturday from 9.30 am to 7 pm (9 pm on Thursday). There's a fine view from the rooftop restaurant.

La Samaritaine – in four buildings between Pont Neuf and 142 Rue de Rivoli (1er; M12; ☎ 01 40 41 20 20; metro Pont Neuf). A colour-coded brochure in English is available; arrowhead-shaped Building 1 is devoted solely to toys, stuffed animals and games. It is open Monday to Saturday from 9.30 am to 7 pm (10 pm on Thursday). You can drink in the outstanding rooftop view for free (see the Things to See & Do chapter).

RACHEL BLACK

Inside Galeries Lafayette

RACHEL BLACK

La Samaritaine

BHV – 52 Rue de Rivoli, 4e (M15; ☎ 01 42 74 90 00; metro Hôtel de Ville). The Bazaar de l'Hôtel de Ville is a straightforward department store apart from its world-class hardware section in the basement, with every type of hammer, power tool, nail, plug or hinge you could ask for.

CLOTHES & FASHION
ACCESSORIES

New collections are released twice a year – for spring/summer and autumn/winter. There are city-wide end-of-season sales from the end of June until sometime in August and from late December through February.

Triangle d'Or

Some of the fanciest clothes in Paris are sold by the *haute couture* houses of the Triangle d'Or (M6 & M7). The clients, including (as you'd expect) elegantly dressed women accompanied by immaculately trimmed poodles, are at least as interesting as the garments.

Along the even-numbered side of Ave Montaigne (1er; metro Franklin D Roosevelt or Alma Marceau) you'll find Inès de la Fressange at No 14, Christian Lacroix at No 26, Christian Dior at No 30, Celine at No 38 and Chanel at No 42. On the odd side, you'll pass Valentino at No 17, Guy Laroche at No 29, Nina Ricci at No 39 and Thierry Mugler at No 49. Givenchy (metro Alma Marceau) is nearby at 3 Ave George V (8e).

Rue du Faubourg Saint Honoré & Rue Saint Honoré

There is another grouping of couture houses and exclusive clothing and accessories stores just north of Place de la Concorde along Rue du Faubourg Saint Honoré (metro Madeleine or Concorde) and its eastern continuation, Rue Saint Honoré (metro Tuileries). Hermès (8e; M7; metro Madeleine), at 24 Rue du Faubourg Saint Honoré, is in the middle of a cluster of exclusive boutiques.

Place des Victoires

Trendy designer boutiques at Place des Victoires (M8; metro Bourse or Sentier) include Kenzo at No 3, Cacharel at No 5 and Thierry Mugler at No 8. Adjacent to Rue Étienne Marcel (1er & 2e; metro Les Halles) is the home of Comme des Garçons (M8) at No 42, Dorothée Bis at No 46, Yohji Yamamoto at No 47 and Chevignon Trading Post at No 49.

The postmodern designs of Jean-Paul Gaultier are on sale a few blocks west of Place des Victoires at 6 Rue Vivienne (2e; metro Bourse). Towards Forum des Halles on Rue du Jour, near Église Saint Eustache, the modern, casual styles of Agnès B (1er; M11; metro Les Halles) are available in the shops at No 3 (for men) and No 6 (for women).

Marais

In recent years, Rue des Rosiers (M15; metro Saint Paul) has attracted a growing number of fashionable clothing shops. Tehen and Apparence are at No 5, L'Éclaireur at

No 3, while Lolita Lempicka is not far away at No 2bis. Under the exclusive arcades of Place des Vosges, Issey Miyake is tucked away at No 3. There are other interesting shops along Rue des Francs Bourgeois, leading out of the Place des Vosges.

For more everyday clothing, there are lots of shops along Rue de Rivoli, which gets less expensive as you move east from the 1er into the 4e.

6e Arrondissement

The largest grouping of chic clothing boutiques in the fashionable 6e – many of them run by younger and more daring designers – is north-west of Place St Sulpice (M11 & M14; metro Saint Sulpice or Saint Germain des Prés). Ultra-chic clothing, footwear and leathergoods shops along Rue du Cherche Midi include Il Bisonte at No 17. Along Blvd Saint Germain, Sonia Rykiel has shops at No 175 (for women) and No 194 (for men). Rue de Rennes has a Kenzo Studio at No 60 and several Benneton shops, including one for kids. At Place Saint Sulpice, you can pop into Yves Saint Laurent Rive Gauche at No 12.

A bit to the south-west, just south of Au Bon Marché, Rue Saint Placide (M11; metro Sèvres Babylone) has lots of attractive shops selling clothes and shoes, mainly (but not exclusively) for women.

Reasonably priced clothing and shoe shops are legion along the southern half of Rue de Rennes (6e; metro Rennes or Saint Placide).

Rue d'Alésia

The part of Rue d'Alésia (M1; metro Alésia) between No 54 (just east of Place Victor & Hélène Baschand) and No 149 is lined with places that sell relatively inexpensive brand-name clothes and accessories, including discounted designer seconds with their labels removed (dégriffés). Most of the shops are cramped and chaotic, with poorly displayed merchandise and disinterested staff – this is especially true west of Nos 110 and 125. More shops can be found on Ave du Général Leclerc, both north and south of Place Victor & Hélène Baschand.

JEWELLERY

Around Place Vendôme (1er; M8; metro Tuileries), Cartier has shops at Nos 7 and 23, Philippe Patek is at No 10 and Van Cleef & Arpels is at No 22. There are more expensive jewellery shops along nearby Rue de Castiglione (1er) and Rue de la Paix (2e).

Less expensive jewellery is sold at various places around the city. Funky items, many of them imported, can be found in the Marais, including along Rue des Francs Bourgeois (3e & 4e). Costume jewellery is available at the flea markets.

MUSIC

A vast selection of recorded music is available at Paris' two Virgin Megastores, three FNAC department stores and one FNAC Musique store – for the addresses and hours of the two main outlets, see Booking Agencies under Entertainment. CDs are generally more expensive in France than in North America – count on paying 90 to 140FF. Virgin lets you listen to many of the CDs before buying them.

Second-hand CDs (49 to 69FF) can be purchased from two shops on Rue Linné (metro Jussieu) in the 5e: Jussieu Classique (M12; ☎ 01 47 07 60 45) at No 16 and Jussieu Music (M12; ☎ 01 43 31 14 18) at No 19. Both are open Monday to Saturday from 11 am to 7.30 pm and on Sunday from 2 to 7 pm.

CAMPING & SPORTS EQUIPMENT

Au Vieux Campeur (5e; M14; ☎ 01 43 29 12 32; metro Maubert Mutualité) has 17 shops in the Latin Quarter just east of Rue Saint Jacques between Blvd Saint Germain and Rue des Écoles. Each specialises in equipment for a specific kind of outdoor activity: hiking, mountaineering, cycling, skiing, snowboarding, scuba diving etc. Camping equipment is sold at several shops, including those at 18 Rue du Sommerard, 2 and 3 Rue de Latran and 6 Rue Thénard. All are open Monday to Saturday from 10.30 am to 7.30 pm (7 pm on Monday, 10 pm on Wednesday).

ANTIQUES

For details on Le Louvre des Antiquaires (M8), see the section entitled Louvre Area (western 1er) in the Things to See & Do chapter.

In the 6e, there are a number of shops selling antique maps and antiquarian books around Rue Bonaparte (metro Saint Germain des Prés) and Rue Jacob.

For information on Paris' legendary flea markets, see Flea Markets in this section.

GIFT/SOUVENIR IDEAS

Paris has a huge number of speciality shops offering unique gift items.

Galerie Inard – 179 Blvd Saint Germain, 6e (M11; ☎ 01 45 44 66 88). This gallery sells stunning Aubusson tapestries from the postwar period and imaginative, contemporary glass (open Tuesday to Saturday from 10 am to 12.30 pm and 2 to 7 pm). You won't get much change from 350,000FF for a medium-sized tapestry by a well-known artist.

E Dehillerin – 18-20 Rue Coquillère (1er; M8; ☎ 01 42 36 53 13; fax 01 45 08 86 83; metro Les Halles). This shop carries the most incredible selection of professional-quality cookware – you're sure to find something even the best equipped kitchen is lacking. VAT-free purchases and shipping home can be arranged. It is open Monday to Saturday from 8 am to 6 pm (closed on Monday from 12.30 to 2 pm).

Limoges-Unic – 12 and 58 Rue Paradis, 10e (M8; ☎ 01 47 70 54 49; metro Château d'Eau). One of the many shops along Rue de Paradis, Paris' traditional centre of *arts de la table* (tableware), whose windows are filled with sparking displays of the finest crystal, porcelain and silverware. It is open Monday to Saturday.

Mélodies Graphiques – 10 Rue du Pont Louis-Philippe, 4e (M15; ☎ 01 42 74 57 68; metro Pont Marie). Carries all sorts of items made from exquisite Florentine *papier à cuve* (paper hand-decorated with marbled designs). It is open from 11 am (2.30 pm on Monday) to 7 pm (closed on Sunday). There are several other fine stationery shops along the same street.

RICHARD NEBESKY

Librairie & *galerie* in Rue St Martin

Produits des Monastères – 10 Rue des Barres, 4e (M15; ☎ 01 48 04 39 05; metro Hôtel de Ville or Pont Marie). Sells jams, biscuits, cakes, muesli (granola), honey, herbal teas etc made at Benedictine and Trappist monasteries. It is open Tuesday to Saturday from 10 am to 8 pm, with breaks for prayers from 12.15 to 2 pm and 6 to 7.30 pm; Sunday hours are 10 to 10.45 am and 12.15 to 1 pm. It is closed in August.

Mariage Frères – 30-32 Rue du Bourg Tibourg, 4e (M15; ☎ 01 42 72 28 11; metro Hôtel de Ville). Paris' premier tea shop, with 450 to 500 varieties from 32 countries; the most expensive is a variety of Japanese *thé vert* (green tea) that costs 490FF for 100 grams. It is open daily from 10.30 am to 7.30 pm. The 19th-century salon de thé, where in summer you can cool off with five kinds of tea-flavoured ice cream, is open from noon to 7 pm.

Mariage Frères, founded in 1854, has another shop (6e; M14; ☎ 01 40 51 82 50; metro Odéon) at 13 Rue des Grands Augustins. It is open the same hours.

Galerie Alain Carion – 92 Rue Saint Louis en l'Île, 4e (M15; ☎ 01 43 26 01 16; metro Pont Marie), on Île Saint Louis. This shop has a stunningly beautiful collection of museum-quality minerals, crystals, fossils and meteorites from 40 different countries, some of them in the form of earrings, brooches and pendants. Prices range from 3 to 80,000FF (for a 60-kg meteorite). It is open from 10.30 am to 1 pm and 2 to 7.30 pm (may be closed on Sunday and Monday).

FLEA MARKETS

Paris' *marchés aux puces* (flea markets), easily accessible by metro, can be great fun if you're in the mood to browse for unexpected treasures among the *brocante* (second-hand goods) and bric-a-brac on display. Some new goods are also available, and a bit of bargaining is expected.

Marché aux Puces de Saint Ouen – This vast flea market (M1; metro Porte de Clignancourt), founded in the late 19th century and said to be Europe's largest, is at the northern edge of the 18e arrondissement. The stalls – of which there are over 2000 – are grouped into eight *marchés* (market areas), each with its own specialities (antiques, cheap clothing etc). Details are listed in the annual *Guide Officiel & Pratique des 'Puces'*, which bills itself in English as the *Complete Guide to the Greatest 'Fleamarket' in the World* (50FF), available from the Centre d'Information (4e; ☎ 01 40 10 13 92) at 154 Rue des Rosiers. It is open to the public on Saturday, Sunday and Monday from 8 am to 7 pm (later during summer).

If you arrive by metro, walk north along Ave de la Porte de Clignancourt and cross under the Blvd Périphérique to the inner suburb of Saint Ouen. The market is centred around Rue des Rosiers and nearby Ave

Michelet, Rue Voltaire, Rue Paul Bert and Rue Jean-Henri Fabre. While shopping, watch out for pickpockets.

Marché aux Puces de Montreuil – This market (M1), established in the 19th century, is in the south-eastern corner of the 20e on Ave de la Porte de Montreuil, between the Porte de Montreuil metro stop and the ring road. It is known for having good-quality second-hand clothes and designer seconds. The 500 stalls also sell engravings, jewellery and linen. It is open on Saturday, Sunday and Monday from 7 am to about 7 pm.

Marché aux Puces de la Porte de Vanves – This market (M1; metro Porte de Vanves), in the far south-western corner of the 14e arrondissement, is known for its fine selection of junk. Ave Georges Lafenestre looks like a giant car-boot sale, with lots of items that aren't quite old (or classy) enough to qualify as antiques. Ave Marc Sangnier is lined with stalls selling new clothes, shoes, handbags and household items. It is open Saturday and Sunday from 8 am to 6 pm (7 pm in summer).

Marché d'Aligre – Smaller and more central than the other three, this market (12e; M13; metro Ledru Rollin) at Place d'Aligre – 700 metres south-east of Place de la Bastille – is one of the best places in Paris to rummage through cardboard boxes filled with old clothes and one-of-a-kind accessories worn decades ago by fashionable (and not-so-fashionable) Parisians. It is open Tuesday to Sunday until about 1 pm.

Excursions

The region surrounding Paris is known as the Île de France (Island of France; M16) because of its position between four rivers: the Aube, the Marne, the Oise and the Seine. It was from this relatively small area that, beginning in around 1100, the kingdom of France began to expand.

The region's exceptional sights and excellent rail and road links with the French capital make it especially popular with day trippers. The many woodland areas around Paris offer outdoor activities such as rambling, cycling, horse riding and (at Fontainebleau) rock climbing.

SAINT DENIS

For 1200 years, Saint Denis (population 97,000) – now an industrial suburb a little north of Paris' 18th arrondissement – was the burial place of the kings of France. Their ornate tombs, adorned with some truly remarkable statuary, and the basilica that holds them – the world's first major Gothic structure – are an easy half-day excursion by metro.

Basilique Saint Denis

The basilica of Saint Denis (☎ 01 44 09 83 54) served as the burial place for all but a handful of France's kings from Dagobert I (ruled 629-39) to Louis XVIII (ruled 1814-24). Their tombs and mausoleums constitute one of Europe's most important collections of funerary sculpture.

The present basilica, begun in around 1135 by the irrepressible Abbot Suger, changed the face of Western architecture. It was the first major structure to be built in the Gothic style, and served as a model for many other 12th-century French cathedrals, including Chartres. Features illustrating the transition from Romanesque to Gothic can be seen in the **choir** and **ambulatory**, which are adorned with a number of 12th-century **stained-glass windows**. The nave and transept were built in the 13th century.

During the Revolution, the basilica was devastated – the royal tombs were emptied of their human remains, which were then dumped in pits outside the church – but the mausoleums, put into storage in Paris, survived. Restoration of the structure was begun under Napoleon, but most of the work was done by Viollet-le-Duc from

1858 until his death in 1879. Saint Denis has been a cathedral since 1966.

You can visit the nave for free, but to get to the interesting bits in the transept and chancel there's a charge of 28FF (18FF for those aged 18 to 25, 15FF for children aged 12 to 17). The basilica is open daily, except a few major feast days, from 10 am (noon on Sunday) to 5 pm (6.30 pm from April to September). The ticket counters close 30 minutes before closing.

Tombs The 800 people buried at Saint Denis include France's kings and queens, their children and close relatives, and a few outstanding servants of the throne. In many cases, the monarchs' bodies were buried here without their hearts and entrails, which were interred at other locations.

The tombs – all of which are now empty – are decorated with life-size figures of the deceased. Figures made after 1285 were carved from death masks and are thus fairly realistic. The oldest tombs are those of **Clovis I** (died 511) and his son **Childebert I** (died 558), brought to Saint Denis during the early 19th century. The finest Renaissance tombs include those of **Louis XII** (1462-1515) and **Anne of Brittany** (1476-1514), **François I** (1494-1547) and **Claude de France** (1499-1524), and **Henri II** (1519-59) and **Catherine de' Medici** (1519-89).

Archaeological excavations in the 12th-century **crypt** have uncovered extensive tombs from the Merovingian era (5th and 6th centuries) and the Carolingian period (late 8th century). The oldest tomb discovered dates from around 570 AD.

Musée d'Art et d'Histoire

Saint Denis' excellent Museum of Art & History (☎ 01 42 43 05 10) at 22bis Rue Gabriel Péri occupies a restored Carmelite convent founded in 1625 and later presided over by Louise de France, the youngest daughter of Louis XV. Displays include reconstructions of the Carmelites' cells, an 18th-century **apothicairerie** (apothecary's shop) and, in the archaeology section, fascinating items found during excavations around Saint Denis. On the 2nd floor, there's an extensive collection of politically charged posters, cartoons, lithographs and paintings from the 1871 **Paris Commune**.

The Musée d'Art et d'Histoire is open daily except Tuesday and holidays; hours are 10 am to 5.30 pm (2 to 6.30 pm on Sunday). Entry costs 20FF (10FF for students, teachers and seniors; free for children under 16).

Getting There & Away

Take metro line No 13 to the Saint Denis-Basilique terminus (don't get on one of the trains going to Asnières-Gennevilliers).

MUSÉE DE L'AIR ET DE L'ESPACE

The venerable Aeronautics & Space Museum (☎ 01 49 92 71 71) in Paris' northern suburb of Le Bourget has almost 150 military and civilian aircraft, dozens of rockets and spacecraft and other displays that chart the history of flight and space exploration. It is open daily except Monday from 10 am to 5 pm (6 pm from May to October). Entry costs 30FF (22, 20 and 15FF reduced rates).

Nearby **Le Bourget Airport**, where Lindbergh landed, hosts the famous Paris Air Show in June of odd-numbered years.

To get to the museum, take RATP bus No 350 (every 10 to 20 minutes until at least 10 pm) from the Gare de l'Est (right out front) or the Gare du Nord bus terminal (behind the station, just off Rue du Faubourg Saint Denis). You can also catch bus No 152 from near the Porte de la Villette metro station (19e).

DISNEYLAND-PARIS

It took US$4.4 billion and five years of work to turn the beet fields 32 km east of Paris into Euro-Disneyland, which opened in 1992 amid much fanfare and controversy. Although Disney stockholders have so far been less than thrilled with the bottom line, the many visitors

OLIVIER CIRENDINI

Euro-Disneyland at night

– mostly families with young children – seem to be having a great time exploring the gleaming facilities and carefully tended gardens.

Euro-Disneyland is open 365 days a year. In summer it's open Monday to Friday from 9 am to 8 pm, and on Saturday and Sunday from 9 am to 11 pm.

Information

The park is totally bilingual, and brochures with details on shows, concerts, parades, restaurants, rides etc are provided at the entrance. There are information booths scattered around the park, including one in City Hall. The complex includes an entertainment centre, two train stations, a camping area and five hotels.

By phone, information is available in France on ☎ 01 60 30 60 30; in the UK on ☎ 01733-335 567; and in the USA on ☎ 1-407-WDISNEY. By Minitel, dial 3615 DISNEY-LAND.

Euro-Disneyland Theme Park

The theme park, isolated from the outside world by clever layout and grassy embankments, is divided into five *pays* (lands). **Main Street, USA**, just inside the main entrance, is a spotless avenue reminiscent of Norman Rockwell's idealised small-town America, circa 1900. The adjacent **Frontierland** is a re-creation of the 'rugged, untamed American West'. **Adventureland**, intended to evoke the Arabian Nights and the wilds of Africa, is home to that old favourite Pirates of the Caribbean, as well as the new Indiana Jones ride. **Fantasyland** brings fairy-tale characters such as Sleeping Beauty, Snow White and Pinocchio to life. And in **Discoveryland**, the high-tech rides (including the new Space Mountain roller coaster) and futuristic movies pay homage to Leonardo da Vinci, H G Wells, George Lucas and – for a bit of local colour – Jules Verne.

Disney engineers have tried to make the 'pre-entertainment areas' – Disney parlance for queues – as pleasant as possible, but a two-minute ride may still require standing in line for 40 minutes of pre-entertainment.

Tickets The one-day entry fee, including all rides and activities, is 195FF (adult) or 150FF (children three to 11 years) in the high season; it drops to 150FF and 120FF in the low season. Two-day, three-day and one-year passes are also available, and there are often special deals, particularly in the low season, available from Disneyland or travel agents. It has been known, on unusually popular holiday occasions, for the park to be closed to anybody who has not booked in advance.

Getting There & Away

Marne-la-Vallée-Chessy (Disneyland's RER station) is served by RER line A4, which runs every 15 minutes or so. Tickets, available at any metro station, cost 37FF (35 to 40 minutes). Trains that go all the way to Marne-la-Vallée-Chessy have four-letter codes beginning with the letter Q. The last train back to Paris leaves Disneyland a bit after midnight.

A taxi to/from the centre of Paris costs about 300FF (450FF from 7 pm to 8 am and on Sunday and holidays); the taxi rank is on the south side of the train station.

VERSAILLES

Paris' prosperous and leafy suburb of Versailles, site of the grandest and most famous château in France, served as the kingdom's political capital and the seat of the royal court for almost the entire period between 1682 and 1789.

Because so many people consider Versailles a must-see destination, the château attracts over three million visitors a year. The best way to avoid the queues is to arrive first thing in the morning; if you're interested in just the Grands Appartements, you can also come around 4 pm. The château is 23 km south-west of Paris.

Château de Versailles

The enormous château (☎ 01 30 84 74 00) was built in the mid-17th century during the reign of Louis XIV to project both at home and abroad the absolute power of the French monarchy, then at the height of its splendour. Its scale and décor also reflect Louis' taste for profligate luxury and his boundless appetite for self-glorification. Some 30,000 workers and soldiers toiled on the structure, whose construction bills wrought havoc on the kingdom's finances.

The château complex consists of four main parts: the palace building, a 580-metre-long structure with innumerable wings, grand halls and sumptuous bedchambers (only parts are open to the public); the vast gardens west of the palace; and two outbuildings, the Grand Trianon and, a few hundred metres to the north-east, the Petit Trianon.

TONY WHEELER

Versailles

GREG ELMS

Detail of the Fountain of Saturn, Versailles

TONY WHEELER

North wing of the Château de Versailles

TONY WHEELER

Hamean de la Reine (Queen's Hamlet), Versailles

The château has undergone relatively few alterations since its construction, though almost all the interior furnishings disappeared during the Revolution and many of the rooms were rebuilt by Louis-Philippe (ruled 1830-48).

Architecture About two decades into his 72-year reign (1643-1715), Louis XIV decided to enlarge the hunting lodge his father had built at Versailles and turn it into a palace big enough for the entire court, which numbered some 6000 people. To accomplish this task he hired four supremely talented people: the architect Louis Le Vau; his successor Jules Hardouin-Mansart, who took over in the mid-1670s; the painter and interior designer Charles Le Brun; and the landscape artist André Le Nôtre, whose workers flattened hills, drained marshes and relocated forests as they laid out the seemingly endless gardens, ponds and fountains.

Le Brun and his hundreds of artisans decorated every moulding, cornice, ceiling and door of the interior with the most luxurious and ostentatious of appointments: frescoes, marble, gilt woodcarvings and the like. The ornateness reaches its peak in the **Galerie des Glaces** (Hall of Mirrors), a 75-metre-long ballroom with 17 huge mirrors on one side and, on the other, an equal number of windows looking out on the gardens and the setting sun.

Gardens The section of the vast gardens nearest the palace, laid out between 1661 and 1700 in the formal French style, is famed for its geometrically aligned terraces, flowerbeds, tree-lined paths, ponds and fountains. The **English-style garden** just north of the Petit Trianon is more pastoral and has meandering paths.

The 1.6-km-long, 62-metre-wide **Grand Canal**, oriented to reflect the setting sun, is intersected by the one-km **Petit Canal**, creating a cross-shaped body of water with a perimeter of over 5.5 km. Louis XIV used to hold boating parties here. From May to mid-October, you too can paddle around the Grand Canal: four-person row boats (☎ 01 39 54 22 00) cost 70FF an hour. The dock is at the canal's eastern end.

The gardens' largest fountains are the 17th-century **Bassin de Neptune** (Neptune Fountain), 300 metres north of the main palace building, whose straight side abuts a small, round pond graced by a winged dragon, and, at the eastern end of the Grand Canal, the **Bassin**

d'Apollon, in whose centre Apollo's chariot, pulled by rearing horses, emerges from the water.

On Sundays from early May to early October, the fountains are turned on at 11.15 am for the 20-minute **Grande Perspective** and from 3.30 pm to 5 pm for the longer and more elaborate **Grands Eaux**. On the days when the fountain shows take place, there is a 25FF fee to get into the gardens.

The Trianons In the middle of the park, about 1.5 km north-west of the main building, are Versailles' two smaller palaces, each surrounded by neatly tended flower beds. The pink-colonnaded **Grand Trianon** was built in 1687 for Louis XIV and his family, who used it as a place of escape from the rigid etiquette of court life. Napoleon I had it redecorated in the Empire style. The much smaller **Petit Trianon**, built in the 1760s, was redecorated in 1867 by the Empress Eugénie, who added Louis XVI-style furnishings similar to the uninspiring pieces that now fill its 1st-floor rooms.

A bit farther north is the **Hameau de la Reine** (Queen's Hamlet), a mock-rural village of thatch-roofed cottages constructed from 1775 to 1784 for the amusement of Marie-Antoinette. You can wander around its gardens for no charge.

Opening Hours & Fees The **Grands Appartements** (State Apartments), the main section of the palace that can be visited without a guided tour, include the Galerie des Glaces and the Appartement de la Reine (Queen's Suite). Except on Monday, they are open from 9 am to 5.30 pm (6.30 pm from May to September); the ticket windows close 30 minutes earlier. Entry costs 45FF (35FF for people aged 18 to 25 and, on Sunday, for everyone; free for under 18s). Tickets are on sale at Entrée A (Entrance A; also known as Porte A), which, as you approach the palace, is off to the right from the equestrian statue of Louis XIV. The queues are worst on Tuesday, when many Paris museums are closed, and on Sunday.

From October to April, the **Grand Trianon** (25FF; 15FF reduced price; free for under 18s) is open Tuesday to Sunday from 10 am to 12.30 pm and 2 to 5.30 pm (no midday closure on weekends). The rest of the year, hours are 10 am to 6.30 pm. The last entry is 30 minutes before closing time. The **Petit Trianon**, open the same days and hours, costs 15FF (10FF reduced price; free for under 18s). A combined ticket for both will set you back 29FF (19FF reduced price).

The **gardens** are open seven days a week (unless it's snowing) from 7 am to nightfall (between 5.30 and 9.30 pm, depending on the season). Entry is free *except* on Sunday from early May to early October, when the fountains are in operation and entrance costs 25FF.

If you have a Carte Musées et Monuments, you don't have to wait in the queue – go straight to Entrée A.

The Town of Versailles

Like the château, the attractive town of Versailles, crisscrossed by wide boulevards, is a creation of Louis XIV. However, most of today's buildings date from the 18th and 19th centuries.

Grandes & Petites Écuries Ave de Paris, Ave de Saint Cloud and Ave de Sceaux, the three wide thoroughfares that fan out eastward from Place d'Armes, are separated by two large late 17th-century stables: the Grandes Écuries (presently occupied by the army) and the Petites Écuries. At the time of writing, the Grandes Écuries, which house a **carriage museum**, could be visited in July and August on Sunday from 2 to 5 pm.

Cathédrale Saint Louis This neoclassical (and slightly baroque) cathedral on Place Saint Louis, a harmonious if austere work by Hardouin-Mansart, was built between 1743 (when Louis XV himself laid the first stone) and 1754. It is known for its 3131-pipe organ and is decorated with a number of interesting paintings and stained-glass panels. Opening hours are 8 am to noon and 2 to 7 pm.

Musée Lambinet Housed in a lovely 18th-century residence, the Musée Lambinet (☎ 01 39 50 30 32) at 54 Blvd de la Reine displays 18th-century furnishings (ceramics, sculpture, paintings, furniture) and objects connected with the history of Versailles (including the Revolutionary period). It is open from 2 to 6 pm (closed on Monday and holidays). Entry costs 24FF (reduced tariffs are 12 and 16FF).

Église Notre Dame Built by Hardouin-Mansart in the late 17th century, this church on Rue de la Paroisse served as the parish church of the king and his courtiers. It has a fine sculpted pulpit. It is generally open in the afternoon from 2 to 6 or 7 pm.

Getting There & Away

Each of Versailles' three train stations is served by RER and/or SNCF trains coming from a different set of Paris stations.

RER line C5 takes you from Paris' Left Bank RER stations to **Versailles-Rive Gauche** station (12FF), which is only 700 metres from the château. From Paris, catch any train whose four-letter code begins with the letter V (eg VAAL, VICK, VONY, VURT). There are 60 trains a day (35 on Sunday); the last train back to Paris leaves at about 11.50 pm. Tickets are not sold at regular metro ticket windows.

RER line C7 links Paris' Left Bank with **Versailles-Chantiers** station (12FF), a 1.3-km walk from the château. From the city, take any train whose code begins with S (eg SLIM, SVEN). Versailles-Chantiers is also served by 36 SNCF trains a day (20 on Sunday) from Gare Montparnasse (14FF; 14 minutes); all trains on this line continue on to Chartres.

From Paris' Gare Saint Lazare and La Défense, the SNCF has about 70 trains a day to **Versailles-Rive Droite** (16FF including a metro journey), which is 1200 metres from the château. The last train to Paris leaves a bit past midnight.

FONTAINEBLEAU

The town of Fontainebleau (population 16,000), 65 km south-east of Paris, is renowned for its elegant Renaissance château – one of France's largest royal residences – whose splendid furnishings make it particularly worth a visit. It's much less crowded and pressured than Versailles. The town is surrounded by the beautiful Forêt de Fontainebleau, a favourite hunting ground of a long line of French kings.

Château de Fontainebleau

The enormous Château de Fontainebleau (☎ 01 60 71 50 70) is one of the most beautifully ornamented and furnished châteaux in France. Every cm of the walls and ceilings is richly adorned with wood panelling, gilded carvings, frescoes, tapestries and paintings. The parquet floors are of the finest woods, the fireplaces ornamented with exceptional carvings, and much of the furniture dates from the Renaissance.

The **Grands Appartements** (State Apartments) feature a number of outstanding rooms, including the spectacular **Chapelle de la Trinité** (Trinity Chapel), whose ornamentation dates from the first half of the 17th century; **Galerie François 1er**, a gem of Renaissance architecture; and the **Salle de Bal**, a 30-metre-long ballroom dating from the mid-16th century.

The **Petits Appartements** were the private apartments of the emperor and empress and are open daily from 9 am to 5 pm (to 8.30 pm in summer); entry is 15FF (10FF reduced tariff).

Museums The **Musée Napoléonien** within the château, also known as the Musée Napoléon 1er, has a collection of personal effects (uniforms, hats, coats, ornamented swords) and knick-knacks that belonged to Napoleon and his relatives. Many of the items are gilded, enamelled or bejewelled.

The four rooms of the **Musée Chinois** (Chinese Museum) are filled with beautiful ceramics and other objects brought to France from East Asia during the 19th century. Some of the items, from the personal collection of Empress Eugénie (wife of Napoleon III), were gifts from a delegation that came from Siam (Thailand) in 1861. Others were stolen by a Franco-British expeditionary force sent to China in 1860.

Gardens On the north side of the château, the **Jardin de Diane** is a formal garden created by Catherine de' Medici, and is home to a flock of peacocks *(paons)*. The formal 17th-century **Jardin Français** (French Garden), also known as the Grand Parterre, is by Le Nôtre. The **Grand Canal** was excavated in 1609 and predates the canals at Versailles by over half a century.

The **Forêt de Fontainebleau**, crisscrossed by paths, begins 500 metres south of the château. This 250-sq-km forest, which surrounds the town of Fontainebleau, is one of the loveliest wooded tracts in the Paris region. The many trails are great for jogging, hiking, cycling and horse riding. Parisian rock-climbing enthusiasts have long come to the forest's sandstone ridges, rich in cliffs and overhangs, to hone their skills before setting off for the Alps.

Hours & Tickets The interior of the château is open daily except Tuesday from 9.30 am to 12.30 pm and 2 to 5 pm (6 pm in July and August); there's no midday closure from June to October. The last visitors are admitted an hour before closing time. Tickets cost 32FF (20FF for people aged 18 to 25 and, on Sunday, for everyone; free for under 18s). The gardens (free) are open daily from early morning until sundown. In winter, parts of the garden may be closed if personnel are in short supply.

Getting There & Away

Between 22 and 25 daily commuter trains link Paris'
Gare de Lyon with Fontainebleau-Avon (43FF; 45 to 60
minutes); in off-peak periods, there's about one train an
hour. The last train back to Paris leaves Fontainebleau a
bit before 9.45 pm (10 pm on Sunday and holidays).

At the Gare de Lyon, tickets are on sale at the Banlieue
(suburban) counters and at Grandes Lignes (long-haul)
counters Nos 47 and 48. Figuring out where to catch your
train can be rather confusing – Fontainebleau-Avon is
served by some (but by no means all) trains going to
Moret-Veneux, Montereau, Montargis, Sens, Laroche-
Migennes and Nevers. And while 'Fontainebleau-Avon'
may appear on the schedule boards, it often doesn't.
Most trains – specifically, those indicated on the schedule boards by alphanumeric codes – depart from the
TGV-Grandes Lignes section of Gare de Lyon, but a few
leave from the Gare de Banlieue (Suburban Station), also
known as the Gare Souterraine (Underground Station),
located three levels below the Grandes Lignes tracks. For
details, enquire at one of the information booths.

At Fontainebleau-Avon train station, the information
office (☎ 01 64 22 38 57, 64 22 39 82) is open from 9 am to
8 pm daily except Sunday and holidays.

CHANTILLY

The elegant town of Chantilly (population 11,300), 48 km
north of Paris, is best known for its heavily restored but
imposing château, surrounded by gardens, lakes and a
vast forest. The château is slightly over two km east of
the train station. The most direct route is to walk through
the Forêt de Chantilly along Route de l'Aigle, but you'll
get a better sense of the town by taking Ave du Maréchal
Joffre and Rue de Paris to Rue du Connétable,
Chantilly's main street.

Château de Chantilly

Chantilly's château (☎ 01 44 57 08 00), left in a shambles
after the Revolution, is of interest mainly because of its
gardens and a number of superb paintings. The **Petit
Château** was built around 1560 for Anne de Montmor-
ency (1492-1567), who served six French kings as
connétable (high constable), diplomat and warrior and
died in battle against the Protestants. The highlight of
the Petit Château is the **Cabinet des Livres** (library), a
repository of 700 manuscripts and over 12,000 other
volumes.

The attached Renaissance-style **Grand Château**, completely demolished during the Revolution, was rebuilt by the Duc d'Aumale in the late 1870s. It contains the **Musée Condé**, whose unremarkable 19th-century rooms are adorned with furnishings, paintings and sculptures. The most remarkable works are hidden away in a small room called the **Sanctuaire** (Sanctuary); they include paintings by Raphael (1483-1520), Filippino Lippi (1457-1504) and Jean Fouquet (1420-1480).

Gardens The château's lovely but long-neglected gardens were once among the most spectacular in France. The formal **Jardin Français**, whose flowerbeds, lakes and Grand Canal were laid out by Le Nôtre in the mid-17th century, is directly north of the main building. There are also English and Anglo-Chinese gardens, as well as the **Hameau** (hamlet), a mock-rural village whose mill and half-timbered buildings, built in 1774, inspired the Queen's Hamlet at Versailles.

Hours & Tickets The château is open daily except Tuesday from 10 am to 6 pm; from November to February, hours are 10.30 am to 12.45 pm and 2 to 5 pm (the same entry ticket is good both before and after the midday break). Ticket sales end 45 minutes before closing time. Entry to the château and its park (open daily) costs 39FF (34FF for children and students, 12FF for under 12s). Entry to the park alone costs 17FF (10FF for children under 12).

Musée Vivant du Cheval

The château's magnificent **Grandes Écuries** (stables), built from 1719 to 1740 to house 240 horses and over 400 hunting hounds, are next to Chantilly's famous **Champ de Course** (racecourse), inaugurated in 1834. They house the Living Horse Museum (☎ 01 44 57 40 40 or, for a recording, 44 57 13 13), whose equines live in luxurious **wooden stalls** built by Louis-Henri de Bourbon, the seventh Prince de Condé. Displays include everything from riding equipment to horsey toys and paintings of famous horses. All signs are in English.

The Musée Vivant is open from 10.30 am to 5.30 pm (6 pm on weekends); it's closed on Tuesday except in June (open on Tuesday afternoons in July). Entry costs 50FF, the students' and seniors' rate of 45FF is available only on weekdays. Children under 16 (under 12 on weekends) pay 40FF.

Forêt de Chantilly

The Chantilly Forest, once a royal hunting estate, covers
63 sq km. Its tree cover, patchy in places because of poor
soil and overgrazing by deer, includes beeches, oaks,
chestnuts, limes and pines. The forest is crisscrossed by
a variety of walking and riding trails. In some areas,
straight paths laid out centuries ago meet at multi-
angled *carrefours* (crossroads).

Getting There & Away

Paris' Gare du Nord is linked to Chantilly-Gouvieux
train station (40FF; 30 to 45 minutes) by a mixture of RER
and SNCF commuter trains, a total of 36 a day (26 on
Sunday and holidays). In the morning, there are departures from Gare du Nord at least once or twice an hour;
in the evening, there are generally trains back to Paris
every hour or so until at least 11 pm.

The dozen weekday RER trains (line B) that are code-
named CODA, CECI and CADE begin their runs at
Châtelet-Les Halles metro station before stopping at
Gare du Nord. The other 24 weekday trains – signposted
for a variety of destinations, including Creil, Amiens,
Compiègne and Saint Quentin – start at Gare du Nord,
where Chantilly-bound trains use both the Grandes
Lignes and Banlieue platforms.

PARC ASTÉRIX

A home-grown alternative to the cultural incursions of
the Euro-Disney resort, the Parc Astérix (☎ 01 44 62 34
44) is 30 km north of Paris, just beyond Charles de Gaulle
airport. Like Euro-Disney it's divided into a variety of
areas – Astérix Village, the Roman City, Ancient Greece
and others – and like Disneyland there are lots of rides.
The park is open from early April to the beginning of
September, every day from 10 am to 6 pm, or longer. The
rest of the year it opens only on Wednesday, Saturday
and Sunday. Entry price to the park and all the rides is
160FF for adults, 110FF for under 12-year-olds.

Getting There & Away

Take RER line B3 just as if you were going to Charles de
Gaulle airport. From the Roissy Charles-de-Gaulle 1
station, Courriers Île de France buses depart for the park
every half-hour from 9.30 am to 1.30 pm. Buses return
from the park every half-hour from 4.30 pm until half an
hour after the park closes.

CHARTRES

The magnificent 13th-century cathedral of Chartres, crowned by two soaring spires – one Gothic, the other Romanesque – rises from the rich farmland 90 km southwest of Paris and dominates the medieval town around its base. It is France's best preserved medieval cathedral, having been spared both postmedieval modifications and the ravages of war and revolution.

The cathedral's collection of relics – particularly the **Sainte Chemise** (Holy Chemise), a piece of cloth said to have been worn by the Virgin Mary when she gave birth to Jesus – attracted many pilgrims during the Middle Ages. Indeed, the town of Chartres (population 40,000, double that including the suburbs) has been attracting pilgrims for over 2000 years. The earliest church on the site, built in the 4th century, was the first in France dedicated to Mary.

Cathédrale Notre Dame

Chartres' 130-metre-long cathedral (☎ 37 21 75 02), one of the crowning architectural achievements of Western civilisation, was built in the Gothic style during the first quarter of the 13th century to replace a Romanesque cathedral that had been devastated – along with much of the town – by fire on the night of 10 June 1194. Because of effective fundraising among the aristocracy and donations of labour by the common folk, construction took only 25 years, resulting in a high degree of architectural and iconographical unity.

The cathedral is open daily from 7.30 am to 7 pm (7.30 pm from Easter to 1 November) except during Mass, weddings and funerals.

Portals & Towers All three of the cathedral's entrances have richly ornamented triple portals, but the west entrance, known as the **Portail Royal** (or Royal Portal), is the only one that predates the fire. The structure's other main Romanesque feature is the 105-metre **Clocher Vieux** (Old Bell Tower), also known as the Tour Sud (South Tower), which was begun in the 1140s. It is the tallest Romanesque steeple still standing.

A visit to the 115-metre-high **Clocher Neuf** (New Bell Tower) or **Clocher Gothique** – also known as the Tour Nord (North Tower) – is well worth the ticket price and the long, spiral climb. Access is via the north transept arm. A 70-metre-high platform on the lacy, flamboyant Gothic spire affords superb views of the three-tiered flying buttresses and the 19th-century copper roof.

Except on Sunday morning, certain major holidays and in icy weather, visits to the Clocher Neuf can be started from 9.30 or 10 to 11.30 am, and from 2 pm to 4 pm from November to February, 4.30 pm in October and March, and 5.30 pm (5.15 pm on Saturday) from April to September. The fee is 14FF (7FF for children 12 to 17, who must be accompanied by an adult).

Stained Glass The cathedral's extraordinary stained-glass windows, almost all of which are 13th-century originals, form one of the most important ensembles of medieval stained glass in Europe. The three most important windows dating from before the 13th century are in the wall above the west entrance, below the rose window. Survivors of the fire of 1194 (they were made around 1150), they are renowned for the depth and intensity of their blue tones, known as Chartres blue.

Trésor Chapelle Saint Piat, up the stairs at the far end of the choir, houses the cathedral's treasury, including the Holy Chemise. From mid-March to mid-October, it is open from 10 am to noon and 2 to 6 pm (closed on Sunday and holiday mornings and on Monday). The rest of the year, hours are 10 am to noon and 2.30 to 4.30 pm (5 pm on Sunday and holidays). Entry is free.

Getting There & Away
There are 36 round trips a day (20 on Sunday) to/from Paris' Gare Montparnasse (69FF one way; 55 to 70 minutes) and Versailles' Chantiers station. The last train back to Paris leaves Chartres a bit after 9 pm (7.40 pm on Saturday, sometime after 10 pm on Sunday and holidays).

Index